Who's Who in H. G. Wells

Who's Who
in H. G. Wells

BRIAN ASH

ELM TREE BOOKS
HAMISH HAMILTON . LONDON

For Diane, Alison (Jane) and Kevin, of
whom H.G. might well have approved—
'with all of Love'.

First published in Great Britain 1979
by Elm Tree Books, Hamish Hamilton Ltd, Garden House
57-59 Long Acre, London WC2E 9JL

British Library Cataloguing in Publication Data

Ash, Brian
    Who's who in H. G. Wells.
    1. Wells, Herbert George—Characters—
    Dictionaries
    I. Title
    823'.9'12   PR5776.A/

    ISBN 0-241-89597-9

Printed in Great Britain by
Willmer Brothers Limited, Rock Ferry, Merseyside

Acknowledgements

Grateful thanks are due to the Executors of the H. G. Wells Estate for permission to quote from the author's works, and also to the following publishers: J. M. Dent, Collins, Longmans, Sphere, W. Heinemann, Pan Books, New Portway Reprints, Corgi, and Greenwood Press (US).

Warm appreciation is also acknowledged of Mr. J. B. Priestley's kindness in allowing the reproduction of the address which he gave on the occasion of Wells's cremation on 16th August, 1946.

About the author

Brian Ash is the author of a variety of books, on subjects including multi-national advertising, the origins of modern music, clinical psychology and science fiction. He has been associated with the International H. G. Wells Society since 1963, having served as publicity officer during the Wells Centenary in 1966, and subsequently as general secretary of the Society until 1970.

He was instrumental in arranging a variety of meetings during the International Year of Human Rights (1968) frequently under the auspices of the Wells Society.

He has been a regular contributor on scientific and psychological subjects to *New Humanist*, and is an editorial contributor to *Psychology Today*. His publications during the next twelve months include a utopian SF novel, a fictional treatment of the Nazi stormtrooper leaders and a performer's view of classic jazz. He is currently engaged in preparing an SF movie scenario.

Contents

'The unknown is full of possible surprises for mankind. There is no more probability of these surprises being dreadful than there is of their being delightful. The chances are strictly even. When everything has gone into either scale, there still remains this fact to tilt the balance in our favour; that here we are with courage in us.'

H. G. Wells : *The Work, Wealth and Happiness of Mankind*

The interested reader may well find a number of discrepancies in spellings and expressions in the following entries, depending whether he has before him the first edition or a subsequent reprint. (Wells made many revisions to his previously published works over the years—the spelling of 'Pierce' later replaced by 'Pearce' and the disparity between Carshot's expletives : 'My Heart and Lungs'—all from *Kipps*—are cases in point.) In general the first editions to appear have been taken as the principal guide in the ensuing text.

Introduction

H. G. Wells can be viewed as a bridge between the Victorian scene of Thackeray and Meredith and the twentieth-century era of speculative fiction. His early stories, which in all probability will be finally viewed as his most enduring contribution to literature, brought him rapid success in his early thirties. But with success, he became increasingly didactic and his later novels—with the occasional notable exception—sometimes deteriorated into little better than sociological tracts and vehicles for Wellsian propaganda.

In considering his characters, therefore, the reader will soon be aware that many of them are barely-disguised extensions of Wells himself, preaching his enheartening message of one world and the mutual interdependence of all sentient life.

It is not the purpose of this introduction to review his work or life in a critical or biographical sense. Many such studies are already available and a number of the more noted are listed in the concluding bibliography which follows the appendices. However, it is necessary to sketch in an outline of Wells the man as an essential ingredient to the understanding of the characters with which he peopled his tales.

He came from a relatively humble background, his father being a failed gardener and shop-keeper, who later played cricket as a professional. His mother was, off-and-on, housekeeper to a large English mansion and essayed her best to force her son into a life of drudgery as a draper's apprentice. A great deal of his early experiences can be found in his own *Experiment in Autobiography*, a work in which he was, for many varied reasons, rather less than frank regarding the personal details of his later life. Winning a scholarship to the Normal School of Science, in London, he studied for a year under the Darwinian apostle, Thomas Henry Huxley—an experience which was to influence him notably when he came to write, as also were the platonic ideas which he had discovered in *The Republic* as a boy of thirteen.

In essence, he became a revolutionary. He developed a passionate concern for social reform, largely motivated by his own experiences as a child and as an impoverished student, and subsequently as a struggling school-teacher. Reference to these early influences will appear in the following entries where appropriate as an aid to the better appreciation of his characters. His *dramatis personae* can be categorized basically under three main headings, all stemming from his own observations and predilections. First is the eternal 'Little Man', the Kipps and Pollys of the late-Victorian world battling against improbable odds to reach self-fulfilment—a reflection of Wells's own struggle.

Second come the women, the Ann Veronicas and Lady Harmans, espousing a liberation and freedom for their own sex which owed much to Wells's childhood dislike of his mother's enforced, but almost happily accepted, servitude.

In the third category fall the scientists, business entrepreneurs, educators and dreamers for mankind—the majority of them Wellsian self-projections, and increasingly vocal in the particular messages which their creator wished to convey.

Outside these principal groupings appear the major allegorical figures, the Moreaus and Blettsworthys, and, of course, the many relatively sketchy personalities of the short stories.

For one who consistently urged a modernist outlook, Wells adopted a paradoxically antiquated tradition when it came to naming his characters—to the extent that in many cases he failed to name them at all, or seemed reluctant to reveal their forenames. As a consequence the reader will find substantial variety in the form of entry headings in the subsequent pages, ranging from 'The Man with a Nose' to 'Christabel, the Girl on the Wall'. Since Wells chose to describe them in no other way, neither can the Compiler; but where they are of significance to the narrative they clearly warrant inclusion.

However, it is beyond the realms of practicability to cover in a volume of this size many of the very considerable host of minor personages who have crossed Wells's pages. In the main they feature only as passing sounding-boards, and occasionally as punching-dummies, for his central protagonists, and they can be viewed generally as an incidental feature in the background scenery.

Wells has never been regarded in the critical field as a master of characterization, although it is difficult to see how such as Mr. Polly could be described if not as a great character. The evidence of the comic tales suggests that Wells felt more at home with the creation of humorous figures once he had begun to enjoy good health in his late thirties. In the same period the marked key-change from the relatively bleak visions of his early years to the beginnings of an optimistic outlook can also be noted.

Again, this is not the place for a continuation of the still unresolved debate as to whether Wells was a natural optimist who lapsed into pessimism towards the end of his life, or whether he was at heart a pessimist who virtually forced himself into the more than twenty years of cautiously optimistic writing which constitutes his middle period. What can be said with certainty is that the state of his health influenced his work considerably. In the late 1890s, when he thought he would not live long, he produced the sombre prophecy of *The Time Machine* (1895) and the chilling accounts of Man's inadequacy which can be found in *The Island of Dr. Moreau* (1896), *The War of the Worlds* (1898), and a good many of his short stories. With the exception of *The Wheels of Chance* (1896), there is no major work in this early period that is without its darker side.

The appearance of *A Modern Utopia* in 1905, and *Kipps* in the following year, can be said to mark the opening stages of Wells's middle period. He had still to evolve the type of 'discussion' novel (the first being *The New Machiavelli* in 1911) which many have suggested led to a serious decline in the quality of his main characters. The books of the middle years, too numerous to mention here, can be found listed in Appendix One. While it is less easy to identify the beginning of the final stage, *Mr. Blettsworthy on Rampole Island* (1928) might be taken as a possible starting point, if only for its return to the darker view. Its elements of pessimism were reflected in the accounts of human stupidity and self-delusion presented in *The Autocracy of Mr. Parham* (1930) and *The Bulpington of Blup* (1932), and most particularly in *The Croquet Player* (1936) and *The Camford Visitation* (1937).

During his very last years, Wells wrote no major fiction. His final novel, *You Can't Be Too Careful* (1941), found him in caustic vein, although surprisingly it also shows a partial reawakening of his ability to create genuinely comic scenes.

In the descriptions of Wells's characters, as can be seen in the following entries, a good many similarities will be found—not merely in the type of person described but also in those particular physical features on which the author chose to elaborate. As an example of the former trait, the reader will be struck by the preponderance of socialist aunts—all engaged in some kind of reformist work—who adorn his stories. Another familiar character, particularly in the discussion novels, is the loquacious middle-aged writer or man of science who is prone to deliver Wellsian messages at almost every opportunity. Yet a third is, of course, the young woman struggling to assert her rights in a predominantly masculine world. None of these is necessarily a major character; in many cases they could be regarded as virtually interchangeable, so striking is the similarity.

Of the physical features with which they are endowed, it is remarkable how many have been granted either squints or unevenly sized eyes. There are frequent descriptions of broad brows, notably among the heroines who are usually also dusky and dark-haired. It will be seen that Wells regularly, and curiously, paid considerably more attention to the physical details of his less important characters than to those of his central figures. In some cases he hardly bothered to describe his leading men at all; and this odd lapse is not merely confined to those stories where the narrative is conducted in the first person.

As might be expected in an author, so much of whose work is autobiographical, the topography of Wells's novels is almost exclusively devoted to those places he knew well. Settings along the Kent coast are extremely frequent, for he had lived overlooking Folkestone for a decade. Indeed, all the Home Counties of Southern England feature prominently in his work, while his descriptions of London itself, where he lived at intervals throughout his life, are usually finely drawn. He also enjoyed a fondness for the Continental Alps, and many of the holidays and retreats of his characters can be found among those mountains. In his fifties he spent several years in France, a country which provides the background for one or two of his later books.

He also travelled extensively in the United States and Soviet Russia (in fact, his first trips to the latter country pre-dated the Bolshevik Revolution). His earliest visit to the USA occurred in 1907 when he interviewed President Theodore Roosevelt. Twenty-seven years later he was to have a long discussion with Franklin Delano Roosevelt in the White House. In the meantime he had achieved a degree of notoriety by his various encounters with Lenin, Trotsky, Stalin, Pavlov and Gorki, in the USSR, as a result of which he was obliged to cross swords in the columns of the *New Statesman* (and elsewhere) with his old friend, George Bernard Shaw. The interested student can refer to these encounters, and subsequent disagreements, in the substantial body of literature already available. All that needs to be said here is that Wells's descriptions of expeditions to Russia (as recorded in several of his novels) are frequently vivid. His accounts of his characters' sojourns in North America are generally less well-outlined.

In much the same fashion the leisure-time pursuits of his principal characters reflect Wells's own interests. Chief among these in his youth was cycling, and the humble bicycle is pedalled through a large number of his early tales—even the Time Machine bears a marked resemblance to this means of propulsion. Later he came to love motoring, so that car journeys subsequently played an often significant part in his stories. He was also a great enthusiast for games, particularly the more vigorous variety, and many of these found a place in his works. In less energetic moments he would resort to playing miniature wars with toy soldiers or to indulging in charades; examples of these pastimes can be discovered in *The New Machiavelli* and *Brynhild* respectively.

Wells's love of the road clearly brought him into contact with many of its habitues. He had an especial gift for depicting tramps and other wanderers, investing them with a range of vivid personalities, from the sly and dishonest to the resigned and philosophical. Above all they were human, comic, mischievous, and sometimes absurd. Wells shared with these vignettes of his own creation the same mischievous sense of fun; he had a ready eye for the absurd. He suffered the compulsion on many occasions to swap hats with his friends, knowing full well what the result was likely to be. For all its contents, his head was small. A photograph in Sir David Low's autobiography bears witness to one such exchange; the cartoonist's homburg has settled around H.G.'s ears. In his long and argumentative friendship with G. K. Chesterton he became intrigued by the considerable disparity in their physical size, a difference emphasized by the fact that they both spoke in high almost squeaky tones, so that a newcomer to their argument might easily have imagined that they were imitating one another. Lance Sieveking tells in *The Eye of the Beholder* (1957) how they arranged to be photographed together in the nude, to record for posterity the comic absurdity of their respective bulk, although posterity is still hunting for the print.

Another common feature of many of his novels is the convoluted love-lives of his leading male characters. More often than not they first enter into relationships with women for whom they experience overwhelming physical desire but to whom they subsequently find they are mentally entirely unsuited. Later they encounter a more appropriate partner; but the web of circumstances—or the incidents of fate—frequently stand between them and the lasting attainment of familial peace. Such was Wells's own experience in his personal life, and a great number of his stories are infected with his own restless search for an ideal which he was realist enough to know was unlikely to exist. There can be few writers who have portrayed more broken marriages, more misunderstandings and petty antagonisms which ultimately assume the proportions of insurmountable obstructions. It can be argued that Wells was mistaken in ascribing to many of his creations the essential character-traits of a writer: necessary isolation (and therefore loneliness), self-centredness accompanied by regular bouts of deep introspection, and working-hours and habits to which only the rare woman can find herself able—or willing—to adjust. He tended to judge all men by his own yardstick; he seemed to assume that every serious-thinking person had run a similar gamut. He was quick to denounce those who professed an unwillingness to share the same point of view. But that is the mark of a writer. In a writer of genius, which Wells undoubtedly was—if not always consistently—the tendency is apt to become disproportionate.

Perhaps more than any other author of his generation, Wells mirrored his times. In his fiction there live the aspirations, dashed hopes, disillusionment, social unrest and international ferment which characterized his life-span from 1866 until 1946. Encoded there, too, are the explosive ideas—on sex, education, religion, republicanism, and visions of the culminating World State. It is perhaps no coincidence that he was born in the same year that dynamite was invented. 'I doubt', George Orwell wrote in his essay, 'Wells, Hitler, and the World State,' 'whether anyone who was writing books between 1900 and 1920, at any rate in the English language, influenced the young so much. The minds of us all, and therefore the physical world, would be perceptibly different if Wells had never existed.'

He wrote with haste, and his judgments likewise proved often hasty. He was quite unabashed at contradicting himself when events overtook his prognoses, but his general overriding message is astonishing in its consistency. Although at times it verged on the kaleidoscopic, its two basic elements have never been in doubt : 'Adapt or perish' and 'The outlook for mankind is a race between education and catastrophe.' If some of his stories have now fallen into the discard, there is one area of literature, at least, where his name is accorded almost universal reverence—the realm of science fiction. Every one of his scientific romances remains in print, and few enthusiasts of the genre would contest the labelling of Wells as 'the Father of Modern Science Fiction'. Far better than Verne, who tended to become embroiled in technical details, Wells demonstrated his mastery of the 'imaginative jump'. Ever alive to the process of change, he knew that whatever the future held in store, it would be vastly different from anything that most people expected. He allowed his imagination to 'play about' prospects. The result, in the view of Robert A. Heinlein—a leading American science-fiction author—'was a flood of some of the most brilliant speculative stories about the future ever written. As prophecy they are all hopelessly dated . . . which matters not at all; they are as spellbinding now as they were in the Gay Nineties and the Mauve Decade.'

Since his death Wells has been called 'The Man Who Invented Tomorrow', a soubriquet he would have undoubtedly loathed. Nevertheless, he set down a series of plot ideas—new ways of looking at things to come, at science and technology, at human society and all its institutions—which have proved immensely fertile in the hands of his heirs, the science-fiction writers of today. Brian Aldiss has named him 'the Prospero of all the brave new worlds of the mind, and the Shakespeare of science fiction'. Thus the characters of his scientific romances take their place here beside those of his 'discussion' works and the enduring figures of his four 'true' novels: *Love and Mr. Lewisham*, *Kipps*, *The History of Mr. Polly* and *Tono Bungay*. Many have the stuff of survival in them.

There is a final element which is so widespread in Wells's writing that it is curious how many commentators should have chosen to overlook it—his constant opposition to élitist culture. The Big House at Up Park, where his mother was housekeeper, provided him with a vision of an élite society which he came to despise. As his son Anthony (by Rebecca West) has remarked in 'My Father's Unpaid Debts of Love' (*Observer* 11th January, 1976) :

'H.G.'s attack on James in the novel 'Boon', published in 1915, is normally represented as a caddish young man's attack on a dear old boy, but the substance of the book (which dealt only incidentally with Henry James) was a sustained assault on élitist culture as such, one of the few that had been made in the English language by a writer of any stature.'

West argues that it is necessary to return to Up Park and to see it again through his father's eyes—'the unchallengeably beautiful thing by aesthetic standards which is a monument to selfish indifference, to injustice and human suffering'. He suggests that *The Time Machine* shows how Wells viewed Up Park as an eventual self-destructive mechanism in its revelation of the disparity of life between the above and below stairs inhabitants. The underground Morlocks of the novel were the descendants of a serving and working class who had been so degraded that they finally became the destroyers of the effete Eloi who passed an idyllic existence on the surface. In effect Wells was saying that an élitist culture was a menace to civilization because it caused those whom it held in subjugation to hate both it and anything with which it seemed to be connected. West continues :

'My father recognized that he had a choice to make at about the same time that he recognized the beauty of Up Park by being given the run of its library. He could either make use of his gift as a creative writer to produce *objets d'art*, crafted pieces for incorporation into the décor of the existing establishment, or he could rise to the challenge of the times and make himself a contributor to the great debate about the way in which the unfinished business of the French Revolution should be handled, and a new social order brought into being that would be responsible and just. I can only respect him for making the choice that he did, and for having devoted his talents to what has been in our time the honourable cause.'

The Compiler can do no more than add his own endorsement to that final sentence.

A few words as to how this compilation has been devised will help guide the student and interested reader. All H.G.'s identifiable novels and short stories are listed in Appendices One and Two, together with their original publishers and (in the case of the novels) full sub-titles and dedications. In each instance the name of the leading character is also given, and in the entry under that name a synopsis of the story will be found. Every synopsis generally contains the names of those other characters for which entries have been compiled (or else they are mentioned in adjoining entries under the same surname), so that the reader may—if he or she chooses—make a logical progression from the plot to the leading personalities involved. Details of stage adaptations have also been included, but not of the musicals which have been based on a number of Wells's tales. Among these may be mentioned *Half a Sixpence* (1963), based on *Kipps, Ann Veronica* (1969) and *Mr. Polly* (1977).

Film productions, of which there have been more than twenty since 1909, have been excluded, as have several British television adaptations. Details of these may be found in *H. G. Wells: A Comprehensive Bibliography* (Third Edition 1972) published by the H. G. Wells Society. Numerous radio versions have been broadcast during the past five decades, of which the most memorable—if only for its notoriety—was Orson Welles's production of *The War of the Worlds* in the United States on 30th October, 1938. Its realism persuaded a great many listeners that an invasion from Mars was genuinely in progress. Their alarmed reaction prompted Wells to cable : 'Unwarranted liberties were taken with my work.' It is hoped that a similar response, dispensed perhaps through the medium of a Wellsian Time Machine, will not be the fate of this present book.

Brian Ash
Summer 1978

A

ADYE, COLONEL : Chief of the Burdock police force who answers a
call from Dr. Kemp when the Invisible Man has blundered into
his house. Adye attempts to arrest the interloper with the help of
two constables, but is overpowered. Following Kemp's advice he
organizes a substantial manhunt and places the local countryside
under near-curfew restrictions. He is again visiting Kemp when
the Invisible Man returns to kill the doctor, and he is shot in the
ensuing siege. Kemp believes him dead, but he is referred to as
still at work in the epilogue which Wells added for the American
edition of the tale. *The Invisible Man*, 1897

ALBERT, PRINCE KARL : Son of the German Emperor, 'darling of the
Imperialist spirit in Germany', and commander of the zeppelin
fleet which attacks North America in *The War in the Air*. Something of a stock character in the then prevailing English appraisal
of the Teutonic personality—hard, arrogant, aloof and ruthless.
He destroys the better part of Broadway, in New York City, before his craft is damaged and drifts aimlessly to Canada. He
survives the destruction of his relief flagship during a losing battle
with the Asian fleet, and he is finally shot by Bert Smallways on
Goat Island beside the Niagara Falls. *The War in the Air*, 1908

ALIMONY, AGATHA : A spinster friend of Lady Beach-Mandarin
whose awareness of women's rights and needs does much to
decide Ellen Harman upon her course of action. She is 'one of
that large and increasing number of dusky, grey-eyed ladies who
go through life with an air of darkly incomprehensible significance'. She first meets Lady Harman at a Shakespearian luncheon where she immediately adopts a conspiratorial tone,
hinting that 'they'—meaning men—know very little of the
deeper secrets of a woman's nature. Once women get the vote,
she argues, they will achieve autonomy. When Ellen later confronts Sir Isaac with her demand for 'autonomy', he is at a loss to
understand what she means. On her escape from the country

I

house where she has been kept a virtual prisoner, she calls on Agatha in the hope that she will give her refuge. Unexpectedly, Miss Alimony appears horrified that Ellen has run away from her husband and insists that she return to continue the fight within her own home. Her rejection leads to the window-breaking incident which results in Lady Harman's imprisonment. *The Wife of Sir Isaac Harman*, 1914

AMERTON, FATHER : A Roman Catholic priest of some renown, he is a member of Cecil Burleigh's car party during its unwitting elevation into Utopia. A well-nourished man in appearance, with a round and plump clean-shaven face—he proves the bane of Mr. Barnstaple's open-minded appreciation of a world in which religion has been consigned to the former 'Age of Confusion'. Amerton's condemnation of the Utopians' enlightened view of their own Messiah is but one of many accusations with which he attempts to berate them. He is aghast at their disinclination to worship what he interprets as their own world's personification of the universal Christ. At one point his diatribes become so offensive that Burleigh is obliged to apologize on behalf of the Earthlings, while the Utopians themselves issue a muted threat that he is liable to be 'taken away ... examined and dealt with'. *Men Like Gods*, 1923

ANARCHIST, THE : A student who burns down the house of a police inspector in Wells's only known story of crime detection. When he steals the explosive from his college laboratory, he leaves his fingerprints on a jar wetted by colourless starch mucilage. Treated with a weak solution of iodine, the starch turns blue, revealing the prints. On discovery, the anarchist hurls bottles of acid at his instructor and colleagues, who retaliate by driving him off with two obnoxious gases—sulphuretted hydrogen and ammonium sulphide. He escapes through a window. The technique of fingerprinting was in its early stages at the time of writing, and the author took full advantage of its potential for identifying criminals. 'The Thumbmark', 1894

ANGEL, THE : The extraterrestrial visitant to the English country village of Siddermorton. His arrival is witnessed by a number of villagers in the locality who consider him no more than a strange bird. This also is the view of the vicar, Hillyer, who shoots him down before recognizing what he truly is. After the bandaging of his injured wings a discussion between the Angel and the vicar ensues, in which it is revealed that the former's world is populated by the mythical beasts of antiquity. The visitor, for his part, is astonished to discover that what are common animals to men are regarded as mythological in his own sphere. He is quite unfamiliar with the necessity for eating, has had no former experience of pain, and is unaware of the process of death.

The curate's wife and daughters express alarm at the Angel's appearance on his being brought into the vicarage, but are rapidly calmed. Doctor Crump is fetched to attend to the wounds, only to be intrigued by the presence of angelic wings. To the Angel's disconcertion he suggests that it might be desirable to amputate them, assuming them to be merely an extraordinary development on what is an otherwise normal man. He remains unconvinced by the vicar's assertion that this is a genuine angel. Others of the inhabitants, including the curate, form a similar opinion. In this light the vicar is concerned regarding the Angel's reception by the larger world.

The following day the vicar continues the education of his charge into the ways of men. He is enraptured by the Angel's performance on the violin, having never heard music so ethereal, and declaring that he himself will never play the violin again. In the Angel's later explorations of the area, various misconceptions arise from his own ignorance and from the wary suspicions of those he encounters. He is rejected by some as an odd-looking hunchback, since his wings are now concealed beneath a coat. He is challenged to fight by a truculent drunk whose condition he cannot understand. A number of small boys jeer at his shoulder-length hair and pelt him with beech-nut husks.

Later he is accompanied by Hillyer to meet Lady Hammergallow, the ancient resident of Siddermorton House, who is interested in his musical skills and suggests to the worried vicar that she make him her protegé. In a further consultation with the doctor, that worthy now accepts his story, assuming him to be the soul of a departed. Grump asks whether new arrivals in his world complain about their former medical attendants. The Angel is obliged to explain that he is unaware of the existence of a life after death and that therefore he has clearly not come from what the doctor regards as the true Angelic Land.

Further encounters in the village include a philosophical discussion with a very typical Wellsian tramp, until the Angel discovers his attraction for Delia, the vicar's waiting maid. In the

3

meantime Lady Hammergallow has arranged his musical debut at her home, where he enchants the invited audience but puzzles them by his inability to read music or to perform conventional works. At the same gathering the Angel's misunderstanding of the refined habits of the gentility creates considerable indignation and the evening ends in fiasco. Further trouble is in store when it is disclosed that he has destroyed the barbed-wire fence of a local landowner, Sir John Gotch. Depressed, he confesses that he must be putting the vicar to a terrible inconvenience.

Returning to the vicarage, he again plays, but for his own comfort, and is also overheard by an enchanted Delia. The following day the Angel is warned by Dr. Crump that he is causing unrest in the village, and that unless he leaves soon the doctor will ensure that he is either imprisoned or committed to an asylum. This threat is reinforced by Gotch, in an interview with the vicar. He reveals that the Angel has been preaching socialism to the inhabitants, in addition to committing various acts of trespass. Much disturbed, Hillyer agrees to expel his guest within a week. To him it is an agonizing decision, for he realizes that the Angel will prove incapable of finding employment or even looking after himself unassisted. However, when even his own housekeeper insists that the Angel must go, he comes to the reluctant conclusion that there is no alternative. Learning of the decision, the Angel grows increasingly disconsolate. He attempts several efforts at flight on the vicarage lawn, but his wings have become shrivelled and useless. Collapsing in grief, he is comforted by Delia whom he now recognizes as a kindred spirit.

As a final demonstration of his horror of human society, he savagely assaults Gotch, leaving him for dead. Once his anger has abated, and given way to remorse, he returns to find the vicarage on fire and is told that Delia has run back into the conflagration to rescue the violin. Impetuously, he joins her and they both perish. A child onlooker later claims to have seen two winged figures rising together in the flames. The vicar himself becomes progressively withdrawn and dies within the year.

The story, which appeared in the same year as *The Time Machine*, continues the criticism of the established order of late Victorian society which Wells began in the earlier work. It contains further examples of social injustice and of man's inhumanity to man. Many years later the author collaborated with St. John Ervine in dramatizing the novel for a stage production at the St. Martin's Theatre, in London, during 1921. *The Wonderful Visit*, 1895

4

ANGEL OF GOD, THE : The guide of Edward Scrope during his First and Second Visions when the Bishop is experiencing the effects of an hallucinogenic drug. A 'figure of great strength and beauty, with a smiling face and kindly eyes', he is first mistaken by Scrope for God Himself. During the First Vision he enters into a metaphysical discussion with the Bishop, dismissing almost off-hand the complexities of the Athanasian Creed. To end the Vision he takes the troubled cleric into the actual presence of the Almighty.

In the Second Vision he presents Scrope with a dazzling view of the entire Earth, allowing him to overhear the arguments and convictions regarding the nature of God by people of many different countries. The general impression given is of the universal brotherhood of the human race and the coming unity of mankind, in other words the Kingdom of God on Earth. *The Soul of a Bishop*, 1917

ANTHONY, MASTER : A young boy whose encounter with a German airship is told in a very short story which was illustrated by Wells himself. Master Anthony subdues the aggressive dirigible, encouraging it to make a nest and produce eggs ! The little piece was done for *Princess Marie-José's Children's Book* in 1916, and the volume was published for the Vestiare Marie-José, a society devoted to the provision of milk, food and clothes for babies behind the firing line in Flanders. 'Master Anthony and the Zeppelin', 1916

ARCHBISHOP, THE : The only character in a very short story which Wells wrote at the time of the abdication of King Edward VIII. The exalted cleric finds himself suffering from loss of confidence and a failure of nerve, from which the reassurance of his friends cannot relieve him. For the first time in many years he directs a personal plea to God, in place of the countless stereotyped prayers which his office has demanded of him. When he addresses himself to his maker, he is met by a genuine voice answering coldly : 'Yes. What is it?' The Archbishop is found dead the next morning, his face contorted in an extremity of terror and dismay. 'Answer to Prayer', 1937

ARTILLERYMAN, THE : A stoical and resourceful soldier possessing a strong instinct for self-preservation. He first meets the narrator of *The War of the Worlds* when he takes refuge in the latter's house in Surrey. He is the sole survivor of a gun troop which has just been destroyed by a Martian fighting machine and, having recovered some of his composure, he is able to bring his host up to date on the progress of the invasion. The following day they venture out, to be encountered by a Lieutenant of Hussars who orders the artilleryman to report to a General at Weybridge.

The two men meet again, and for the last time, some two weeks later on Putney Hill, from where they can view a large area of a desolated London. The artilleryman is building a tunnel from the cellar of a house and outlines his plans for a resistance movement to occupy the London sewers. He dreams of a day when underground guerrillas will capture a fighting machine and confront the Martians on an equal footing. But it is clear his proposed campaign *is* only a dream; though resourceful, he lacks the character to carry it out himself. Instead, he resorts to gluttony by raiding the house's well-stocked larder and wine cellar, and wastes valuable time playing cards. Disillusioned, and still anxious to reach Leatherhead in search of his wife, the narrator leaves him to his reveries. *The War of the Worlds*, 1898

AZUMA-ZI : The simple-minded native from the Straits Settlements who tends the great machine which is the true central character in the short story, 'The Lord of the Dynamos'. He sees the machinery as a god, and, after sacrificing the drunken supervisor, Holroyd, to his deity, he martyrs himself by throwing his body against the naked terminals. 'The Lord of the Dynamos', 1894

B

BACTERIOLOGIST, THE : The narrator of 'The Stolen Bacillus', who has developed a drug which affects the pigmentation of the skin and turns it blue. An anarchist, assuming the drug is a plague virus, steals a phial of the chemical and swallows it hoping thereby to infect the population of London, a method of protest which he feels more effective than throwing bombs. In fact, as the plot of the story reveals, the only effect is that he himself turns blue. 'The Stolen Bacillus', 1894

BAILEY : The incapacitated hero of 'Through a Window', who witnesses from his bed an extraordinary chase when a Malay servant from a nearby estate runs amok with a huge knife. Eventually the Asian arrives in Bailey's room, where he is shot by one of his pursuers only moments before adding the invalid to his list of victims. 'Through a Window', 1894

BAILEYS, THE : Oscar and Altiora, a leading intellectual couple in the Liberal revival through whom Remington is re-united after an interval of five years with his future wife. A political journalist, Oscar is of Anglo-Hungarian extraction and a brilliant scholar, collecting degrees in several provincial universities before proving at Balliol to be 'the most formidable dealer in exact fact the rhetoricians of the Union had ever had to encounter'. In his attention to detail he is the perfect complement to his wife, whose ability to bring together a great variety of people in public affairs secures a wide audience for the results of their mutual research. They first meet Remington when he is taken to one of their 'evenings' by his friend Willersley; they express no little interest in his recent book, *The New Ruler*. Thereafter he becomes a regular visitor to their home and receives their wholehearted encouragement in his political endeavours.

They are instrumental in his successful candidature as a Liberal Member of Parliament; and Altiora, in particular, is delighted with his marriage to Margaret—a union she has done much to promote. But it is she, also, who is to prove the most recriminating opponent when Remington foregoes his seat after a relatively short term to become editor of a right-wing weekly paper. When he re-enters Parliament as a 'New Imperialist', she engineers his downfall by deliberately spreading the scandal of his affair with Isabel Rivers, a liaison of which she has obtained details from Remington's former, and untrustworthy, male secretary.

There can now be no argument, and there was little at the time of the novel's publication, that the Baileys were intended as cutting portraits of Sidney and Beatrice Webb, the real-life leaders, together with Bernard Shaw and others, of the Fabian Society and founders of the *New Statesman*. Wells was settling an old score which arose from his failure to oust the Fabian 'Old Guard' a few years earlier, and when his own sexual adventures had been one of the weapons turned against him. His depiction of Beatrice as Altiora can only be described as malicious : '. . . her soul was bony, and at the base of her was a vanity gaunt and greedy !' He was also aggrieved that she had once suggested he was unsuitable for a certain public post because 'he had not the

7

manners for it'. However, she accepted the attack with some equanimity, even recommending her friends to read the book. *The New Machiavelli*, 1911

BALCH : A freelance journalist in his early fifties who befriends Stella Kentlake and Gemini Twain during their first stay in Suffolk. 'A large bluff face with an enormous loose mouth, large grey eyes with a slight cast, and quantities of iron-grey hair not only on the scalp but bursting generously from brows and ears'—his physical appearance is combined with an air of anxious benevolence as if he is relieved to discover things no worse than they are. He refers to the young couple as his *'wunderkinds'*, while they in turn describe him privately as 'the unquenchable Balch'—an epithet earned by his penchant for interminable harangues once launched on the subject of the vast possibilities which might be Man's. At the outbreak of the Second World War he joins the Ministry of Propaganda, with responsibility for Brazil, a post he discharges by providing the South Americans with a subtle indoctrination into such essential aspects of the British as Keble's 'Christian Year', the heroines of Jane Austen, and the nonsense verse of Edward Lear. *Babes in the Darkling Wood*, 1940

BARNET, FREDERICK : Author of *Wander Jahre*, an autobiographical novel published in 1970 which chronicles the writer's exploits during the Last War. A short, sturdy man, running to plumpness, with a 'rather blobby' nose and large protruding blue eyes. An able linguist, he has studied in Heidelberg and Paris before entering the classical school of London University. His father is ruined in the financial crash of 1956 and, reduced to penury, Barnet earns a meagre living by teaching and journalism. He describes the poverty which is widespread throughout the country during the final days of peace. As a volunteer reservist in the Army, he is mobilized at the beginning of the war and sent to France. His narrative depicts aerial dogfights and the effects of bombing. Later in Holland he witnesses the destruction of the dykes and the flooding of great areas of the countryside. He passes out of the story on his return to a devastated Britain when hostilities have ceased. *The World Set Free*, 1914

BARNSTAPLE, ALFRED : A liberal journalist who is unexpectedly propelled into Utopia while driving outside Slough. His journey through time and space has been caused by experiments in the fourth dimension conducted by Utopian scientists, and two other cars which had recently overtaken him arrive at the same destination. Barnstaple has originally set out to take a solitary holiday as a respite from his family and the disappointments of the international situation. At one time a firm believer in President Woodrow Wilson's 'Fourteen Points', he can see nothing but futility in the League of Nations in its finally established form (elsewhere Wells described the League as a little 'Balfourian corner of jobs and gentility').

Barnstaple is therefore all the more impressed with the Utopian order of things. In essence it is the same world as that of *A Modern Utopia*, but a further millennium forward in its development. The most noticeable difference from the earlier society is the complete absence of any ruling élite. The samurai have disappeared; or, more appropriately, everyone has risen to join their ranks. A further thousand years of selective breeding have banished criminality and dissidence for ever : 'Nearly all the greater evils of human life had been conquered; war, pestilence and malaise, famine and poverty had been swept out of human experience. The dreams of artists, of perfected and lovely bodies and of a world transfigured to harmony and beauty had been realized : the spirits of order and organization ruled triumphant.'

The Utopians have dispensed with the encumbrance of clothes and communicate, both between themselves and to their visitors, by telepathy—two aspects of their enhanced way of life which prove disconcerting to the majority of the newcomers. Of the occupants of the other cars, the chief are Lord Barralonga, a property magnate; the Conservative leader, Cecil Burleigh; and the Secretary of State for War, Rupert Catskill (the two last are respectively caricatures of Arthur Balfour and Winston Churchill). The remainder of their parties consist of an odd assortment of characters representing the clergy, the stage and the cinema, journalism and high society, together with a pair of oafish chauffeurs. Of these, only the socialite Lady Stella appears to share Barnstaple's favourable impression of Utopia, and then only on a superficial level. In one way or another the others demonstrate their inflexibility of outlook and their resistance to the process of change.

Father Amerton, from Burleigh's car, offers so vociferous a

9

condemnation of the Utopians' lack of ritual and religious worship that he is threatened with corrective treatment. Burleigh himself subjects them to a characteristically political harangue; while his chauffeur Penk is felled by a single blow from a young girl with whom he has attempted to interfere.

Most disruptive of all, however, is the man of action, Catskill. Determined to show that the everyday human species is superior to what he sees as a degenerate society, he marshalls the Earthlings—against all Barnstaple's inclinations—for an armed stand in the 'castle on the crag' where two of the Utopian spokesmen are shot by Barralonga's chauffeur Ridley. The Utopians respond by 'quarantining' the castle in the fourth dimension, and several of its occupants, including Barralonga, are killed by falling into infinity when they attempt to escape. The survivors are returned in due course to Earth. But Barnstaple, who requires nursing, remains.

On his recovery, he spends many hours with the ancient Sungold, in discussion of the evolution and philosophy of Utopia. He continues to be awestruck by its beauty and eventually departs for his own world, refreshed and cautiously hopeful : 'Some day here and everywhere, Life of which you and I are but anticipatory atoms and eddies, Life will awaken indeed, one and whole and marvellous, like a child awaking to conscious life. It will open its drowsy eyes and stretch itself and smile, looking the mystery of God in the face as one meets the morning sun. We shall be there then, all that matters of us . . .'

The novel is a more dramatic treatment of an ideal society than its predecessor by eighteen years, *A Modern Utopia*. But just as the earlier work had brought a reaction against the Wellsian technological paradise in E. M. Forster's 'The Machine Stops' (1909), so *Men Like Gods* prompted Aldous Huxley to attack its concepts in his noted *Brave New World* (1932). Both writers freely admitted that they had deliberately set out to criticize what they regarded as Wells's mechanistic view of a perfect world. *Men Like Gods*, 1923

BARRACK, DR. ELIHU : A general practitioner at Sundering on Sea who is consulted by Job Huss when the headmaster experiences a pain in his side. Cancer is suspected, a diagnosis which later proves unsound, and the doctor arranges for an operation to be performed by the surgeon, Sir Alpheus Mengo. Barrack is in his thirties, a round-headed, clean-shaven and determined man who has lost a leg (possibly in the First World War which is drawing to its close). He joins in the discussion between Huss and his three visitors while they await the arrival of the surgeon, siding with Job in many of his arguments.

Acting out the earlier rôle of Elihu the son of Barachel the Buzite, he questions Job's concept that the Spirit of God exists in every man and finds the idea of universal brotherhood on this basis distasteful. Agreeing that personal immortality is probably a myth, he sees no overriding meaning in individual existence other than what a man will make of it at his own will. While egotistical, he is clearly dedicated to his vocation, and as a realist he sees the value of extending education to embrace religion and politics as a proper preparation for adult life. *The Undying Fire*, 1919

BARRALONGA, LORD AND PARTY : The travellers in the first car to be precipitated through the space-time continuum to Utopia. Their violent arrival is a cause for consternation among that world's inhabitants, for they run down and kill a silver cheetah and subsequently a Utopian named Gold with little inclination to stop. A business entrepreneur, Barralonga is small, youngish, with thinning hair, 'who suffers very gravely from a disordered liver and kidneys'. A fortune accumulated by property speculation has enabled him to 'buy' his title. He dies by falling into limbo when the castle in which the Earthlings have been confined is plunged into quarantine through another dimension.

Of the other members of his party, Hunker is an American movie magnate who remains very much in the background. Émile Dupont introduces himself as a Gallic journalist with a particular interest in the educational and propaganda uses of the cinema. Unaware of the telepathic nature of the Utopians' form of communication, he asserts that the *linqua franca* of their world can hardly be other than French! The feminine interest is represented by Greeta Grey, a popular actress of vacuous mentality who attempts to emulate the Utopians' lack of attire, but has neither the figure nor the complexion for such pretence. Her sole concern is to return to Earth in time to fulfil her next theatrical engagement.

Ridley, the chauffeur, is a comparable, if more articulate, character to his counterpart in Cecil Burleigh's party, Penk. His reaction to the blow with which a Utopian girl discourages Penk's unsolicited attentions is characteristic :

' "Why! If there's one sign more sure than another about degeneration it's when women take to knocking men about. It's against instink. In any respectable decent world such a thing couldn't possibly 'ave 'appened. No 'ow."

"No 'ow," echoed Penk.

"In *our* world, such a girl would jolly soon 'ave 'er lesson. Jolly soon. See?" '

In response to the aggressive exhortations of Rupert Catskill, Ridley shoots the Utopian spokesmen Cedar and Serpentine when they approach the castle for what was intended as a peaceful talk. *Men Like Gods*, 1923

BATES, MASTER TOMMY : Not his real name, of course, as the author assures the young reader for whom he wrote and personally illustrated this children's story while he was ill towards the beginning of his writing career. Out fishing one day, Tommy saves a rich man from drowning. Refusing to accept money as a reward, he asks instead for a pet. To his surprise and delight, he is presented ostentatiously with an elephant.

The manuscript of the tale remained in the possession of the family with whom Wells had stayed during his illness at the turn of the century, and it was not published until some thirty years later. *The Adventures of Tommy*, 1929

BAYNES, EDWIN PEAK : A very young aspiring poet whose manuscripts are typed by Ethel Lewisham in an attempt to supplement her husband's income. Unbeknown to him, he very nearly becomes the cause of Lewisham leaving his wife. She guiltily assumes that the roses, which Lewisham has sent as a gesture of reconciliation, are a gift from Baynes and hides them under her bed. A bitter row ensues when Lewisham learns of her misapprehension, although she is quite innocent of any of his charges. *Love and Mr. Lewisham*, 1900

BEACH-MANDARIN, LADY : An effusive friend of the author Brumley and a champion of Lady Harman's struggle for freedom. A 'gallant full-rigged lady', blue-eyed and pink of complexion, she gives the impression of 'a broad abundant billowing personality with a taste for brims, streamers, pennants, panniers, loose sleeves, sweeping gestures, top notes, and the like that made her altogether less like a woman than an occasion of public rejoicing'. Her chin, brows and nose all appear 'racing up to the front of her as if excited by the clarion notes of her abundant voice'. She is particularly keen to involve Lady Harman in her efforts to establish a Shakespearian theatre, much to Sir Isaac's disapproval. Attempting to call on Ellen Harman when Sir Isaac has virtually incarcerated his wife in the country, she is turned away; but her support during the subsequent flowering of Ellen's social and altruistic ambitions proves valuable. She is also mentioned in *The Research Magnificent*. *The Wife of Sir Isaac Harman*, 1914

BEALBY, ARTHUR : Stepson of the gardener at Shonts, the country home of Sir Peter and Lady Laxton. Forced into service understairs at the age of thirteen, he adopts a truculent attitude which makes him the target of abuse by the other servants. Tormented beyond endurance, he stabs a footman, Thomas, with a toasting fork and flees to the upper part of the house where he cannons headlong into the back of the Lord Chancellor, Moggeridge, an accident that leads to dire consequences for the head butler, Mergleson. Unaware of the furore this simple accident will cause, he escapes through a secret passage and leaves the house in the morning. Thus begins a chain of adventures, each more disastrous than its predecessor.

Within hours of deserting Shonts, he is befriended by three women holidaying in a horse-drawn caravan who employ him as a boy Friday. Much taken with one of the trio, the actress Madeleine Philips (the others being Winifred Geedge and Judith Bowles), Bealby performs his tasks with an enthusiasm he failed to display in the Laxton household. However, when the party's menfolk arrive after a few days, he feels it is time to move on. Inadvertently, he disturbs a chock restraining the wagon on the brow of a hill, watching in dismay as it hurtles downward and through the village below carrying its disagreeable driver, William, with it.

Fearful of the woods at night, he seeks refuge at the campfire of a tramp, Billy Bridget, who not only relieves him of his meagre shillings, but also insists on taking him into partnership. Reluctantly, Bealby is forced to attempt a burglary, in a house where he discovers a dead man. Conscience-stricken by the experience, he resolves to part from the tramp, and does so at the first opportunity. Coming across a notice in a shop, he discovers there is a price on his head and assumes it is a result of the burglary (in fact it is no more than an effort by Lady Laxton to ascertain his whereabouts, having overturned Shonts in a futile search). He is quickly recognized by a shopkeeper and a hue and cry begins. In its course, Bealby hurls tiles at his pursuers from a rooftop and leads a disorganized collection of tradesmen, police and hangers-on—including the tramp—across the strawberry beds of a market gardener, much to that person's dismay. Evading capture, he spends a lonely night in a shed, interrupted by the tramp who also shelters there briefly, unaware of Bealby's presence, and is rescued next morning by Captain Douglas just as a fresh pursuit is about to begin. Returned to Shonts, he promises his mother that, given another chance, he will try harder to succeed as a serving-boy.

Wells sub-titled the story 'A Holiday', and it is clear it was as much a holiday for himself as for the reader, for he was busily engaged, among other things, with intensive journalism during the First World War. Much of the background of the tale is drawn from his own experience—he, too, was the son of a gardener, and at the age of thirteen spent some time in the servants' quarters at Up Park, near Petersfield, where his mother was housekeeper. Bealby's final acceptance of his lot, a fate against which the young Wells would almost certainly have continued to rebel, is uncharacteristic and suggests that other work may have compelled the author to contrive a hasty ending. *Bealby: A Holiday*, 1915

BECHAMEL : A writer and reviewer, some thiry-five years of age, who entices Jessica Milton to flee from her stepmother and join him on a bicycling escapade through the South-East of England. Fair-haired and moustached, he has a pale face, an aquiline nose, and a demeanour of marked self-importance. Although married, he has prevailed on Jessie to accompany him on the pretence that he can help her to establish herself as a writer—his true intentions are less innocent. They stay at a number of wayside inns posing as a brother and sister named Beaumont, he becoming increasingly irritated by the apparent pursuit of Hoopdriver whom he eventually mistakes for a private detective employed by either his wife or Mrs. Milton. His announcement in Bognor that he has Jessie in his power prompts her to enlist Hoopdriver's aid in escaping. *The Wheels of Chance*, 1896

BEDFORD, MR. : A young aspiring playwright and the narrator of an extraordinary journey to the moon. Unsuccessful business speculations have forced him into bankruptcy and he has retired

14

into virtual hiding at Lympne, on the South Coast, at the opening of the story. There his solitude is disturbed by the nightly excursions of Cavor, a local eccentric and inventor with whom he becomes friendly. Cavor explains his theory of gravity and the means he is devising to overcome its effects. Basically this is a substance which will act as a gravity-shield.

Bedford is intrigued by the commercial prospects for Cavor's projected invention and persuades the reluctant physicist to take him into partnership. The first experimental manufacture of cavorite comes near to universal disaster. It creates a roaring vortex of air which is hurled into space and would, if continued indefinitely, dissipate the Earth's entire atmosphere. Fortunately, the cavorite itself is carried up in the turbulence, but not before half the village has been wrecked. Bedford and Cavor are happy to acquiesce in the general assumption that the cataclysm has natural causes. The next experiment proves successful.

Bedford is now prepared to begin commercial exploitation and is astonished when Cavor announces his intention of using the discovery to power a spacecraft. Against his better judgement he assists in the construction of a metal sphere which is encased in cavorite in the form of roller-blinds. Motive force is applied to the craft by the simple process of opening and closing the blinds. The pair embark for the moon with much trepidation on Bedford's part, although Cavor remains supremely confident. The journey passes uneventfully, a graphic and realistic account of the lunar terrain being given before the sphere lands.

Viewed from the craft, the moon's surface appears inhospitable and largely covered with snow. But with the coming of day a unique transformation occurs. Before the incredulous watchers the snow boils off to form an atmosphere, revealing a carpet of seed-pods which germinate instantaneously. A lush vegetation rises within minutes and obliterates the rocky landscape, so rapidly that Bedford draws a parallel with the opening of Genesis :

'So, one must imagine, the trees and plants arose at the Creation and covered the desolation of the new-made earth.

'Imagine it! Imagine that dawn! The resurrection of the frozen air, the stirring and quickening of the soil, and then this silent uprising of vegetation, this unearthly ascent of fleshiness and spikes. Conceive it all lit by a blaze that would make the intensest sunlight of earth seem watery and weak. And still around this stirring jungle, wherever there was a shadow, lingered banks of bluish snow.'

Venturing out of the sphere, the pair find the atmosphere breathable, and they pass some while in the heady pursuit of running and jumping under the moon's reduced gravity. They are amazed by their first sight of a mooncalf, a vast lumbering beast two-hundred feet in length and eighty feet around. Even more unexpected is the appearance of its herder, a lowly type of Selenite whose humanoid form, but insect-like structure, excites Cavor's imagination. In the dense undergrowth the explorers lose sight of the sphere and realize they are lost. During their search, and overcome with hunger, Bedford eats an innocuous seeming fungus; finding it palatable, he persuades his companion to do the same. Both become thoroughly intoxicated, and in this condition they are captured and taken beneath the surface.

They awake to find themselves chained hand-and-foot and guarded by a noseless, earless Selenite. After being fed, they are forced at spearpoint along a series of passageways until they come to the brink of a chasm. Illumination is provided by a strange liquid running in gulleys along the floor and glowing with a blue light before it falls in a cascade into the depths. Bedford recoils at the attempts of his captors to force him over a narrow plank bridging the void and, wrenching off his chains, he turns to attack them. To his surprise, he finds their bodies can literally be smashed by the impact of a single blow. When they retreat in terror he and Cavor escape to a higher level, and a further affray takes place in the chamber where the mooncalves are butchered. Finally regaining the surface, Bedford discovers that the chains and a spear he has seized are solid gold. The revelation persuades him that a conquest of the moon could prove highly profitable. Cavor, in his turn, is more concerned to learn of the lunar civilization, convinced that beings of high intelligence must exist in the deeper levels. They decide to separate in an effort to find the sphere, and shortly before the onset of night Bedford comes in sight of it. His efforts to locate Cavor fail; he realizes, on discovering a blood-stained note, that the other has been recaptured. He struggles back to the sphere as the first snow begins to fall.

By good fortune, the inexperienced Bedford manages to pilot himself to a random landing in the sea at Littlestone, off the Kent coast, fortuitously close to their launching point. The gold he has retrieved enables him henceforth to live with some ease, but the sphere is accidentally activated on the water's edge by an inquisitive boy who, together with the vehicle, disappears into space. So far as Bedford is concerned the adventure is at an end and he assumes Cavor to be dead. He is therefore taken aback to hear from a Dutch electrician who is receiving radio messages from the inventor. These arrive in disjointed instalments, but taken together they convey an intelligible account of Cavor's subsequent experiences inside the moon. He describes at some length the structure of the Selenite society, explaining how each individual is shaped—often by force—to equip him for the task he has been allotted. Perhaps the most unusual Senenite feature is the enlargement of the brain-case in the higher intellectuals and 'memory-carriers', some being so distended that the individuals concerned must be carried on litters. Most pronounced of all is the ruling Grand Lunar, whose brain-case measures many yards in circumference and requires the constant support of a host of attendants and the application of cooling sprays. One of the more advanced of the Selenites has learned Cavor's language and acts as an interpreter during an audience with the moon's supreme intelligence.

The Grand Lunar questions Cavor closely on the ways of men and is astonished to learn of their lack of proper organization. It seems clear that Cavor also betrays the secret formula for the manufacture of the anti-gravity shield. His last message ends abruptly in a futile attempt to pass the same knowledge to Earth, and it marks the end of the tale.

Some commentators have seen the novel as a warning against the dangers of specialization, citing the Selenite civilization as a soulless society in which the *sole* function of the citizen is to serve the state. In one passage Cavor comes across a group of Selenites lying insensible on the ground : they are workers whose services are temporarily un-needed. There is no alternative to the duties for which they have been moulded but oblivion. One noted critic of the story was Jules Verne himself, who objected on the grounds of scientific plausibility to the method of the sphere's propulsion. 'I sent my characters to the moon with gunpowder', he wrote, 'a thing one may see every day. Where does Monsieur Wells find his cavorite? Let him show it to me !' For Wells, however, as he was to indicate on many occasions, the experience of arrival was more important than any amount of hopeful journeying. *The First Men in the Moon*, 1901

BELLACOURT : World Air Director under Rud Whitlow and the

man chiefly responsible for the overthrow of Marshal Reedly's attempted coup. He is a brilliant aeronautical engineer who has fought against Franco in the Spanish Civil War and consequently developed a hatred of aerial bombing. He has written many pamphlets calling for a 'World Control of Aviation' and he allies himself with Rud, believing that the Common-sense Party is the most likely movement to achieve it. He assumes control of the Allied air forces in the final disintegrating stages of the Second War to End War, and his bombers obliterate Reedly's head-quarters in Poland where the Marshal has independently, and contrary to orders, accepted the German surrender. *The Holy Terror*, 1939

BELLOWS, MR. : The narrator of the short piece 'Le Mari Terrible'. Actually more of a vignette than a story, it gives a brief glimpse of the relationship between a flighty woman and her cynical husband. The sketch remains as yet uncollected in the U.K.; it appeared in the U.S.A. in 1897 as the twenty-first item in the collection, *Thirty Strange Stories*. 'Le Mari Terrible', 1897

BENHAM, AMANDA : The wife of William, whom he meets during his solitary walking-tour of Sussex. She is nineteen at their first encounter, when Benham is bitten by one of her dogs—a tall, slim girl with dark brown hair and glowing face, 'half childish imp, half woman'. Above her honest hazel eyes her eyebrows are 'like the quick stroke of a camel's-hair brush'. Her voice is 'music' and her decision of character 'manifest'. Taken back to her home for treatment to his hand, he meets her mother and socialistically-minded aunt; but it is to Amanda Morris that his attention is drawn. His courtship is rapid, and his mother's revelation of the late Mr. Morris's disgrace leaves him undeterred.

After their marriage and honeymoon, Amanda is distressed by his persistent need to journey abroad. At first she assumes that she is to accompany him, only to find that he wishes to go alone, or occasionally with his friend, Prothero. Her letters to him, origin-ally warm and loving, grow increasingly trite, until he realizes that he has lost her. When he finally discovers her in the arms of Sir Philip Easton she begs him to forgive her, beat her, even kill her, insisting that there should be no divorce. With the passage of time, however, and in the light of Benham's continuing absence, she begins to suggest it would be 'better' for their marriage to be legally ended and asks that Benham take the blame. Initially his reaction is one of anger, but shortly before his death he is resigned to letting her have her way. *The Research Magnificent*, 1915

BENHAM, THE REVEREND HAROLD : Father of William and the headmaster of a high-class preparatory school at Seagate. In appearance he is very much 'the average of scholastic English gentlemen'. He is good-looking in a rather worn way, has a high narrow forehead, a large moustache, and tired brown eyes behind powerful glasses. He speaks somewhat formally with a sonorous voice. At first his school is extremely successful, but its fortunes decline when his wife elopes and he sues for divorce. His remarrying does little to improve matters, and his introduction of science teaching and the provision of a school library fail to attract the anticipated influx of new pupils.

Granted legal custody of his son, he intends to devote himself to the moulding of the boy by a process of moral and intellectual training, the subject of several stimulating articles he writes for *School World*. However, the constant worries about his own establishment lead to his neglect of the scheme, and he feels that his former wife exercises more influence on the young Benham than he does himself. His caution when pursuing his favourite sport of mountaineering proves irksome to the reckless William, who also grows weary of his father's regular resorts to Greek quotations. With minor exceptions he passes out of the narrative on Benham's departure for Cambridge. *The Research Magnificent*, 1915

BENHAM, WILLIAM PORPHYRY : The schoolmaster's son whose pursuit of the 'Research Magnificent' ruins his marriage and leads him across the world to an untimely death. His life-story is revealed in disjointed fashion by White, a former schoolfellow who is attempting to assemble Benham's many papers in the hope of book publication. Throughout the novel long quotations are given from Benham's manuscripts, interspersed by comments from White and sections of narrative written in the third person.

Benham is born in the 1880s at Seagate, on the South Coast. His early life is disrupted by his mother's elopement with a wealthy young adventurer who dies in Wiesbaden a few days after the senior Benham's divorce has been made absolute; later she marries a noted London surgeon, to become Lady Marayne. Benham is allowed to visit her quarterly as a boy, when he compares her warmth and affection favourably with the dutiful attentions he receives from his step-mother, for his father has also remarried. From his mother's deceased lover he has inherited an income of several thousand pounds a year, a sum which ensures his independence when he comes of age. His early education is acquired at Minchinghampton, a school at which his father once taught, and where he first meets a life-long friend, William Prothero.

Benham and Prothero go up to Cambridge together as undergraduates; the latter is to remain there as a don. He is first drawn to Benham by the other's display of courage, in such incidents as the challenging of an irate bull. In fact, Benham considers himself a coward and attempts feats of daring in an effort to overcome his natural fear. On one of the mountaineering holidays which he regularly spends with his father during his adolescence, he deliberately braves his horror of heights to cross the worn planks at the Bisse of Leysin, in France, where a single slip would hurl him over a precipice. Other characteristics which identify him as unusual at Minchinghampton are his atheism, his general dislike of animals, and his open hostility towards many of the masters.

On learning of his friendship with her son, Lady Marayne invites Prothero to stay at Chexington Manor. She suspects him of being a socialist and resolves that he should be 'thoroughly and conclusively led on, examined, ransacked, shown up, and disposed of for ever'. In the event she fails, and if anyone suffers a loss of esteem during Prothero's visit, it is Benham himself—by virtue of his atrocious handling of a horse-and-gig. At about this time the youth has begun writing essays, in which he endeavours to crystallize his view of life. The first of these, which White finds among his papers, is 'True Democracy', produced very much under Prothero's influence. In it Benham argues that men are by nature and in the most various ways unequal; thus true democracy can at the most secure the removal of artificial inequalities.

In a later, more mature, exposition he discusses his concept of a natural aristocracy, an idea which is to obsess him for the remainder of his life :

'I know there is a better life than this muddle about us, a better life possible now . . . If I had no other assurances, if I were blind to the glorious intimations of art, to the perpetually widening promise of science, to the mysterious beckonings of beauty in form and colour and the inaccessible mockery of the stars, I should still know this from the insurgent spirit within me . . .

'Now this better life is what I mean when I talk of Aristocracy. This idea of a life breaking away from the common life to something better, is the consuming idea in my mind.'

On leaving Trinity College, Benham takes a flat in London, which he furnishes according to his mother's advice, also accepting the manservant she has selected for him. The following twelve months are unproductive. He talks much, mixes with the hunting set where he meets young men whose minds are 'as flabby as Prothero's body', and begins an affair with Milly Skelmersdale, an attractive and sympathetic widow who grows much attached to him. There are hints that he might stand for Parliament, but he remains uncertain which political party he might represent. Finally, in a mood of intense dissatisfaction, he decides to go on a walking tour of Sussex, hoping that solitude will help him to plan his life.

He indeed comes to certain positive conclusions during the early part of his self-imposed isolation. He resolves to stand aside from the main body of politics and to join, if possible, with like-minded people in an effort to bring the two main opposing parties back to the consideration of sensible issues and away from what he regards as the irrelevancies of Home Rule for Ireland and Tariff Reform. He also determines to break with Milly Skelmersdale and, as a realization of his concept of natural aristocracy, to travel the world, learning how its diverse nations think—and how they are governed. It will be, he convinces himself, a 'Research Magnificent', with its end in the attainment of the larger life. Before the tour is over, however, he has fallen in love with Amanda Morris, who lives with her widowed mother and aunt at Harting Coombe, close to the country mansion Up Park. As a parting gift before his return to London, he gives her a copy of Plato's *Republic*, in support of his argument that socialism is inadequate.

The end of his affair with Milly is achieved without rancour, but Lady Marayne is distressed by his new romance, discovering that Amanda's father had committed suicide after being sentenced to seven years imprisonment for fraud. Benham's urge to go abroad is another cause for her concern; she cannot understand his—in her eyes—odd compulsions and regards her efforts to guide him towards a distinguished career a failure. Many of her reservations disappear when she actually meets Amanda, for she finds the girl enchanting. Benham has proposed to Amanda by suggesting that she accompany him around the world as his wife. The couple are married quietly at South Harting church, an occasion marred only by the obvious grief of the curate, whose devotion to Amanda necessitates his withdrawal to the vestry where 'an uproar of inadequately smothered sorrow' comes as 'an obbligato accompaniment to the more crucial passages of the service'.

A protracted honeymoon takes them on a journey through Switzerland, the Austrian Tyrol, North Italy, and along the Adriatic coast. Amanda discovers a hitherto concealed side of Benham's character when, in a fit of anger, he seizes the reins from the Italian driver and negotiates their carriage down a perilous mountain road. From the Adriatic they pass briefly into the Balkans, where they are deeply disturbed by the sight of a Bulgarian village in which the inhabitants have been massacred and mutilated as traitors. Soon afterwards Benham contracts measles, and it is with something approaching relief that they finally return to England.

Amanda, who has coined the nickname 'Cheetah' for her husband, and 'Leopard' for herself—an animal whose colour she sees rather mysteriously as black—is determined that they shall have a house in London. She is unfamiliar with the city and is excited by the notion of 'taking it by storm'. To Benham, who has learned to detest the capital, this fixation comes as a surprise, and he begins to realize how very far are Amanda's goals from his own predilections. In due course she gets her house, flinging herself wholeheartedly into the social round with the encouragement of Lady Marayne. Reluctantly she accepts Benham's suggestion that she remain in London while he visits Russia with Prothero, a course of action which dismays his equally indignant mother. Amanda begs him to make her pregnant, hoping that a child will dampen his wanderlust; but Benham will not be swayed from his intentions.

He finds Prothero in a state of considerable agitation : the don is tormented by his enforced celibacy. Their stay in Moscow is complicated by Prothero's attachment to a prostitute whom he wishes to marry and take back to Cambridge, a step which both Benham and the woman concerned know could only lead to unhappiness. In the event, she disappears. Benham pays a fleeting visit home to discover Amanda esconced in his mother's manor at Chexington, where she is expecting their child. He is noticeably galled by the familiarity shown by both his wife and Lady Marayne to Sir Philip Easton, a man of his own age who hardly troubles to disguise his sentiments towards Amanda, but whom he is assured is entirely honourable. His suspicions are justified when he next returns, having travelled through Russia and down as far as Karachi. Amanda has given birth to a son, but it is evident that she and Easton are lovers.

Benham strives to overcome his jealousy by appealing to his own sense of the aristocratic nature which should be capable of rising above such commonplace emotions. Eventually he succeeds, but not before contemplating killing his wife. Amanda asks his forgiveness, declaring that she does not want a divorce but only his presence. 'Cheetah', however, is adamant. He says he will continue to support her and she is free to continue her relationship with Easton. Having eased his feelings by wrecking an hotel bedroom, he departs to continue his travels. They take him far and wide : from Germany to the United States, to Haiti where he is imprisoned for assaulting a policeman who had been ill-treating a native woman, and on into China in the company of Prothero.

Over the years his actions have become progressively more hazardous and impulsive. Alone he braves the terrors of nights in the jungle, rescues ghetto Jews from persecution near Kiev, in Russia, until at last he is shot dead while trying to intervene in a clash between demonstrating strikers and the militia in Johannesburg. His final years have seen the passing of Prothero who, having succumbed to opium in China, is stabbed to death when Benham refuses to settle his debts with a gang of drug-pedlars, and also a change of mind on the part of Amanda who has begun to request a divorce. It is in South Africa that he renews his acquaintance with the journalist, White, who is with him when he dies. His final words are a plea to his former school-friend to make a book of his papers—a task which White is later to find almost impossible because of the diffuseness of the material.

So ends the inconclusive pursuit of the 'Research Magnificent', a passion that has proved more powerfully attractive to Benham than his love of his wife. Before its close he has identified what for him are the 'Four Limitations' to the soul of man : Fear, Indulgence, Jealousy and Prejudice. All these, he claims, may be overcome by an adherence to the 'Life Aristocratic' and he attributes the last of the quartet to human muddle-headedness : 'Man, I see, is an over-practical creature, too eager to get into action . . . He

23

takes conclusions ready-made, or he makes them in a hurry. Life is so short that he thinks it better to err than wait. He has no patience, no faith in anything but himself. He thinks he is a being when in reality he is only a link in a being, and so he is more anxious to be complete than right.'

Designed as a 'discussion' novel (although in this particular case the arguments are presented more in monologue form), the book was not particularly well received and its sales probably suffered as a result of the outbreak of the First World War shortly before its publication. Wells himself retained a high opinion of it and in later years was to lament that it had been largely forgotten. The mansion, Up Park, was the real house in which his mother had been housekeeper, and it was in its library that Wells first read Plato's *Republic* when he was a boy. *The Research Magnificent*, 1915

BENSINGTON, MR. : The co-developer, with Redwood, of 'Herakleophorbia', the growth-inducing chemical better known as 'the Food of the Gods'. A bald, shortish man, he is a Fellow of the Royal Society and one-time President of the Chemical Society, by virtue of his research into toxic alkaloids. When the outcry against the drug is at its height, it is assumed by many that Bensington is solely responsible for its discovery and his life is put in jeopardy. He promptly disappears from public view, and from the story, by securing refuge with his cousin Jane in Tunbridge Wells. *The Food of the Gods*, 1904

BERNSTEIN, RACHEL : Together with her brother Melchior, an ardent communist—and the first woman to introduce Theodore Bulpington to the experience of sexual fulfilment on his arrival in London. In effect, she seduces him, but with little resistance on his part despite his self-sworn loyalty to Margaret Broxted. Rachel tires of him rapidly, and her originally ardent physical overtures soon become perfunctory. A few years older than Theodore, she tends rather to toy with him during their brief liaison, summoning him by notes when the whim takes her until he acquires a flat of his own and reverses the procedure. On one occasion she expresses her conviction that almost any Gentile face is more interesting than a Jew's; that, however, does not prevent her eventually marrying a Zionist and emigrating to Palestine. *The Bulpington of Blup*, 1932

BESSEL, MR. : The amateur psychic researcher who finds himself in a dire predicament when he attempts an 'out-of-the-body' experiment with his fellow enthusiast Vincey. Bessel succeeds in attaining his non-corporeal objective, but on attempting to return he is horrified to find that one of the evil phantoms, which have swirled about him in whatever limbo he has entered, has taken possession of his body. Vincey hears disconcerting reports of Bessel running amok through London, causing untold injury and damage, but always evading capture. He witnesses one such episode himself in Covent Garden and frequently sees a distraught Bessel appealing to him in his dreams. In due course a message is received from Bessel, via a spiritualist medium, saying he is at the bottom of an excavation off Baker Street—where he is duly found, the fiend having taken its leave. 'The Stolen Body', 1898

BETTERAVE, W. B.: A vituperative literary critic and supposed author of 'The Betterave Papers', best described—and it has been—as a bitter opusculum among the last pieces of writing which Wells sent to press. It appeared on both sides of the Atlantic : in the British *Cornhill Magazine* and the American *Virginia Quarterly Review*. Betterave (the name derived from the French for 'beetroot') outlines the career of Harold Swansdown, 'who lived elaborately aloof from all the stresses of these vehement days'. The transparent design of the piece shows Wells attacking his detractors, but it is also noted for revealing passages on his personal appraisal of his parents, most particularly his mother; however, it added little to the disclosures made more than a decade earlier in his *Experiment in Autobiography* (1935). 'The Betterave Papers', 1945

BETTS, MR. : An enterprising young man who buys and assembles an aeroplane in the village of Mintonchester. His first flight creates havoc; for someone has attempted to secure the machine by tying its wings to two metal posts. These are trailed during the flight, causing a variety of damage before the eventual crash-landing which puts paid to a number of pigs. The second (and last) attempt is equally disastrous, and ends in an abrupt invasion of the vicar's drawing-room. Thereafter Betts declares himself bankrupt and disappears to Italy, leaving his mother to fend off the irate villagers. 'My First Aeroplane', 1910

BIRKENHEAD, EVANGELINE : The first Mrs. Edward Albert Tewler, who meets him while they are both in residence at Mrs. Doober's

25

boarding-house in Kentish Town. A sallow, dark girl, displaying thin arched eyebrows above alert hazel eyes. Her manner towards Tewler becomes notably more intimate when she learns of his Scottish inheritance, and she rapidly elicits a proposal of marriage. Physically leading him on, but as sexually inexperienced as he is, she finds his first inept effort at lovemaking completely distasteful and refuses to see him again until she discovers she is pregnant.

Having spent some time working in Paris, she has acquired a penchant for extravagance and a habit of ordering goods and services on account, much to her husband's consternation when he receives the bills. After the birth of their son she denies Tewler access to her bed and assigns the care of the infant entirely to their housekeeper, Mrs. Butter. She deserts within a matter of weeks, returning to her former employer—an admirer —the middle-aged owner of a glove-making concern to whom she bears several subsequent children. *You Can't Be Too Careful*, 1941

BIRKENHEAD, INSPECTOR : Father of Evangeline, a C.I.D. man at Scotland Yard and the innocent party of a disastrous first marriage of his own. He is a large weighty man whose very presence is sufficient to intimidate Tewler. He finds much in his daughter to remind him of her mother's errant ways and is consequently not without sympathy for his prospective son-in-law. At the same time, he is determined that his name shall not be shamed again, insisting that Tewler honour his obligations : 'That girl is going to be decently and properly married, whether she likes it or not, whether you like it or not, whoever likes it or don't like it—or not.' *You Can't Be Too Careful*, 1941

BLATCH, DESMOND : A literary agent who handles the affairs of Mr. Rowland Palace; later he also takes on the rising new writer, Alfred Bunter. His demeanour fluctuates between that of a family solicitor and a commercial traveller in fancy goods. When he talks of art he tends to use his glasses as a baton with which to conduct his expositions. He proves unhelpful when consulted with a view to improving the author's public image, a consideration which he sees as falling outside his particular terms of reference. So far as he is concerned, 'the real maker of an author's personality is the author himself'. *Brynhild*, 1937

BLETTSWORTHY, ARNOLD : The narrator of an allegorical tale which describes his experience of an extraordinary delusion. Born in Madeira in the 1880s, he is the legitimate son of a much-travelled, and much-married, Englishman of a noted family and a woman of mixed Portuguese and Syrian origin. Raised in England by his uncle and educated at the expense of his father's sister, he graduates from Oxford and subsequently sets up a book business there with a fellow graduate, Lyulph Graves. During this period he becomes engaged to an attractive local girl, Olive Slaughter, but the relationship—and his business partnership—end when he discovers Olive and Graves about to make love.

Graves disappears forthwith, leaving a debt to Blettsworthy of some three thousand pounds. Having settled his affairs in Oxford, Arnold is advised by the family solicitor, Ferndyke, to take a long sea voyage, which he does with disastrous consequences. He embarks as sole passenger on the cargo vessel *Golden Lion* where he finds himself ostracized by most of the crew and a target of the captain's animosity. Off the coast of South America he witnesses the beating to death of a young deckhand whose funeral is interrupted by the onset of a violent storm. During its course, the ship's engines fail, as a result of the captain's neglect, and the vessel develops a fatal list. Abandoning the craft, the captain locks Blettsworthy below and leaves him to drift to his death.

Weak with hunger, he lapses into semi-consciousness—to be aroused when savages board the ship and carry him off to Rampole Island. There he is first imprisoned and seems likely to be sacrificed. Instead he is designated the tribe's 'Sacred Lunatic' and is released on sufferance. To some extent he is befriended by the soothsayer, Chit, who familiarizes him with the ways of the Islanders.

Blettsworthy is appalled by the tribal customs. The natives are devoid of industry and their hierarchy is maintained by means of the 'Reproof', a blow with a ceremonial club which usually kills the victim and indirectly provides the meat that, with roots, is their staple diet. They worship the *megatheria* (sloths) with which the island abounds, the largest of these being prehistoric and exceeding the bulk of an elephant. The Sacred Lunatic is obliged to wear a rotting sloth skin and attends meetings of the sages at which the prospects of war with a neighbouring tribe are discussed, particularly by Ardam, the chief warrior.

During his enforced stay on the island Blettsworthy is prone to odd flashes of illusion when he imagines he can see the outside world looming through his repellent surroundings. He comes to compare the squalid purposelessness of the savages with what he sees as the selfishness and futility of civilized Man, and he likens the *megatheria* to the ponderous, almost immovable institutions which impede human progress. Following the outbreak of war, he discovers a concealed gorge through which he believes a surprise attack could be led. While investigating he dives into the torrent to save a drowning girl, later claiming her as his woman. Wounded in the shoulder by a spear, he is overcome by fever, from which he awakes in astonishment to find he is in New York.

The mental specialist, Minchett, who resembles Chit, explains that Blettsworthy was rescued from the *Golden Lion* by a scientific expeditionary party of which he was a member. Consequently, he has been treating Blettsworthy in the United States for nearly five years, where, while capable of day-to-day activity, Arnold has actually been in a state of profound reverie. The injured shoulder, which appears to have triggered the end of his illusion, was in reality caused by a motor accident.

The talk, and outbreak, of war experienced on Rampole Island, prove to be a reflection of the genuine advent of the First World War; and Blettsworthy is reminded by Ferndyke, who comes to visit him, that his family has a long record of heroism in the championship of civilization. Despite his newly-wed wife Rowena's protestations, he returns to England and joins up. At the front he sees in the horror of the trenches a revelation that Rampole Island *is* the real world and that he has never properly escaped it. His active participation in the fighting ceases when he loses a leg in a shellburst.

While convalescing he is reunited with Lyulph Graves who has been nearly scalped by a shell. The episode with Olive Slaughter is forgiven and Graves insists that he is determined to repay his debt. Their old friendship is resumed. After the war Blettsworthy establishes a wine company, appointing Graves to handle the marketing, which he accomplishes with considerable success.

While outwardly prosperous, the post-war Blettsworthy continues to suffer lapses when he fears the return of his delusion.

He admits to the element of fascination : 'However much my fellow-mutilated may forget the war and the ugly face life turned upon them, I do not forget ... If some mental specialist made me an offer to clear every trace of that interpretative reverie out of my mind, if he assured me that this present life would lose its translucency and become completely real for me and safe in appearance as the life of a young animal seems safe to that young animal, certain I am that I should not accept. I have read that men who have nearly died in the desert, or men who have passed as explorers through the indescribable hardships of an Arctic winter are for ever afterwards possessed by an irrational craving to return to the scene of their endurance. It has made common life trivial for them, it has enslaved their imagination by its intenser values. So it is with me. Rampole Island calls to me in much the same fashion. It is as if I felt my real business was there, and that all my present swathings of comfort and entertainment were keeping me back from essential affairs. I have never to forget Rampole Island, I feel, I have to settle my account with it. Until that account is settled, the island lies in wait for me.'

At the close of the story he becomes intensely disturbed by the execution in the U.S. of the radicals, Sacco and Vanzetti (on what many regard historically as a trumped-up charge), and he experiences several visions of Rampole Island during which the unfortunate pair are subjected to the Reproof. He confesses as much to Lyulph Graves, who endeavours to reassure him, and the book ends with a discussion on the outlook for a new society.

Wells saw Rampole Island as 'a caricature-portrait of the whole human world', and in that context it represents a more extensive reflection on the faults of civilization than Dr. Moreau's island, although there are several similarities between the two works. It met with a tepid reception from the critics of the day, but it can now be more properly regarded as a forerunner of the type of psychological drama which is classed in recent science fiction under the heading of 'Inner Space'. *Mr. Blettsworthy on Rampole Island*, 1928

BLETTSWORTHY, ROWENA : The wife of Arnold whom he rescues from a suicide attempt in the Hudson River, in New York, believing that he is saving her from a gorge on Rampole Island. Like Wena—the girl of his illusion—her prettiness is emphasized by her black hair, level brows and 'exquisite' mouth. She is by his side when he eventually emerges from his reverie in her flat, where he has lived since saving her.

Her previous history is chequered. She was born of a poor family in Georgia and raised in 'a simple, old-fashioned Protestant way'. At college she read voraciously, at the same time deciding that she could exercise her physical appeal to secure herself some advantage over men. In New York she began an affair with a senior police official, whose jealousy of her other men friends led to her being hounded by half his department and brought her to the banks of the Hudson.

At first she resists Blettsworthy's offers of marriage, considering herself not good enough. However, on the insistence of Dr. Minchett, who describes her as a medicine he is prescribing for his patient, she finally agrees. Unable to persuade her husband against enlisting, she accompanies him to England where their son is born. After the war she settles with him in comparative tranquillity, although she is apprehensive of the occasional flashes of his old delusion and disapproves of his continuing friendship with Lyulph Graves. *Mr. Blettsworthy on Rampole Island*, 1928

BLETTSWORTHY, THE REVEREND : The uncle of Arnold who looks after him in Wiltshire during his boyhood and adolescence while his father travels abroad. A short, round and rosy man, wearing rimless spectacles and dressing like the rich and happy rector he is. His influence on Arnold's development is considerable, particularly in matters of kindliness and tolerance. The 'good broad churchman' is singularly accommodating in his faith :

' "At bottom we are all the same thing" he said to me, preparing me for confirmation. "Never get excited about forms or formulae. There is only one truth in the world and all good men have got it."

"Darwin and Huxley?" I reflected.

"Sound Christians both," said he, "in the proper sense of the word. Honest men that is. No belief is healthy unless it takes air and exercise and turns itself round and about and stands upon its head for a bit." '

He dies shortly after his nephew's graduation from Oxford, and within a few days of his own wife's death. *Mr. Blettsworthy on Rampole Island*, 1928

BODISHAM : A disgruntled member of Lord Bohun's Popular Socialist movement who joins forces with Rud Whitlow to overthrow his former leader. A graduate from the London School of Economics, he is to become the intellectual driving force behind the party's revival at Rud's direction and the most potent influence in its gradual rise to world domination. If Whitlow is the motive power behind the final establishment of the World State, Bodisham is unquestionably its detailed planner. A born director and co-ordinator, he is a strong advocate of 'parallel independent co-operation' by which collaboration can be sought with outsiders in areas of mutual interest (a characteristically Wellsian idea that the author had already propounded on many occasions). The enlistment of Bellacourt in the move towards a World Aviation Control is a typical example of the process.

Bodisham's genius as an organizer is fully stretched once the revolution is won and, if his painstaking methods frequently arouse Rud's impatience by their leisurely pace, his sudden death at the age of fifty-two marks the beginning of Whitlow's decline into paranoia. Bodisham's doctors are publicly tried and executed (in an exact parody of Stalin's persecution of Gorki's physicians), marking the beginning of a wave of progressively less discriminating purges. *The Holy Terror*, 1939

BOHUN, LORD HORATIO : Boss of the Popular Socialist Party whom Rud Whitlow ousts at an early stage in his own bid for power. A tall, excessively vain man, he gives Rud at their first meeting 'the benefit of his profile, the ruddy forelock, the Corinthian nose, the rather underhung jaw'. The expression of his closely-set eyes is 'designed to convey hypnotic penetration'. Initially his party gains a substantial following in the depressed Britain of the 1930s, but it loses momentum when Bohun reveals himself increasingly as a leader without ideas. He is incensed when Rud takes over his regular platform at Speakers' Corner at Hyde Park, in London, but agrees to a closed meeting at which criticisms of policy can be aired. He invades the hall with hired thugs, only to be defeated in the ensuing skirmish, although Rud himself is briefly kidnapped and locked in a cell in Bohun's headquarters. A search of his house discloses his penchant for sado-masochism, and he leaves his party, and the country, forthwith. *The Holy Terror*, 1939

BOLARIS, RICHARD : One of the identical twins, in their early thirties, who plays a leading role in his nation's civil war during which the brothers find themselves on opposing sides. Short in stature but broad-shouldered, with a fine head, clear hazel eyes and a slightly impish grin, he was separated from the rest of the family when New Orleans was flooded in his infancy. Presumed an orphan, he was adopted by General Bolaris and taken from America to the country (which remains unidentified) where the story is set. At the opening of the narrative he has succeeded in capturing Robert Ratzel, a leader of the left-wing enemy forces who is brought to Bolaris's headquarters for interrogation.

The remarkable likeness between the two men leads to the realization that they are twins, and Ratzel is able to tell his brother of the parents Bolaris cannot remember; he himself left the U.S.A. as a young man to become an immigrant mineworker. In their first discussion they talk more of literature and culture than of their conflicting policies, discovering similar tastes and warming to one another's company. Bolaris is reluctant to order his brother's execution and holds him prisoner while he stages a *coup d'état*. He elicits the help of his mistress, Catherine Farness, in the hope of engineering Ratzel's escape.

Further discussions between the two men ensue, again illustrating the similarity of their points of view. Each is idealistic and dedicated to the well-being of his countrymen. They come to the conclusion that they represent the right and left halves of the same picture and that each agrees with the best of the other's aims. Bolaris reviews the situation with his new cabinet, none of whom he entirely trusts. They are astonished to learn he has Ratzel a captive and oppose the suggestion that he should be set free to persuade his forces to surrender the city they hold.

A plan for Ratzel's escape, involving each brother impersonating the other, proves unworkable, and events overtake any further machinations. Ratzel's forces discover his whereabouts and attack in a bid to rescue him. He breaks loose from the H.Q. but is shot by Bolaris's aid, Handon, in ignorance of his master's intentions. In anger Bolaris struggles to wrest the rifle from Handon and is himself killed when it fires by accident. The story closes with a despairing lament by Catherine on the lost possibilities of a rational peace.

The novel is among Wells's shorter pieces of fiction and was evidently designed as a comment on the Spanish Civil War, then in its mid-way stage. The backgrounds are hastily sketched and deliberately vague, but references to the killing of priests and other similar allusions reinforce the connection with the Spanish conflict. The work also provides a further opportunity for the author's advocacy of Republicanism. *The Brothers*, 1938

BOMBACCIO : Head servant at Casa Terragena and a model of impeccable tact and efficiency whose gestures say more than his words. His innate sense of orderliness is disturbed on more than one occasion by Mrs. Rylands's guests, particularly the unconventional departure of Miss Puppy Clarges, but he is unaware of the cause of her need for so rapid a leave-taking. Care is taken to keep him similarly ignorant of the presence of the refugee, Signor Vinciguerra, in case his sympathies might lie with the pursuing Blackshirts, but he proves later to be an admirer of the former minister. *Meanwhile*, 1927.

BONOVER, GEORGE : Headmaster of Whortley Proprietary School, under whom Mr. Lewisham is an assistant master. He elevates vast black eyebrows on discovering Lewisham escorting Ethel Henderson for a walk during his free afternoon. Bonover later attempts to draw out his assistant regarding his relationship with the girl, but without success. Further put out by Lewisham's refusal to stand in for another master, Dunkerley, so that the latter can join him for croquet, the headmaster gives him a term's notice when he finds that Lewisham, distracted by Ethel's charms, has also failed to appear for the supervision of his pupils' preparation. *Love and Mr. Lewisham*, 1900

BOON, GEORGE : A fictitious writer whose 'literary remains' first appeared as collected under the pseudonym 'Reginald Bliss', prefaced by 'an ambiguous introduction by H. G. Wells'. (That Wells was the author of the entire book became apparent almost immediately, and he confessed as much in the 1920 second edition.) Boon is a man whose physical presence can rarely be captured by a camera '. . . so much of him was movement, gesture, expression, atmosphere and colour, and so little of him was form'.

He writes nothing with his own hand, preferring to dictate to an amanuensis. His last two projected works, *The Mind of the Race* and *The Wild Asses of the Devil* are left uncompleted on his death from fatigue and depression during the early stages of the First World War. They are, however, discussed in the book—often with the critically-minded acquaintance Wilkins—and ap-

33

pear as thinly-disguised Wellsian indictments of human folly, coupled with what was to become a familiar call for worldwide co-operation. A short story, allegedly written by Boon, concludes the collection (*see under entry for* Parchester, the Rev. Mr.).

The book also contains a skilfully satirical eavesdropping on an imagined conversation between Henry James and George Moore regarding their respective literary designs, followed by a diatribe against James which precipitated a celebrated argument between that writer and Wells. Boon attacks James's elaborately constructed sentences and likens him to an overblown hippopotamus endeavouring at the cost of its dignity to pick up a very small pea.

The criticism deeply wounded James, who had hitherto expressed genuine admiration for Wells's earlier novels. A long correspondence ensued, in which James defended his position as an artist while Wells, becoming increasingly impatient and already embarked on his series of novels of discussion and ideas, sought to justify the purpose of fiction in less aesthetic terms. In critical and educational circles the dispute is generally regarded as a victory for James, whose remarks have been much quoted : 'It is art that *makes* life, makes interest, makes importance, for our consideration and application of these things, and I know of no substitute whatever for the force and beauty of its process . . . If I were Boon I should say that any pretence of such a substitute is helpless and hopeless humbug; but I wouldn't be Boon for the world . . .' Wells retaliated with a final dismissive statement which has also been frequently repeated in judgment of his later books : 'I am a journalist, I refuse to play the artist. If sometimes I am an artist it is a freak of the gods. I am a journalist all the time and what I write *goes now*—and will presently die.' *Boon*, 1915

BOTANIST, THE : The companion of the narrator of *A Modern Utopia*—his contributions to what is basically a novel of dialogue are few and his occasional interpolations are frequently expressions of captious or narrow-minded views. He is lean, tall, and a 'graver and less garrulous man' than the narrator. 'His face is weakly handsome and done in tones of grey, he is fairish and grey-eyed, and you would suspect him of dyspepsia. It is a justifiable suspicion.' He is one of those men who are 'romantic with a shadow of meanness. They seek at once to conceal and shape their sensuous cravings beneath egregious sentimentalities, they

34

get into mighty tangles and troubles with women, and he has had his troubles.' Much of his time in Utopia is occupied with thoughts of a woman of the everyday world whose sufferings at the hands of her husband cause him distress. He has proved incapable of helping her, and his discovery of her double in Utopia only adds to his histrionic laments. *A Modern Utopia*, 1905

BOWLES, MRS. JUDY : The leader of the caravan party of three women who befriend the fleeing Bealby and employ him briefly as their willing slave. A professor's wife, businesslike and brisk, she expresses what the boy considers unhealthy concern over his untidy appearance. She persuades him to buy a fresh collar which her husband, on his arrival, immediately insists that Bealby remove. *Bealby: A Holiday*, 1915

BREAM, THE VICAR OF ST. HIPPOLYTUS : A friend of Trumber at Camford who attempts to explain the Voice, which the don hears, in psychological terms. He sees it as a manifestation of Trumber's inner distress at the pressure and direction of modern living, an 'upthrust of the sub-conscious'. The don remains unconvinced, but Bream later makes use of his friend's experience as the basis of a book, *Extra-Terrestrial Disturbances of Human Mentality*, which, while hardly a best-seller, does much to enhance his reputation. *The Camford Visitation*, 1937

BRETT, KITTY : A noted leader of the Suffragette movement who attempts to define its goals for the benefit of a quizzical Ann Veronica. In her early twenties, slightly plump and lively eyed, she is 'about as capable of intelligent argument as a runaway steam roller'. To her the vote is the symbol of everything; all other considerations, such as women's economic freedom, are secondary and will fall into place when the franchise has been won. She allocates Ann Veronica to the band of suffragettes who are to storm the House of Commons, a raid which leads to Ann Veronica's imprisonment. *Ann Veronica*, 1909

BRIDGET, BILLY : A tramp who entertains delusions of playing Fagin to Bealby's Oliver. Excessively dirty and unkempt, he is appalled at the boy's apparent unwillingness to steal, a pastime which he regards as universal. While providing Bealby with some degree of security during nights in the open, he adds to his distress by forcing him to join in a burglary. He spends Bealby's remaining few coins on drink, after which he discourses at length on the ways of the road. His favourite ruse is to simulate a fit, foaming at the mouth with the aid of a bar of soap—the only use he makes of that commodity. Bealby deserts him during one such performance, and although they are not to meet again, the tramp joins unsuccessfully in the chase after the boy when he learns of the offered reward. *Bealby: A Holiday*, 1915

BRIGHTON-POMFREY, DR. : The regular physician of Edward Scrope who finds to his alarm that his patient has accepted a hallucinogenic drug from his locum, Dale. A round-faced, blue-eyed man, with 'an unsuitable nose for the glasses he wears'. He flaunts, for some unaccountable reason, enormous side whiskers. Called away to an inquiry into the treatment of gas gangrene, he is absent at the time of Scrope's insomnia and nervous debility, and as a consequence the Bishop is treated by Dale. On his return, he is horrified to learn of the drugs which his locum has provided for many of his other patients and of their far-reaching results. He correctly suspects that Scrope's break with the Church is connected with Dale's treatment and is obliged to listen to the Bishop's account of his illusions :

'The Doctor suddenly gave way to botryoidal hilarity. "To think that one should be consulted about visions of God—in Mount Street ! And you know, you know you half want to believe that vision was real. You *know* you do." '

He suggests that Scrope was administered some type of morphine derivative, but since Dale has been killed, and has left no notes, he is unable to identify it precisely. He refuses to prescribe anything similar. *The Soul of a Bishop*, 1917

BRISHER, MR. : A character of little means who unearths a chest of coins while building a rockery in his fiancée's back-garden. Hampered by the puritanical honesty of her father, he makes several efforts to remove his find before escaping when disturbed during his last desperate attempt. Far from declaring the treasure, the father appropriates it for himself and, ironically, is arrested for passing counterfeit money. 'Mr. Brisher's Treasure', 1899

BRITLING, EDITH : The second wife of Hugh Britling who bears him two sons. A tall freckled woman with bright brown eyes and pretty, similarly coloured hair; she gives the impression of an air of preoccupation. Very much the mistress of her household, she expresses doubt regarding the wisdom of the tutor Heinrich's filling his room with trees for the accommodation of his pet squirrel. She has brought her own money into the home, yet her cool estimate of her step-son leads to a widening rift between herself and her husband. On Hugh junior's death in the war, she feels strongly moved to comfort Britling, but realizes quite soon that she is failing miserably, confessing as much. In the event it falls to Britling to console her and to reassure her of her value to him. *Mr. Britling Sees It Through*, 1916

BRITLING, HUGH JNR.: The only son of Mr. Britling's first marriage, and his father's favourite, possibly because of his frailty in early youth. A shock-headed young man, having Britling's nose and freckles, but of darker complexion. There is a look about his arms and legs which suggests overnight growth. His early interest in crystallography has been dashed by an uninspiring professor at the University of London, so that he subsequently turns to the study of art. It is only after considerable soul-searching that he reaches the conclusion that he should join the army. Once posted to Flanders he writes many long letters to Britling which include graphic accounts of the conditions in the trenches, so that his father concludes that Hugh could well become a writer. His death puts an end to Britling's hopes for any such promise. *Mr. Britling Sees It Through*, 1916

BRITLING, HUGH SNR.: The writer whose reaction to the First World War was recorded in one of the most emotive stories to be published during that conflict. To some extent it is a self-portrait : 'His was a naturally irritable mind; this gave him point and passion; and moreover he had a certain obstinate originality and a generous disposition. So that he was always lively, sometimes spacious, and never vile. He loved to write and talk. He talked about everything, he had ideas about everything; he could no more help having ideas about everything than a dog can resist smelling at your heels. He sniffed at the heels of reality. Lots of people found him interesting and stimulating, a few found him seriously exasperating. He had ideas in the utmost profusion about races and empires and social order and political institutions and gardens and automobiles and the future of India and China and aesthetics and America and the education of mankind in general . . . And all that sort of thing . . .'

Originally a critic and essayist, he has achieved international prominence as an author of books on national relationships and social psychology. Red-faced and freckled, he has small hazel eyes, and moustache, hair and eyebrows which appear to 'bristle'. He frequently wears the expression of 'a wire-haired terrier disposed to be friendly', and his mode of attire is 'miscellaneous'. He is first seen at his home, Dower House, in the village of Matching's Easy in Essex, to which he is welcoming a young American visitor, Direck. He alarms his guest by the eccentricity of his driving, and their journey from the local railway station in his new car, 'Gladys', terminates in a ditch. Thereafter Direck tactfully attempts to decline any further offers of a lift.

The American has come to England to invite Britling to lecture to the Massachusetts Society for the Study of Contemporary Thought, an organization of business men of which he is the Secretary. Initially the Britling household is portrayed through his eyes, and he delights in its informality. Basically it consists of the writer's second wife, Edith; his eldest son by his first marriage, Hugh Jnr; two young boys born by Edith; and their German student-tutor, Herr Heinrich. At his first meal, lyrically taken at a long table out-of-doors in the shade of sycamore trees, Direck also meets Britling's secretary, Teddy, who with his wife Letty and baby lives in a cottage in the village, and Letty's sister, Cecily Corner, to whom he is immediately drawn.

Britling's early conversations with Direck tend to be voluble and distinctly one-sided; the visitor has difficulty in interjecting any of his own views into his host's long expositions. Britling introduces him to a number of local dignatories, and the resulting discussions centre on Wellsian themes. He also subjects him to a vigorous game of hockey, at which Direck surprisingly excels. However, the American is more concerned to pursue the company of Cecily Corner, believing they may be distantly related. Later he is incautious enough to allow Britling to drive him again, only to suffer concussion and a dislocated wrist which delay his departure from Dower House—a circumstance he welcomes, since it prolongs his acquaintance with Cecily.

For some time Britling has been engaged in an extra-marital liaison with a Mrs. Harrowdean, an emotional woman who feels he should devote his talents exclusively to his artistic work—such as his unfinished poem 'The Secret Places'— and avoid becoming embroiled in current affairs. She is intensely jealous of

Edith; and this sentiment, coupled with the attentions paid to her by another man, finally persuade Britling to end the relationship. He sets out to visit her one night, but loses his way and returns to Matching's Easy.

The outbreak of war rapidly disrupts Britling's comfortable circle. Herr Heinrich, whose mildly comic Teutonic manner has endeared him to the family, goes back to fight for Germany. Teddy enlists, and later Hugh Jnr. Britling reluctantly accepts his son's decision, for he can readily appreciate the youth's underlying convictions. His own reaction to the hostilities is one of outrage against the enemy—a common feeling of the time. He embarks on a series of articles expressing this view, but as the war drags on his mood changes, influenced partly by his boy's letters from the front. He begins to write a pamphlet, 'And Now War Ends', with which he becomes increasingly dissatisfied, finding it an inadequate expression of his thoughts.

News is received that Teddy is missing, and Letty spends anguished months anticipating confirmation of his death. Direck, who has joined the Canadian Army so that he will be able to fight, an action which secures his engagement to Cecily, endeavours to discover the secretary's fate. But eventually Teddy reappears, minus an arm, although the joy of his welcome is muted in the case of Britling, who in the meantime has heard that Hugh has been killed. Within days he receives a letter through an intermediary in Norway to say that Herr Heinrich has also died. Abandoning an essay, 'The Better Government of the World', he spends the night penning a long and moving reply to Heinrich's father which occupies the closing pages of his story: 'Let us pledge ourselves to service. Let us set ourselves with all our minds and with all our hearts to the perfecting and working out of the methods of democracy and the ending for ever of the kings and priestcrafts and the bands of adventurers, the traders and owners and forestallers who have betrayed mankind into this morass of hate and blood—in which our sons are lost—in which we flounder still . . .'

Britling's anguish was to awaken a response in many British parents who had suffered similar loss. Many wrote personally to Wells assuming, erroneously, that he had actually had a son killed in the war. The book became a best-seller and remains a noted example of the change in attitude of an intelligent man with the growing realization of the futility of the war's conduct.

In the war's initial stages Wells had coined the phrase 'The

War that Will End War', a slogan that was to haunt him for the rest of his life. His subsequent tours of the French battlefields convinced him of the true horror of the hostilities, and his reaction to this experience was recorded in the advocacy of a just peace and a genuinely effective League of Nations—ideas which he put into print, as Britling might well have done, in such books and pamphlets as the *Elements of Reconstruction* and *What Is Coming: A Forecast of Things after the War* (both 1916), *War and the Future: Italy, France and Britain at War, A Reasonable Man's Peace* (both 1917), *In the Fourth Year: Anticipations of a World Peace*, and *British Nationalism and the League of Nations* (both 1918), and, with eight collaborators, *The Idea of a League of Nations* and *The Way to a League of Nations* (both 1919). Many subsequent books were to reiterate the same arguments, e.g. *The Salvaging of Civilization* (1921), and *Washington and the Hope of Peace* (1922). He became Director of Propaganda against Germany in Lord Northcliffe's Ministry towards the end of the war, not without the usual differences of opinion which accompanied all his attempts to collaborate with other people.

In the event he was disgusted by the treaty of Versailles, recognizing it as France's vindictive rejection of President Woodrow Wilson's Fourteen Points. As he wrote in *Washington and the Hope of Peace* : 'The peace imposed upon the young German republic was a punitive peace, exactly as punitive as though there were still a Kaiser in Berlin : it was a vindictive reversal of the Franco-German treaty of 1871 without a shred of recognition or tolerance for the chastened Germany that faced her conquerors. The Germans were dealt with as a race of moral monsters, though no one in his senses really believes they are very different, man for man, from English, French or American people; every German was held to be individually responsible for the war, though every Frenchman, Englishman and American knows that when one's country fights one has to fight, and it is quite natural to fight for it whether it is in the right or not; and a sustained attack of oppressive occupations, dismemberment, and impossible demands was begun and still goes on upon the shattered German civilization . . . It is high time that this barbaric insanity, this prolongation of the combat after surrender, should cease and that the best minds and wills of Germany and the very reasonable republican government she has set up for herself should be called into consultation. I could wish that Washington could so far rise above Versailles as presently to make that invitation. Sooner or later it will have to be made if the peace of the world is to be secured.'

Such might Britling have written, had the novel had a sequel. The letter to Heinrich's father includes much criticism of Germany, but its tone is enlightened, indicating the direction in which Wells's ideas were moving. At the time of writing he was living at Easton Glebe, in Essex, on the estate of Lady Warwick; and the environment of Dower House at Matching's Easy, while clearly not an exact replica, is obviously based on the author's own home surroundings. *Mr. Britling Sees It Through*, 1916

BRITTEN : A student friend of Remington at City Merchants School, and much later in life his assistant in the editorship of the highly successful political magazine *Blue Weekly*. Ruddy-faced, short and thickset, with dark curly hair, he shares with Remington an enthusiasm for socialism and Darwinism, and together they attend meetings at William Morris's home in Hammersmith. Britten is also initially interested in the new school magazine originally to be a combined venture between himself, Remington and Shoesmith, but cannot condone the style proposed by its ultimate overseer Cossington, later to become a press magnate.

While working under the anonymous editorship of Remington on *Blue Weekly*, he covers for the former's absence when Remington virtually flees to America in an effort to overcome his affection for Isabel Rivers. When the scandal of the couple's subsequent affair persuades Remington both to abandon his magazine and political career and to elope, Britten makes an overwhelming but unsuccessful appeal to his friend to reverse his decision.

Another common interest between Britten and Remington in their schooldays was the playing of War Games using toy soldiers. Wells's description of this pastime so intrigued another publisher Frank Palmer that he invited the author to produce a book setting out the details. The result was *Floor Games* (1911), followed by a sequel in 1913, *Little Wars*. *The New Machiavelli*, 1911

BROWNLOW, MR. : The recipient, through his letter-box in 1931, of a 1971 edition of the London *Evening Standard* newspaper, although it is then spelt *Even Standrd*. Brownlow, having overcome his initial disbelief, is astonished by the quality of paper and

41

colour reproduction, and no less by the news conveyed : the death of the last gorilla, the attempt directly to tap the Earth's energy seven miles down, a massive reduction in birth-rate, a complete absence of reference to any of the world's major nations but repeated mention of federal boards, federal police and other such organizations. The reader is left with the impression that the Wellsian world state has come to pass. Unfortunately for Brownlow, his housekeeper throws the paper away in the morning while he is still asleep—only a single page remains as evidence of an extraordinary experience. 'The Queer Story of Brownlow's Newspaper', 1931

BROXTED, MARGARET : Daughter of the professor and the physical personification of Theodore Bulpington's 'Delphic Sibyl'. Her broad-browed, soft-eyed resemblance to Michelangelo's ceiling depiction moves Theodore to a flurry of imaginative fantasies in which she figures inseparably at his side. But in reality her nature is enigmatic. She becomes increasingly fond of him, yet reluctant to enter fully into a physical relationship, although she takes the initiative in an evening of abandoned kissing on the occasion of a neighbour's fancy dress ball. It is as if she senses the nature of his amorphous personality, and hesitates to commit herself to so shifting a lover.

In London, she accompanies her brother Teddy to Fabian and like-minded meetings, inveigling Theodore deeper into the same circles. By the beginning of the war, she has resolved to become a doctor; and, although she gives her body to Theodore before he enlists, she declines on the pretext of her studies to join him later behind the lines in France. After the armistice Theodore finds her noticeably changed; she has qualified, and become involved with a young doctor, Laverock, with whom she works. While moved by Theodore's pleas, she refuses to make love with him again. Finally, Haverock takes it upon himself to dissuade Bulpington from any further pursuit. *The Bulpington of Blup*, 1932

BROXTED, PROFESSOR : An eminent biologist at Kingsway College and a member of the Rationalist Press Association, described dismissively by Enoch Wimperdick as the 'little brother of Huxley and Haeckel'. He is a short stocky man, red-haired, brown-eyed and heavily freckled. A champion of the scientific approach to every area of life, he exercises a profound influence over both his children. He argues bitterly with his son regarding the causes, conduct and outcome of the First World War, seeing the conflict —idealistically—as a necessary precursor to the establishment of a world state. After the war he directs his energies beyond his own scientific discipline and joins in the public debate on reconstruction. His *Human Association from the Point of View of General Biology* is quoted at Theodore Bulpington by an argumentative young man on Bulpington's return to England at the end of the 1920s. *The Bulpington of Blup*, 1932

BROXTED, TEDDY : A childhood friend of Theodore Bulpington who introduces him to the realm of science and the mysteries of his father's laboratory. In complexion, both physical and philosophical, he resembles the professor; but he falls out with him dramatically at the outbreak of the war. His prediction of the unpreparedness and subsequent incompetence of the army general staff is accurate enough, and no argument can shift his conviction that Britain should have refused to become involved. He passes the war period as a conscientious objector and is gaoled for his resistance to conscription. Later he becomes a professor of Social Biology and the youngest Fellow of the Royal Society. *The Bulpington of Blup*, 1932

BRUMLEY, GEORGE : A successful author and widower who conducts something of a one-sided romance with Lady Ellen Harman. The story opens with their first meeting when she comes to see his country home, 'Black Strand', with a view to purchase. Of medium height, stout, artistically-clothed, he has a round, good-looking amiable face, brown hair and a fine profile. His eyes are expressive, his mouth 'very passable'. His wife has been dead for a little over three years, and he has a young son at boarding-school in Margate. His most popular books are those in his 'Euphemia' series, that being his late wife's forename. In general his work is light and he has also written travelogues. He feels he must move from his old home, with its many memories, before he can fully resume his career.

Brumley is immediately attracted to Lady Harman, becoming progressively concerned for her welfare as he learns more of her husband's nature and the realities of her marriage. After a Shakespearian luncheon, which she had been forbidden to attend, he takes her to visit the gardens at Hampton Court Palace, finding to his dismay that he has insufficient cash on him for her return taxi-fare. She arrives home very late, an incident which provokes Sir Isaac Harman to buy 'Black Strand' forthwith and more-or-less incarcerate her there. Brumley visits her, with a vague idea of effecting her rescue, and awkwardly declares his love. He attempts to return to the rear of the house through the adjoining woods, but only succeeds in reducing himself to a dishevelled condition. In fact, a great many of his endeavours in the course of the tale verge on the ineffective or comical.

He cherishes the notion of carrying Ellen off abroad, quite forgetting the existence of her four young children. His continuing attentions, when she seeks his advice on the running of her hostels, irritate Sir Isaac who insists she must choose between seeing Brumley and her work. When her husband dies, Brumley is convinced she will marry him and is all the more taken aback by her resolve to remain free. Close friendship is the most he can hope for and he pleads rather lamely for a single kiss, which is given more ardently than he expected. *The Wife of Sir Isaac Harman*, 1914

BUGGINS, CARSHOT AND PIERCE : Fellow colleagues of Kipps at the Folkestone Drapery Bazaar who suffer, like him, under the remonstrances of the proprietor, Shalford. Carshot is the window dresser, a persistent nagger and sufferer from chronic indigestion. A fat man, with a large nose, he constantly appeals to his 'visceral economy', a favourite expletive phrase being 'My Heart and Liver!'

Buggins is young and thick-set, bald, and possessed of a 'round, very wise face'. He is probably the closest to Kipps, advising him against replying to the advertisement concerning his inheritance and recommending courses of action once Kipps has been dismissed.

Pierce is Kipps's immediate senior, who pays much attention to his personal attire (in popular parlance, 'a Masher'). Under his influence Kipps visits a tailor and buys an outfit which will meet with Pierce's approval.

Both Buggins and Pearce express genuine pleasure when Kipps inherits his fortune. They regularly spend evenings at his house, drinking and singing to the accompaniment of Kipps's banjo. Deeply offended by their off-hand dismissal by Chester Coote, who considers their company unsuitable for his protégé, they call no more until Kipps has severed his ties with the Walshinghams. *Kipps*, 1905

BULLACE, COLONEL : A choleric member of Mrs. Rylands's house party at Casa Terragena. To his hostess he is reminiscent of a Belgian griffon, with a large eyeglass and an extraordinarily canine face. His opinions of the British trade unions and the possibility of a general strike are representative of his class, and he prompts a number of caustic remarks from the writer Sempack and Philip Rylands, both of whom are inclined to regard him as an English fascist. He leaves the villa with imprecise suggestions that he is being recalled to Britain to join in the definitive confrontation between the Establishment and the workers. *Meanwhile*, 1927

BULPINGTON, CLORINDA : Mother of Theodore, a dark, sturdy woman taken to dressing untidily in an assortment of flowing robes and art gowns. Originally she intended simply to live with Raymond, but her father saw the matter differently. She has a finer brain than her husband, and a more constructive approach to creative work. She frequently travels to London for the day to take stock of the latest intellectual and cultural movements, leaving Raymond to tinker at his *magnum opus*. It is clear the marriage is a loosely-knit affair; on one occasion Theodore surprises his mother in an intimate embrace with a fair young man whose interests also include folk-dancing and cottage industries. She is never particularly close to her son, and in later years he ascribes his emotional condition partly to her lack of affection. By the time of her death she has seen through his posturing, attempting to give him some belated guidance in two last disjointed letters addressed to him while he is serving in France. She dies during an operation. *The Bulpington of Blup*, 1932

BULPINGTON, RAYMOND : Husband of Clorinda—he earned a reputation for brilliance at Oxford which is never fulfilled. He has a dark querulous face and copper-red eyes; his hair, blown about by the south-west wind during his frequent solitary walks, is rarely tidy. One of his favourite words is 'sensuous'. After a raffish bachelor life in London, he makes his home in the Channel resort of Blayport. There he edits classics, writes hostile reviews and advises 'a particularly scoundrelly publisher'. His life's work, which he discusses incessantly, is a monumental history of the Varangians—the Scandinavian race which once reached as far as Vinland and Constantinople. Like his wife, he shows little affection for Theodore, but is kind to him in a condescending

45

way when he feels so disposed. After his death from pneumonia during Theodore's adolescence, his son discovers that the writing of the great history was a sham—nothing more than chapter outlines and a few pages of actual text exists. *The Bulpington of Blup*, 1932

BULPINGTON, THEODORE : An outlandish dreamer and fantasist whose progress through life leaves a trail of either puzzled or disillusioned acquaintances in its wake. Unprepossessing in appearance as a child, he grows in adulthood into a tall, lean dark-haired man, with a military leaning which his actual wartime service has done little to justify. As a boy he is precocious, echoing the opinions of his father, mother, and their friend Wimperdick, to any available audience. At first irreligious, he later becomes confirmed in the Anglican faith, but his conversion is merely a further pose. In childhood he meets the Broxted siblings, Margaret and Teddy. With the latter he forms an uneasy friendship, for even at a youthful age Teddy has adopted his father's scientific and rational outlook, an attitude which hardly accords with Theodore's undisciplined day-dreams. In Margaret he finds the personification of the 'Delphic Sibyl', come down into life from Michelangelo's great ceiling. He seeks out her company, and in his fantasies consigns to her the rôle of eternal helpmate and companion.

From his earliest days Theodore has thought of himself as 'The Bulpington of Blup'. Derived from the name of his home town, Blayport, 'Blup' figures in his imagination as a mystical kingdom which shifts its location according to his whim, but always with himself as its titular head. This inner product of self-aggrandizement remains with him for life, subtly assuming greater control of the face he presents to the world—a front for every occasion. In his adolescence he takes lodgings in London, under the supervision of his Fabian aunt, Lucinda Spink, and studies at the Rowlands School of Art. He encounters Margaret and Teddy at a socialist meeting and is introduced to Rachel and Melchior Bernstein, both ardent communists. To better them, he announces himself an 'Ultra-communist', without ever precisely defining what that label implies. He is seduced by Rachel while her brother is away one weekend, and this experience of his first physical relationship prompts him to plead with Margaret for her to become his mistress. Though moved, she refuses him; they eventually become lovers for a brief spell be-

46

fore he enlists during the First World War.

The outbreak of war presents Theodore with a dilemma. His keen instinct for self-preservation tells him manifestly to stay at home. But the Bulpington of Blup is already envisaging heroic actions, particularly in the light of Teddy Broxted's determination to register as a conscientious objector. For a year Theodore pretends to have been rejected from the forces on medical grounds, but finally he prevails upon himself to join. As a private in the trenches he does not acquit himself well. Later, with the help of an influential uncle, he returns to England to obtain a commission, and then serves briefly behind the lines and close to Paris. From Paris he writes to Margaret that the prostitute with whom he has spent the night (for once a statement of fact) knows more than she will ever do of love.

Returned to the front, he flees in terror from the final all-out German offensive and feigns shell-shock. Only the humaneness of the examining doctor, Laverock, who later becomes Margaret's fiancé, spares him from execution for cowardice. After the war he spends some time in a psychiatric hospital before attempting to resume his former life in London. His efforts to revive his affair with Margaret fail, and when he pesters her he is physically threatened by Laverock. His attitude to her rejection is a good example of his quality of mind : ' "And she could betray me like this ! She could take my letters and run off with them to this man, this interloper in our affair, this scuffling imbecile ! She could bolt to him because she could not trust herself to meet me again. My God ! And this is the woman to whom I would have given my life ! The staggering disproportions in things ! The inadequacies of existence ! This is how my love, the one great love I shall ever experience is to end !" ' He returns to France, motivated by a fleeting desire to renounce the world and set up a new Jesuit order. Instead he becomes co-proprietor of a ludicrous *avant garde* magazine, *The Feet of the Young Men*, which he edits for ten years.

He returns to England to live in a Devonshire cottage left him by another aunt. The end of the story sees him increasingly adrift from reality, regaling his neighbours with accounts of his fictitious war exploits and with his extraordinary delusion that, on one occasion, he captured the Kaiser more or less single-handed.

Wells described the novel as a 'very direct caricature study of the irresponsible disconnected aesthetic mentality' and in Theo-

47

dore Bulpington he magnified the problem faced by some individuals as to the establishment of their true identities. The gulf between the scientific-minded Broxteds and the drifting Theodore, who forever extols the necessity of 'values', provides a keen insight into the dichotomy between science and art. Wells, who had been both a biologist and a creative artist, spoke of Bulpington's character as 'friendship's offering to the world of letters from the scientific side'—a euphemistic indication of which of the two states of mind he personally preferred. He also made an attempt in the story, by the depiction of Teddy Broxted's conscientious objection, to make amends to the pacifists whom he had savaged unmercifully in *Mr. Britling Sees It Through* during the actual time of the First World War. *The Bulpington of Blup*, 1932

BUNTER, ALFRED : The publicity-shy author whose rapid rise to success arouses the envy of Rowland Palace. A tall, brown-haired man, of ruddy complexion, he excites the interest of Brynhild Palace when they first meet at a house party where he appears singularly out of place. Later they are drawn closer together, and Bunter confesses to the real identity of David Lewis. He has assumed a new name to escape his second wife and a possible charge of murdering his brother-in-law, Gregory. He is distraught when his ruse is exposed by Immanuel Cloote in an effort to end his challenge to Rowland's reputation. To console him, Brynhild makes love with him and later bears his child. Eventually he clears his name, grows a beard and settles in Dubrovnic. *Brynhild*, 1937

BUNTING FAMILY, THE : The befrienders of the Sea Lady after she emerges from the waves at Folkestone, principally under the instigation of Mrs. Bunting, who virtually accepts her as a third daughter until late in the tale. The main action of the novel takes place in the Bunting home where the mermaid is confined to a wheelchair. *The Sea Lady*, 1902

BUNTING, THE REV. : Vicar of Iping, in Sussex, whose home is burgled by the Invisible Man. Bunting and his wife surprise the intruder but cannot account for his escape from a room where they thought they had him trapped. Earlier the vicar has heard of his friend Cuss's strange experience with a bandaged stranger at the local inn. Subsequently, when the Invisible Man has been unveiled, Bunting and Cuss search his room—only to be relieved of their clothes on his unexpected return. *The Invisible Man*, 1897

BURLEIGH, CECIL : The Conservative leader whose entourage finds itself translated into Utopia while travelling by car along the Maidenhead road. Tall, slender and grey-haired, he has 'a small upturned face with a little nose', the latter barely sufficient to support his gilt *pince-nez*. He addresses the Utopians for all the world as if they were one more political gathering, but appears a mere dilettante in the face of the determined action advocated by Rupert Catskill. He survives the displacement of the castle on the crag and the Utopians express their intention of returning him safely to Earth. The character is a further caricature of Balfour, whom Wells had earlier depicted in *The New Machiavelli* (*see under* Evesham), the same personality traits being again described. *Men Like Gods*, 1923

BURLEIGH'S PARTY : The other occupants of Cecil Burleigh's car, namely Amerton and Catskill (*see separate entries*), Freddy Mush and the chauffeur Penk. Lady Stella, well-known in London society, proves the most sympathetic to Barnstaple's championship of the Utopians; she tends to seek his company and he finds reassurance in her attractive presence. However, her loyalties lie ultimately with her other companions, as Barnstaple is eventually to realize.

Mush is Catskill's secretary, a monocled figure at ease in the literary world and a diligent discoverer of raw young poets. He is drawn from the real-life Sir Freddy Marsh, who was an ardent supporter of Winston Churchill.)

Penk illustrates a number of the characteristics which Wells found least likeable among the lower social orders. His views on the Utopians' nudity complement those of Barralonga's driver, Ridley. He attempts to make advances to a Utopian girl when she wakens him on the visitors' first morning and regards the blow with which she fells him as a further sign of degeneracy. *Men Like Gods*, 1923

BURNET, SUSAN : A young woman regularly employed by the Harman household to renovate their curtains and furniture covers, and who also helps to stimulate Lady Harman's ideas in the direction of feminine rights. Short and sturdy, she has open blue eyes and a frankness of manner which Ellen Harman finds particularly engaging. Her father was a small independent baker who was found drowned after being driven out of business by the onset of Sir Isaac's chain stores. Initially, Susan finds it hard to accept that Ellen is the wife of the man whom she regards as her father's murderer, but she warms to the other's friendliness and is soon her willing accomplice. She pawns a valuable ring for Ellen, only to be nonplussed by the Harmans' sudden disappearance from Putney. Eventually she succeeds in handing over the money raised on the pledge, which enables Ellen to return by herself to London. Latterly, Susan has much advice to offer regarding the organization of the Harman hostels for the company's female employees. Her sister Alice is turned out of one, under the officious supervision of Mrs. Pembrose. *The Wife of Sir Isaac Harman*, 1914

BURROWS, SIR ELIPHAZ : The modern counterpart of Eliphaz the Temanite in *The Undying Fire*, and, indeed, it is in the manufacture of Temanite building blocks that he has made his fortune. A governor of Woldingstanton, Job Huss's school, and a thin old man with a vulturine head, he visits the sick headmaster in company with another governor and Farr, the head of the school's technical department. Although hardly a religious man, he is shocked to hear Huss speak of the ingratitude of God. In response to the headmaster's catalogue of the cruelties of Nature, he lists some of the marvels of God's creation. Passing to the subject of immortality, he quotes descriptions of the Hereafter he has gleaned from some speculative book, much to the disquiet of Huss's doctor. His argument fails to convince the sick man, and his plans to have Huss replaced by Farr are ultimately foiled. *The Undying Fire*, 1919

BUTCHER : The narrator of 'Aepyornis Island', who recounts his experiences of his unwilling exile on a desert island in the company of a presumably extinct, but decidedly carnivorous bird. Wells added a footnote to the tale : 'No European is known to have seen a live Aepyornis with the doubtful exception of MacAndrew, who visited Madagascar in 1745'. 'Aepyornis Island', 1894

BUTTER, MRS. MARY : Originally hired as housekeeper by Evangeline Tewler, she becomes to all practical purposes the mother of the infant Henry from the time of his birth. She has not enjoyed a happy life. Orphaned when young, she has been raised by a neglectful aunt and been previously married to a violent drunkard whose beatings resulted in the pre-natal injury and subsequent death of her own child. She is younger than Evangeline, light-complexioned, brown-haired and unobtrusively good-looking. She yields with an air of resignation to Tewler's sexual demands once his wife has left him, and consents to marry him more out of love for Henry than his father. Nevertheless she is a loyal wife, although always of an independent bent. Her attitude to Tewler is one of long sufferance rather than genuine affection. She is fatally wounded during a bombing raid in Brighthampton on Sea during Edward Albert's absence in London for the investiture of his George Cross. He reaches the hospital in time to proffer his cherished medal, but she gives every appearance of dying unimpressed. *You Can't Be Too Careful*, 1941

BUTTERIDGE, ALFRED : The inventor of the only reliable flying machine to date in *The War in the Air*. By all accounts an eccentric, but forceful character; heavily moustached and possessed of a booming voice with which he announces his name with monotonous regularity during his one and only flight from London to Glasgow and back. Subsequently, he dismantles his aircraft and offers its secrets to the British government. When negotiations appear to drag, he corresponds with German interests. During an accident on a ballooning outing at Dymchurch, accompanied by a large lady whom he claims society has much maligned, he inadvertently vacates the basket in favour of a reluctant Bert Smallways, who is immediately whisked skywards and across the Channel. *The War in the Air*, 1908

C

CADDLES, ALBERT EDWARD : The giant grandson of Mrs. Skinner, who feeds him 'Herakleophorbia' on her escape to the village of Cheasing Eyebright. The boy is slow-witted, and grows to a progressively lonelier existence commensurate with his increasing size. His meagre education is acquired by squatting outside the classroom window; and he comes near to creating a famine in the already destitute village by his constant demands for food. In his play, he dams the local river, unwittingly causing a ruinous flood. Finally, on the insistence of the autocratic Lady of the Manor, upon whose sparing charity the villagers depend, he is put to work in the local chalk quarry which he digs single-handed. On an impulse he walks to London at a time when the anti-giant propaganda is at its height; and, unable to comprehend the law prohibiting him from the city, he is killed by police. *The Food of the Gods*, 1904

CAMPBELL, CLEMENTINA : The final companion of William Clissold and the woman whom he intended to be his second wife. He literally accosts her in the Champs Elysées, in Paris, where she is dawdling in the hope of being picked up. In her late twenties—thirty years younger than Clissold—she has a graceful body and an 'abstracted countenance, elfin and pensive, infantile and sage'. Her eyes are intelligent and hazel, under long slanting brows. She is the daughter of a Scottish engineer who worked with tramways in Athens and Asia Minor before lapsing into alcoholism. Her mother was Greek. At the age of twenty-one, after her father's death, she became infatuated with an aristocratic French subaltern and lived with him in Paris until his family chose him an appropriate wife. Subsequently she was kept by a number of men of means, having just finished such a liaison when she meets Clissold.

He, however, is in no mood for an affair, but, liking her, he commissions her on the strength of an evening's company to find him a house in Provence. This she does, and he settles her in a *pension* nearby. He has taken the villa in order to write his book and intends keeping her at a distance, although she shares his meals. As he begins to know her better, he discovers her prone to a great variety of moods. She can be rhetorically argumentative, swift and fierce in her opinions, and with a streak of the pagan, but at heart she is affectionate, whimsical and generous.

Imperceptibly almost, she falls deeply in love with her employer, and he with her. He has provided her with the anchor she has sought. She cannot bear the thought of his returning to London when the book is done, and confesses as much. Realizing his own feelings for her, Clissold resolves that they shall marry; but both are killed when his car overturns on a narrow mountain road. They are buried side-by-side in the cemetery at Magagnosc. *The World of William Clissold*, 1926

CAPES, GODWIN : Biology demonstrator under the anti-Mendelian Professor Russell at Imperial College in London. In his early thirties, ruddily blond, he strikes Ann Veronica as perhaps the most variable personality she has yet encountered. His manner of expression is at times clumsy, at others exceptionally vivid. He illuminates by 'darting flashes', throwing light into corners which Russell tends to neglect. His moods and demeanour fluctuate between brilliance, kindliness, irritability and malignant wit. A Fellow of the Royal Society, he is also a regular contributor to the monthly reviews.

Initially Capes appeals to Ann Veronica on a mental level, his arguments adding to the ferment of her own mind. She finds him distinctive, unlike other men, but she is unaware at first that this might indicate that she is falling in love with him. Capes's own appreciation of his student runs along similar lines; and it is only when she announces her engagement to Manning that he realizes the nature of his feelings towards her. During a meeting at the Zoo it becomes clear to them both that they belong together, although Capes, restrained by the presence of her engagement ring, aspires only to the role of life-long friend. Later, when she has broken with Manning, he tells her with painful honesty of his infidelity to his wife, of their separation, and of her refusal to divorce him.

An elopement with Ann Veronica will, he realizes, put an effective end to his scientific career, obliging him to turn full-time to his writing. They both consider the risk worthwhile, and pass an idyllic 'honeymoon' in the Swiss Alps. For one extra-ordinary moment on the brink of a chasm they consider, at Capes's suggestion, hurling themselves to their deaths in each other's arms, but the call of life proves too strong. Within four years he has become a successful playwright and effected a reconciliation between Ann Veronica and her father.

Much of Wells himself can be observed in the history and personality he bestowed on Capes, from the teaching of biology and the contributing to reviews, to the elopement with a student while he was still married to his first wife. The figure of Russell would appear a thin disguise for T. H. Huxley, under whom Wells studied for a year at what, by coincidence, is now Imperial College. *Ann Veronica*, 1909

CAPTAIN OF THE GOLDEN LION, THE : Master of the cargo ship in which Arnold Blettsworthy sails from England to South

America. He remains unnamed, other than the soubriquet, 'the Old Man', but his personality is evident enough—he hates both his vessel and his crew. In appearance he is squat, square-faced, with ginger hair, a bitter mouth, and small grey-green eyes beneath sandy lashes. He ridicules Blettsworthy's erudition, addressing him as 'Miss' and is incensed by his passenger's imitation of his noisy method of consuming soup.

Having beaten to death a young deck-hand after leaving Rio, he abandons ship following a storm during which the engines fail. But he leaves Blettsworthy locked below to await his fate. He reappears in the tale in London during the First World War, when Blettsworthy encounters him in a Pimlico restaurant (his soup-drinking habits have remained unchanged). On this occasion he is almost affable, recounting his experiences of mine-laying and hunting German submarines. *Mr Blettsworthy on Rampole Island*, 1928

CARNABY, LORD : A man of sixty-five who has 'sinned all the sins' but retains a 'remarkable vestige of his own brilliant youth'. Small and lean, he has a tanned face and grey-blue eyes. In appearance fresh and fit, Carnaby shows little evidence of the dissolution which has 'laid waste to the most magnificent political debut of any man of his generation'. Although he appears little in the narrative, he plays a significant rôle in the plot as the keeper of Beatrice Normandy, and thus a major reason why she eventually refuses to marry George Ponderevo. *Tono Bungay*, 1909

CARSTALL, DR. : Father of Richard and the physician who delivers Rud Whitlow to an unexpecting world. Large in appearance and deliberate in manner, he had been made a widower early. He is asked to examine Rud as a result of the latter's aggressive behaviour, but he declares there is nothing abnormal about the boy, except perhaps his tenacity. Privately, however, he considers Rud a little monster, and the effects of Rud's early public speeches only confirm his opinion. Somewhat shy of his own son, he nevertheless indulges in a long conversation with him on the nature of democracy which forms the basis of a chapter. *The Holy Terror*, 1939

CARSTALL, RICHARD : The head boy at Hooplady House school while Rud Whitlow is a junior student there. Taciturn, fair-haired and good-looking, he is idolized by the younger boy, but later becomes the instrument of his death. Carstall approves of Rud's policies as World Director, and is a signatory to a declaration to that effect; however, he is quick to realize that the man's growing paranoia is endangering his very real achievements. Now a noted doctor himself, he takes the opportunity to poison Whitlow with arsenic when the latter has come to Carstall's clinic for treatment. At the rigorous post-mortem examination he substitutes tissue from another body so that the crime remains undisclosed until he confesses a decade later to a former student, Krause, who conducted the post-mortem. Krause agrees to keep silent, and the novel closes with a conversation between Carstall and his eight-year-old son on the personality of the man who brought about the World State. *The Holy Terror*, 1939

CATERHAM, JOHN: 'Jack the Giant-Killer'—the British Prime Minister who comes to power on a pledge to outlaw the growth-promoting drug developed by Redwood and Bensington. Although given to somewhat hysterical public pronouncements on the subject of the giant children, he appears to Redwood, whom he meets towards the story's close, as a more sober individual genuinely aware of the social consequences of the drug's widespread use, and with some concern for the welfare of the giants. *The Food of the Gods*, 1904

CATSKILL, RUPERT: The Secretary of State for War, who is accompanying Cecil Burleigh when the latter's car is spirited to Utopia. A sandy-complexioned man, distinguished by a 'grey top hat with a black band that the caricaturists had made familiar', he entertains the dream that the small band of Earthlings can conquer what he regards as an effete world. He organizes an armed stand from the castle in which they have been quarantined and is scathing in his condemnation of Mr. Barnstaple as 'a conscientious objector'. The character is an easily recognizable lampoon of Winston Churchill, made obvious by his manner of address and such details as the slight impediment in his speech. That Wells had difficulty in containing this particular creation is evident from his later remarks: 'One of the characters got out of my control, and began to speak and act in a way so like Mr. Churchill that even I could see the resemblance. I was shocked and alarmed. I had to stun the character and hustle it out of the way, but not before it made a long characteristic speech and started a war.' *Men Like Gods*, 1923

CAVE, C. : The naturalist and dealer in antiquities who is able to see visions of Mars through the medium of a crystal egg. His unsympathetic family, unaware of its unique properties, insist that he offers the egg for sale. As a consequence, he smuggles it out of the shop and into the care of a hospital demonstrator, Jacoby Wace. Together they record Cave's views of the Martian landscape and its inhabitants. Unhappily, Cave dies with the egg in his hand, and it is subsequently sold by his widow to a buyer who cannot later be traced. 'The Crystal Egg', 1807

CAVOR, MR. : The inventor of cavorite, the anti-gravity material which proves the means by which he and his companion, Bedford, embark on a journey for the moon. A small, rotund and thin-legged man, he proceeds in jerky motions and is given to expansive gesticulation. Vocally, he affects a peculiar buzzing sound. When first encountered by Bedford at Lympne, on the Kent coast, he has 'seen fit to clothe his extraordinary mind in a cricket cap, an overcoat, and cycling knickerbockers and stockings'; a curious sartorial assemblage, since he never cycles or plays cricket. He discourses with Bedford on the nature of gravity, announcing his intention of developing a material which will act as a shield against it.

Cavor's prime motivation is the quest for knowledge, and he remains largely unconcerned with Bedford's speculations on the commercial possibilities of his potential discovery. He also displays little remorse for the extensive damage to the local community caused by the explosion with which his first experiment ends. Once on the moon, he is more interested in investigating the nature of the Selenite civilization than in his personal safety, and he is horrified at his partner's wild attacks on the lunar inhabitants. Having escaped from the Selenites, due mainly to Bedford's efforts, he is recaptured while the other returns to Earth.

He is allowed some freedom in captivity and an opportunity to study the strange alien culture, radioing his observations to the world. Most impressive of these is his description of an audience with the Grand Lunar, the ruler of the moon. Ever naive, he discusses the faults and frailties of Man's organization with that exalted personage and, it seems, is unwise enough to reveal the formula of cavorite. His last message to Earth is hastily sent and broken off before he can also impart the secret of his discovery to his own race. It is assumed that, having provided the information required for an invasion from the moon, his continuing existence is no longer regarded necessary. *The First Men in the Moon*, 1901

CHAFFERY, MR. : The medium exposed by Smithers and Lewisham, and the step-father of Ethel Henderson. A benevolent-looking man with generous side-whiskers and a chin 'like the toe of a boot'. He expresses not the slightest remorse for his fraudulent career, going so far as to justify his trickery by arguing, not altogether unconvincingly, that society and civilization itself are largely based on varying degrees of dishonesty. While complaining that the Lewishams' secret marriage has disorganized his household, he finds his step-son-in-law a useful sounding-board for his anti-social philosophy and pays him frequent visits. He is anxious to involve Ethel in mind-reading experiments, but meets with Lewisham's heated objection. Finally, he disappears, having persuaded his patron Lagune, under hypnosis, to put his name to a blank cheque on which he draws some five thousand pounds.

His attitude to Lagune, recorded in his farewell letter, can well be taken as a summary of his attitude to life as a whole : 'I marvel at the man, grubbing hungry for marvels amidst the almost incredibly marvellous. What can be the nature of a man who gapes after Poltergeists with the miracle of his own silly existence (inconsequent, reasonless, unfathomably weird) nearer to him than breathing and closer than hands and feet? What is *he* for, that he should wonder at Poltergeists?' *Love and Mr. Lewisham*, 1900

CHAFFERY, MRS. : Mother of Ethel Henderson by a previous marriage and wife of the fake medium. Middle-aged and continuously nervous, she has a weak mouth beneath a thin nose and perplexed eyes. Her general appearance is of 'a queer little dust-lined woman with the oddest resemblance to Ethel in her face'. She seems to go in daily dread of her husband, but without elaborating why. When he leaves her after robbing Lagune, she takes Ethel and Lewisham—since married—into her home in Clapham. *Love and Mr. Lewisham*, 1900

CHAMBLE PEWTER, MR. : A lodger at Mrs. Doober's boarding-house who tends to attach himself conversationally to a gratifyingly receptive Edward Albert Tewler. He professes a 'confounded sense of humour', which frequently appears to his listener as an apology for the sceptically vernacular 'I don't fink!'. He decries science and its achievements, and misses no opportunity to debunk Darwinism. His influence over Tewler's limited mental outlook is enduring; in later years the echo of his destructive comments is to be found in Tewler's frequent use of such expressions as 'Bawls' (a delicate spelling in accord with the publishing ethics of the times), 'Piffle before the wind', 'You can't put that over on me', and 'Forgive me if my sense of humour prevents my swallowing that sort of rot'. He passes the Second World War attached to the Ministry of Reconstruction, where his principal trait does much to restrain 'the extravagances of imaginative people'. *You Can't Be Too Careful*, 1941

CHASER, PHILIP : An undertaker's representative, first cousin by marriage to Evangeline Birkenhead, and the ebullient organizer of Tewler's protracted nuptials. He has alert brown eyes, a pug nose, and 'a large oblique mouth ready to smile'. His mode of attire in his leisure moments is distinctly jaunty. He is not without insight into Edward Albert's sudden loss of nerve at the prospect of marriage, and acts as peacemaker of sorts between Tewler and his future father-in-law. He also becomes a discreet go-between during the almost immediate separation and divorce proceedings. *You Can't Be Too Careful*, 1941

CHATTERIS, HARRY : A physically attractive, somewhat irresponsible parliamentary candidate who is the object of desire for the Sea Lady. Under her spell, he more or less abandons his fiancée and also his constituency campaign. Having finally determined to sever himself from her influence, he immediately reverses his decision and goes to his death with her in the sea. His character is best summed up in his own words to the unwilling intermediary, Melville : 'I cannot sit down to the oatmeal of this daily life and wash it down with a temperate draught of Beauty and water. Art! . . . I suppose I'm voracious, I'm one of the unfit—for the civilized stage. I've sat down once, I've sat down twice, to perfectly sane, secure, and reasonable things . . . It's not my way.' The *Sea Lady*, 1902

CHIFFAN : The original architect of Rud Whitlow's career, later to be murdered on his friend's orders. He has a pale, intelligent face with a prominent nose, grey-blue eyes and dark-brown untidy hair. Some five years Rud's senior, he is very much his mentor in the area of politics. They first meet on a walking tour, visit a mildly revolutionary summer school, and join up again in London when Rud has concluded his studies at Camford University. Chiffan introduces him to a number of like-minded acquaintances and a group is formed which meets regularly at the flat of Steenhold, a rich young Anglo-American whom Rud has cultivated at Camford.

Chiffan admires Rud's abilities as an orator and offers constant advice as to how this gift should be exploited. He remains close to Whitlow throughout the long struggle to bring the Common Man's Party to world power. However, his rôle is principally as an unofficial adviser and he enjoys no major executive function. His dalliance with women has always been a cause of distaste for Rud, but he finally achieves respectability by marrying his twenty-ninth mistress, Pheobe. His concern for Rud, who appears to be growing increasingly miserable and paranoiac as World Director, prompts him to offer further advice. Its effect is to arouse Whitlow's suspicions regarding Chiffan's loyalty, and he is subsequently executed in secret without trial. *The Holy Terror*, 1939

CHITTERLOW, HARRY: An aspiring playwright who is instrumental in the dismissal of Kipps from the Folkestone Drapery Bazaar. Altogether an effusive character, he has a figure of 'slight anterior plumpness', enormous calves, and legs that are 'exuberantly turned out at the knees and toes'. Facially he is clean-shaven, having a bluish, generous chin, dark red hair and bright reddish-brown eyes. His gestures are expansive and theatrical, and his talk voluble; he has a habit of punctuating his sentences with the single word 'bif!' He also rejoices in the habit of consuming unusual quantities of 'Old Methusaleh', a semi-lethal Canadian rye whisky which serves to fuel his enthusiasms.

Chitterlow first encounters Kipps by knocking him down with his bicycle in Folkestone. Taking him back to his lodgings, he plys him liberally with 'Old Methusaleh' and regales him with tales of the theatre. Consequently Kipps is locked out of the Bazaar for the night and finds himself 'swapped' on his return in the morning. The pair meet regularly, with predictably inebriated results. Chitterlow's experiences with women, recounted one evening to Kipps and Young Walshingham, persuade Kipps to be more forward with Ann Pornick—a step which eventually leads to his marriage. Kipps advances Chitterlow two thousand pounds, as a share in the play he is currently writing. After the decline in his own fortunes, he assumes the money has been lost. But *Pestered Butterfly* proves an enduring success, establishing Chitterlow's reputation and restoring Kipps to a position of wealth. *Kipps*, 1905

CHRISTABEL, THE GIRL ON THE WALL : A red-headed vision of loveliness who confronts Mr. Polly during one of his frequent bicycle rides. The wall marks the bounds of her school, and she declines to descend from it. For some ten days Polly pays her court, both of them seeing him as a knight in armour and she an enchanted maiden held against her will. The illusion is shattered on the occasion when he discovers that she has allowed two of her friends to eavesdrop on their conversation from behind the wall. Although only a brief episode, there is a strong hint that, through it, Wells was reliving the kind of idealized vision of womanhood which he admitted to experiencing as a sickly adolescent. *The History of Mr. Polly*, 1910

CHRISTIAN, GUY AND PHILIP : The brothers of Lady Mary Justin who first meet Stephen Stratton during his childhood visits to their home, Burnmore House in Surrey. They play a brief but significant rôle during the immediate consequences of their sister's affair with Stratton. Philip assaults Mary's lover on the steps of a London club and wildly reveals the reason for his action to his fellow members. Guy is cooler in his disapproval of the liaison and accompanies Mary during what, at the time, is assumed to be her final parting with Stratton after his promise to go abroad. *The Passionate Friends*, 1913

CLARGES, MISS PUPPY : A house guest of Cynthia Rylands who causes her hostess pronounced distress when she is discovered in a compromising situation with Cynthia's husband. She is 'strident and hard, a conflict of scent and cigarette smoke, with the wit of a music hall and an affectedly flat loud voice'. She is also graceless, rude, troublesome, occasionally indecent and professes to be unchaste. These various attributes make it all the more shocking to Mrs. Rylands that her own husband could be attracted to such a woman. Puppy departs hastily from the Italian villa as soon as her indiscretion is revealed. *Meanwhile*, 1927

CLARKSON, MARY : A friend of Gemini Twain and Stella Kentlake, who loans them her Suffolk cottage when they decide to spend a week living together. A woman in her early thirties, she is slim, dark-haired, with bright brown eyes and whimsical eyebrows. Something of a cosmopolitan, she moves in vaguely bohemian circles in London with an air of the worldly-wise. She goes to bed with Gemini during his enforced separation from Stella, her attitude to the male sex being exemplified by her amused reaction to his fear that Stella would be hurt if she knew of their liaison : 'Most men keep that sort of pompous puerility, I suppose, all their lives. *Why*, I can't imagine. They don't want to hurt the poor dear innocent little, leetle, *leetle* woman. The female of the species, let me tell you, by the age of fifteen has a clearer sense of reality in these things than most men have to the doddering end of their days. The stuff women in love have to put up with ! Oh ! . . . Well well'. *Babes in the Darkling Wood*, 1940

CLAYTON : The club member who encounters the distressed phantom of 'The Story of the Inexperienced Ghost'. Relating his experience to a gathering of fellow members the next evening, he describes the appearance of an ineffectual little spirit whose lack of success at haunting matches a similar pattern of failure in its worldly life. The ghost has forgotten a particular sequence in the complicated series of gestures and manual passes it must perform in order to return to its own world. With some encouragement from Clayton, it finally achieves its aim and disappears. Clayton then informs his friends that he intends to repeat the same passes, in the hope of attaining the other side. He succeeds only too well, and ends by dropping dead at their feet. 'The Story of the Inexperienced Ghost', 1902

CLERGYMAN, THE : Officiator at the wedding of Miriam and Mr. Polly, who adopts what seems to the bridegroom an indescribably habitual stance and marries them wearily and with an initial deep sigh. And also with a fine disregard for the niceties of English pronunciation :

'Pete arf me,' said the clergyman to Mr. Polly.

'Take thee Mirum wed wife—'

'Take the Mi'm wed wife,' said Mr. Polly.

'Have hold this day ford.'

'Have hold this day ford.'

'Betworse, richypoo'.'

'Bet worse, richypoo . . .'

Then came Miriam's turn.

'Lego hands,' said the clergyman, 'gothering? No! On book. So! Here! Pete arf me "Wis ring Ivy wed." '

'Wis ring Ivy wed—'

At the conclusion he expresses his appreciation of an excellent ceremony and insists on being the first to kiss the bride. *The History of Mr. Polly*, 1910

CLISSOLD, CLARA : William's first love, whom he marries but is unable to divorce when she leaves him. He first encounters her at the home of mutual friends and is soon physically drawn to her, even though originally he does not find her particularly pretty. She is slender, dark-haired, having aquiline features and hazel eyes. By nature restless and talkative, she is intelligent and diverse in her talents. She is much more widely-read than William, introducing him to the work of many authors. She can act, but does not wish to become an actress; she sketches well, but has no ambition to follow art. In spite of her numerous interests and enthusiasms, she really has no desire to do anything seriously other than 'living as a sexual consumer'.

Clara is the second of four sisters and convinces Clissold that her parents are attempting to marry her off to a middle-aged friend of her father. This revelation prompts him to propose, and, although his income as a research student is meagre, they are shortly wed. While they agree to delay beginning a family until their finances improve, Clara finds homelife tedious during her husband's daily absence. She rejoins the Fabian Society and begins to take lessons in drawing and painting from the artist, Philip Weston. Inevitably, for one of her instincts, she starts an affair with him.

Discovering she is pregnant, she leaves Clissold for Weston and in due course gives birth to a daughter. Much later she approaches William for help when the liaison with her lover ends. She is concerned for the welfare of her daughter, who has been the cause of their inability to obtain a divorce. Receiving an allowance from him, she later travels a great deal, usually in the company of either very old or very young men. Eventually she dies of a chill caught while dancing before she has fully recovered from a bout of influenza. *The World of William Clissold*, 1926

CLISSOLD, SIR DICKON, BART : The elder brother of William— an advertising magnate who later works tirelessly for monetary reform. He is a large, loquacious man, running somewhat to fat, round headed, with level blue eyes. He tends to grunt when he moves—this being the description of him in middle age. In childhood there were occasions when he exerted his two years of seniority over his brother, but in general they were happy with each other. He shared William's haphazard education while their father was alive, followed by the more stable period at Dulwich College and the Royal College of Science. Later, when they share lodgings in London, he upbraids William for his dedication to research, although he himself has still to decide what career to pursue.

Becoming progressively aware of the chaotic methods of marketing in the late 1880s, he resolves to enter advertising and abandon science. Nevertheless, he adopts a scientific approach to his work which brings him rapid success. Beginning with such diverse commodities as watches, boots and bicycles, his activities soon cover a very considerable range of products. He is one of the first to see the value of poster advertising, an area which he develops to the full. Because he dislikes falsehoods, his approach is not always popular with others in the same 'profession'. As he tells a meeting of leading advertisers : 'We are the masters of the newspapers and they know it. We and we alone have the ear of the world. We can dictate what shall be known and what shall not be known, what shall exist and what shall not. We can educate the people or degrade the people, exalt right things and humble base things. We can be the guide, philosopher, and friend of the common man—working together. Why should we not rise to the full height of our possibilities?'

During the First World War he serves as a colonel, his knowledge of marketing securing him a leading position in the distribution of equipment and supplies. Towards the end he also becomes involved in Lord Northcliffe's propaganda organization (as did Wells himself), and after the armistice he is offered a baronetcy. Much to the chagrin of the republican-minded William, he accepts it, more to enhance his presence and potential influence than anything else.

His relatively happy marriage ends with the death of his wife

Minnie, and he is much moved by a letter she has left him. They have had two sons, both of whom fought in the war, and a daughter. For his part, William considers that Minnie has held Dickon back, his best work being done once she has gone. Certainly his horizon expands during the period of reconstruction. He agrees with William that a 'new sort of man' is required to put the world to rights, and he determines to bring together the more powerful financiers on the international scene with a view to reforming the world monetary system. As a result, he travels much and sees little of his brother in the final years.

After William's death, Dickon contributes a postscript to his unfinished book as an 'Editorial Fraternal'. It is mainly personal. Apart from some criticism of his brother's view of Minnie, and a few remarks concerning himself, its chief purpose is to describe the circumstances of William's fatal accident. Dickon professes himself substantially in agreement with the wealth of ideas in the long manuscript which he has arranged for publication. *The World of William Clissold*, 1926

CLISSOLD, MINNIE : Wife of Dickon whom he first meets during his Bloomsbury days. The only child of a local doctor, she is 'made upon a delicate scale' and enjoys exquisite features; but she does not dress well. Much given to reading and study, she is nevertheless disinclined to talk. Her husband adores her, but his brother William regards her as a cynic, albeit a gentle one. In his book he describes her as holding only Freedom and Virtue, as defined by the Ancient Greeks, of any worth in life. He feels she is disillusioned about the latent power in the human being and that her own efforts are weak. (This view of her is subsequently rejected by Dickon in his postscript to William's book.) She dies unexpectedly in 1920 while undergoing an operation which was not thought dangerous, although she herself has a strong presentiment of death. *The World of William Clissold*, 1926

CLISSOLD, MR. : Until his flight and arrest, a noted financier— the father of Dickon and William. He is a large man, quick of movement, with red whiskers, a flushed complexion and reassuring smile. His rise in the business world has been meteoric, but after a serious failure he perpetrates a series of frauds in which he becomes increasingly more careless. When these are discovered he disappears to France wearing a false beard, only to be arrested there and brought back to stand trial. Deserted by all his former colleagues and friends, he gives his evidence in a manner which indicates that he hardly thinks he has done anything wrong. The judge, a member of one of his clubs, is obliged to rebuke him for familiarity and sentences him to seven years imprisonment. He kills himself by swallowing potassium cyanide as he leaves the dock. *The World of William Clissold*, 1926

CLISSOLD, MRS. : The mother of Dickon and William who later remarries to become Mrs. Walpole Stent. Dark and slender, she is gentle, but also weak and ineffective. She appears to have an element of fear in her nature which both her sons deem excessive; it robs them of much of the love and confidence which they might otherwise have had for her. She finds, not surprisingly, her husband's exalted business and society acquaintances somewhat overwhelming. The exposure of his crime, and his subsequent suicide, bring her close to a nervous breakdown; she refuses to discuss the matter with her children, other than telling them that their father is dead and that in future they must use her maiden name. In her cousin, Stent, she later discovers a less awe-inspiring companion, and with him she has a further son and two daughters. *The World of William Clissold*, 1926

CLISSOLD, WILLIAM : An expert in mineralogy and a business entrepreneur whose long autobiography remains unfinished at the time of his death. Born in 1865, his early years were spent mainly on the South Coast of England while his father conducted his financial affairs in London. At school he proved brighter than his brother Dickon, so that educationally he maintained the same level, although more than two years younger. Like his brother, he was exceptionally fond of the senior Clissold and resentful that the circumstances of his death should be withheld from him. Returned from France after his mother's remarriage, at the age of sixteen he looks up the account of his father's trial in back numbers of the newspaper at *The Times* offices. What he reads elicits his sympathy rather than any sense of disapproval—the two brothers have already reverted to the Clissold surname, their mother having forbidden them to use it for fear that they might be ostracized.

Later both study at the Royal College of Science, sharing a dingy bedroom in South Kensington. There until late at night they begin to share the serious discussions which are to continue between them throughout William's life. But while Dickon sees

65

his future in the commercial marketing world, and moves to Bloomsbury on his marriage, William elects to continue his researches into metallurgy and mineralogy. Only after he has married Clara does he contemplate a change, and it is not until she has left him that he joins the firm of Romer, Steinhart, Crest and Co., which specializes in raw materials and mineral resources.

Sexually inexperienced until he encounters Clara, he finds the physical aspects of their relationship beginning to dominate his attention. For this reason his research work gradually begins to deteriorate, but not before he has made the discoveries concerning dissimilar crystalline masses in rocks which will later earn him a Fellowship of the Royal Society. He is astounded at the news that his wife is pregnant, since they have taken precautions to avoid starting a family. He assumes her condition must be the responsibility of the artist Weston, for whom she is deserting him. He realizes that he might long since have recognized the signs of her affair, had he but wanted, and is puzzled by his failure to do so. Divorce proceedings are instituted and a decree nisi granted before the Queen's Proctor learns of the pregnancy. It is regarded as evidence of collusion, precluding the award of a decree absolute. In such circumstances Clissold must remain married and accept legal responsibility for the child. Clara approaches him to suggest a reconciliation, an appeal which his disillusionment obliges him to reject.

His rise to prominence in Romer, Steinhart is rapidly achieved, his inventiveness being an invaluable asset to the company. Meanwhile he relieves his sexual inclinations, which once awakened have become fierce, in a series of *passades* until he meets Sirrie Evans. Fully aware of her reputation as a consistently unfaithful wife, he nevertheless supports her throughout her divorce and is named as co-respondent, notwithstanding that several other of her earlier lovers could be equally cited. She becomes his only mistress for the next seven years, and he buys a house for her on the outskirts of London and another in due course at Bournemouth, on the South Coast, in the hope that the sea air will help her health. During the same period his work takes him to many parts of the world, wherever rich mineral deposits are to be found.

Clissold's relationship with Sirrie to some extent limits his movement in British society, because many hostesses will not accept her into their homes. Even his own brother's household falls into this category, and for a while he sees less of Dickon. During her last two years the ravages of tuberculosis reduce Sirrie to the state of a semi-invalid, and for those winters William takes her to Switzerland, where she eventually dies in his arms. Her passing hits him hard; he spends the next decade in what he describes as 'copious low-grade living'.

The interval ends with the onset of the First World War. Too old to be eligible for early enlistment, he undertakes technical work which brings him into close contact with the Ministry of Munitions. There he forms a low opinion of the higher ranks of the Army, Civil Service and armament advisers, regarding them as the moral inferiors of 'a Constantinople tourists' dragoman'. Offered a knighthood for his services to the war effort, he is firm in his refusal and indignant that Dickon should accept a baronetcy. From his early days as an ardent socialist, William has been a republican, avouching a staunch dislike of the monarchy and the pomp and mock servility which accompany it. Dickon, whom his brother describes as an Individualist, finds such trappings less of an affront.

Both involve themselves ardently in the movement for reconstruction at the war's end, joining in many debates and laying individual plans. While the hostilities are still in progress, Clissold has developed a new romantic attachment, in the shape of an ambitious and much sought-after young actress, Helen. He finds her beauty near to overwhelming but her theatrical entourage repellent. She, in turn, shows lack of interest in his own career. The affair endures for a number of years and is brought to a close by his refusal to marry her on the news of Clara's death. He appears to have been independent too long to be prepared to sacrifice his freedom of movement and choice of action.

With Helen's departure he resolves that she shall be his last affair. Therefore, when he meets Clementina Campbell in Paris soon afterwards, he is at pains—much to her disbelief—to make this clear. Instead he employs her to find him a suitable villa in Provence, where he can write the book in which he wishes to set out the distillation of his many ideas. Installed in the house, he provides residence for her in a *pension* a few minutes' walk away, treating her as a companion who may share his table and leisure time, but little else. However, over the period of two years' writing they become intimate friends, although he never fully reveals whether they make love. Distraught at his impending departure as the book nears completion, she accuses him of cruelty, arguing that he can hardly fail to see what she feels for him. In a night of characteristic introspection he examines his own emotions, knowing finally that he is as much in love with her. Although she is thirty years his junior, he is now prepared for remarriage and to take her back to London with him. Tragically, both die when his car overturns off a narrow road descending from the gorge of the Loup towards Thorenc on 24th April, 1926. He has swerved to avoid a child who has suddenly darted into the way. Clementina dies instantly, but Clissold lives for some two hours, his pain deadened by morphine injections given by a local doctor. His last words are : 'Neat of You, Mr. G.'

The cryptic 'Mr. G.' is an expression which both he and Dickon have used since boyhood to denote the Almighty, and Dickon refers to it in his postscript to William's manuscript. The book, of course, is the novel itself. In its form it is highly discursive, sections of argument being interspersed with sections on Clissold family history, and yet others devoted to William's love-life. He opens it by protesting his age (fifty-nine) and lamenting that, with luck, he may have another fifteen years of life : 'I do not want to go yet. I am sorry to have so little time before me. I wish before the ebb carries me right out of things altogether that I could know more—and know better. I came into the world with a clutter of protest; my mind is still haunted by protesting questions too vague for me to put into any form that would admit of an answer.'

The range of ideas which the book contains is indeed considerable. There are passing comments and opinions, not to say arguments, on almost every aspect of modern life. Among these are portraits of the British expatriates inhabiting Provence, described as 'Stratum of Futility', and a dissertation on the growth of the metals and raw materials industries, which he relates to the progress of his own company under the heading of 'the Market Tree'. Karl Marx is 'psycho-analysed' and Lord Northcliffe dissected; 'systems' throughout history—from Feudalism to Capitalism—are reviewed and demolished. And through all this, real-life personages stalk : Carl Jung, Bernard Shaw, David Lubin, even Wells himself is accredited a paragraph. However, the most illuminating section, which occupies the last third of the book, begins with Clissold's concept of 'the Open Conspiracy' —a drawing together of intelligent and aware people from every field of endeavour into an international revolution which will lead to a World Directorate. Included in this manifesto are ideas and blueprints for new social routines, the 'civilization' of the Press, the abolition of racism, and a long and substantial attack on the existing form and content of education. The future rôle of women is also covered in detail, interspersed with appropriate comments from Clementina.

Throughout the entire expansive canvas on which Clissold has chosen to illustrate the variety of his thought there is painted one single centre of focus, to bring the entire fabric of the endeavour into perspective—the process of change. This he portrays by the old Greek palliative Πανγα ρει, everything passes—in the last reckoning it is the struggle, and not the objective, which makes the labour worthwhile : 'Πανγα ρει, flux universal. It is only because I may sit at this window for so brief a time that I do not see this scene dissolve visibly and pass and give place to other unprecedented and equally transitory appearances. Of one thing only can I be sure, that all this goes, peasants and pleasure cities, ships and empires, weapons, armies, races, religions, and all the present fashion of man's life. Could my moment be enlarged to the scale of a thousand years, my world would seem less lasting than a sunset and the entire tragedy of this age the unimportant incident of an afternoon.'

This particular novel by Wells was the longest to appear anywhere in 1926, the first edition being published in three volumes. It marks a high peak in his development of the 'discussion' technique and incorporates less genuine action than all else of his work in this category. In an eight-page 'note before the title page' he warns the reader that the ideas of Clissold are not necessarily those of Wells, albeit there are a great many similarities. Understandably, the personality of Clissold is less ebullient and complex than that of his creator, but his arguments are Wellsian in the extreme. In one sense the book can be seen as a sounding-board for the author's subsequent attempts to present his imagined world revolution in non-fictional form : *The Open Conspiracy: Blue Prints for a World Revolution* (1928) and its revised version, *What Are We To Do With Our Lives?* (1931). It generated no little interest in its time, even attracting a parody, *The World of Billiam Wissold* by H. A. M. Thomson—a curiosity now forgotten. Πανγα ρει! *The World of William Clissold*, 1926

CLOOTE, IMMANUEL : The publicity agent hired by Rowland

Palace to promote his image. A young man, with a broad head of 'the Alpine type' and dark curly hair; 'his features seemed to have been flattened vertically into a permanent frown'. Palace is at a loss to know quite what to make of him but respects his ideas. (In passing he refers to Wells himself, suggesting that a man who allows his friends to address him as 'H.G.' cannot amount to much!). Cloote arranges various publicity ventures for his employer, not all of them successful, but his chief action in the story is to track down Mrs. Freda Lewis and expose Alfred Bunter's true identity in the hope of ruining his reputation which is threatening Palace's own. *Brynhild*, 1937

COMMON, ESAU : The main character in the fragment of a story which Wells intended should open a series of tales about the British Army. He abandoned the project before even the first story was complete. The fragment, which was published in *The Contemporary Review*, February 1902, opens with a brief description of Esau's inadequate education and of his fascination for warfare. However, his country's army holds out no promise to him; he is too clever to endure the life of a private, and not well-born enough to become an officer. Instead he works as a journalist. The fragment ends with a conversation between Esau and a stranger, possibly a spy, while they watch the Aurelian Army undergoing manoeuvres, Esau insisting that for all his criticism of its military unpreparedness, he remains loyal to his country. 'The Loyalty of Esau Common', 1902

COOMBES, JIM : The henpecked husband of 'The Purple Pileus' and an early, but not the first, example of Wells's small army of shopkeepers. Oppressed by the playing of popular tunes by his wife's friend on a Sunday afternoon, he leaves his house for a stroll in a nearby wood, where intent on suicide, he eats a poisonous-looking fungus. Its only effect is to intoxicate him, so that he returns to terrorize his household—an act which finally enables him to reach a proper relationship with his wife. Thereafter his business prospers. 'The Purple Pileus', 1896

COOTE, CHESTER : A prime mover in the Folkestone Young Men's Association who becomes mentor to Kipps in the ways of higher society. A young man of semi-independent means—he has inherited a share in a house agency—he is pale-faced and has light blue eyes above a prominent nose. His voice, which is heard in numerous committees, and on many platforms, is noted for its 'quivering quality'. His characteristic cough is likened to the sound of an ancient sheep at a quarter-of-a-mile's distance being 'blown to pieces by a small charge of gunpowder'. He lives with an unmarried elder sister who paints. Familiar with the Walshinghams, Coote undertakes jointly with Helen to 'improve' the former apprentice once he has inherited his fortune. His manner towards his charge is generally condescending, and he assumes an almost proprietorial rôle in his lectures to the socially inept Kipps. He dwells at length on the use of 'the cut'—the art of haughtily ignoring anyone considered socially inferior or otherwise undesirable. Kipps is distressed when Coote applies this technique to his friends, Buggins and Pierce, but less surprised when he is himself the recipient after he has ended his engagement to Helen. *Kipps*, 1905

CORNER, CECILY : A friend of the Britling family who is courted by Mr. Direck, the visiting American who claims to be distantly related to her. The daughter of a Colchester printer, she has an extraordinarily pretty smile, and there is 'something in her soft bright brown eye—like the movement of some quick little bird'. She grows very fond of Direck, placing her full trust and confidence in him. She is completely won over when he appears in a Canadian army uniform and announces his intention of fighting for the allies in the First World War. As the sister of Letty, the wife of Britling's secretary, she shares her distress at her husband's supposed death in the trenches. *Mr. Britling Sees It Through*, 1916

COSSAR : An acquaintance of Redwood and Bensington, and the father of three of the giant children whose enormous growth is attributable to the 'Boomfood' drug. A civil engineer by profession, he is gaunt, large, clumsily-limbed, while his face resembles 'a carving abandoned at an early stage'. He undertakes the destruction of the experimental farm at Hickleybrow, in Kent, when it becomes overrun by enormous rats and wasps, and later builds a redoubt for his sons at Chislehurst. Here they are often to be seen at play, to the wonderment—or consternation—of passing railway travellers. It is also from Chislehurst that the physical war between the giants and normal-sized men is waged. *The Food of the Gods*, 1904

COSSINGTON, ARTHUR : A contemporary of Remington at the City Merchants School, who quite overpowers the original plans for a new magazine and eventually assumes its direction. Given to sentimentality, and something of a poseur, he nevertheless displays a remarkable grasp of the fundamentals of publishing success. In later life he becomes Lord Paddockhurst, a newspaper magnate of the Right with a certainty of his single-handed ability to 'raise' England. Very possibly he is a veiled portrait of the real Lord Northcliffe, who came to entertain similar notions, and whom Wells knew in person. The author later served as director of propaganda literature aimed at Germany in Northcliffe's Ministry towards the end of the First World War. *The New Machiavelli*, 1911

CRAMPTON, CECIL : A slightly delicate, genteel young man whose supposed ride from London to Brighton forms the basis of one of Wells's bicycling tales. He encounters 'a bounder' more than once along the route, and when he stops to repair a puncture for a particularly attractive girl, it is the bounder who comes to her aid after Crampton has half ruined her machine. Later he discovers that she is a close friend of the girl whom his mother had hoped he would marry—a prospective union that is now doomed. The ride to Brighton is never completed, the last twenty miles being covered by rider and machine in the comfort of a train. 'A Perfect Gentleman on Wheels', 1897

CRUMBS, THE : A young couple in whose flat Christina Alberta and Preemby lodge after they have left Woodford Wells. Harold Crumb is red haired, with a 'rampant profile', and lives by attempting to sell drawings to weekly papers. Fay Crumb reviews books and writes romantic fiction for bookstall magazines. She talks rapidly and indistinctly, in a manner difficult to understand. The couple are not, according to Christina Alberta, 'fearfully married', presumably indicating that they have no wedding lines.

Preemby awakens the maternal instinct in Fay : 'She struggled with a persuasion that he was really a little boy of nine who had been naughty and grown a big moustache and that she had to take care of him and restrain him.' The couple agree to look after Preemby when he first emerges as Sargon, but unhappily they allow him to escape. They search for him ineffectually, and then

pass out of the story until its close when they attend his funeral.
Christina Alberta's Father, 1925

CRUMP, DR.: The physician of Siddermorton who treats the injured Angel and later advocates his departure. A large heavy-looking man, clean-shaven and double-chinned, he regards his patient as an ordinary human whose wings are a mere deformity. Subsequently he is inclined to accept the Angel's tale, until he learns that the visitant has no knowledge of any souls of the departed. When the Angel begins to disturb the local community, Crump threatens him with either prison or the mad-house, now believing him to be either a clever impostor or simply deranged.
The Wonderful Visit, 1895

CUMMINS, EGBERT CRADDOCK: Originally a shy, likeable and conservative young man whose demeanour undergoes an extra-ordinary change on his appointment as a newspaper drama critic. Constant visits to the theatre lead him to adopt the gestures and affectations of the actors he must nightly watch. He loses all concept of self-identity, together with the girl he loves. 'The Sad Story of a Dramatic Critic', 1895, later re-titled 'The Obliter-ated Man'

CURATE, THE: A thoroughly weak specimen of humanity who saddles himself upon the narrator in *The War of the Worlds*. His face tells all that is needed to be known of his personality: a receding chin, crisp flaxen curls lying across a low brow, and pale blue vacant eyes. The Martian invasion has clearly unhinged what little intelligence he might once have possessed and has reduced him to incoherent babblings on the subjects of Sodom and Gomorrah and the Last Judgment. He becomes a distinct liability to the narrator from the moment of their first meeting near Walton-on-Thames, and never more so than when they find themselves trapped in a ruined house at Sheen immediately above the crater formed by the fifth cylinder from Mars. The curate will neither lower his voice, nor confine himself to his own share of their diminishing food supply. After more than a week of imprisonment he becomes completely demented and attempts to address the invaders in the terms of a Jeremiah. Fearful that this outburst will reveal their hiding-place, the narrator kills him with the blunt end of a meat-chopper. His body is rapidly removed by a Martian handling machine which comes to investigate the disturbance, but the narrator survives undetected. *The War of the Worlds*, 1898

CUSS, MR. : A general practitioner at the village of Iping who is intrigued to learn of a visitor swathed in bandages staying at the local inn. His professional interest being aroused, he calls on him on a charitable pretext but finds him uncommunicative. At the end of the interview he is astonished to find the stranger is waving around an apparently empty sleeve—even more so to have his nose pinched by an invisible finger and thumb. He recounts the experience to his friend Bunting, the vicar, and together they later investigate the Invisible Man's room following his tumultuous departure. He surprises them by his return to retrieve his books, robbing them of their clothes before violently disrupting the villagers' Whit-Monday festivities. *The Invisible Man*, 1897

D

DAD, WILLIAM : An updated version of Bildad the Shuhite, and a governor of Huss's school in *The Undying Fire*. A warily alert, silver-haired industrialist from the Midlands, he is a participant in the long discussion which precedes the headmaster's operation and which constitutes the major part of the novel. He regards Huss as ultimately responsible for the deaths of two boys in a fire at Woldingstanton and is anxious to see him replaced by the head of his technical department, Farr. Conservative in his attitude to education, he views Huss's concentration on history as excessive. He is less disposed to argue with Huss than his fellow governor, Sir Eliphaz Burrows, tending merely to support the latter with brief interjections; but he is equally taken aback by Huss's expressed views on the cruelty of God. As a man whose whole thought is orientated towards business, he believes that Woldingstanton should be run with a view to preparing its pupils for a commercial career. *The Undying Fire*, 1919

DALE, DR. : The rogue physician who treats Bishop Scrope in the absence of Dr. Brighton-Pomfrey. His appearance exceeds the Bishop's worst apprehensions—lean, lank, dark-complexioned, with 'long black hair and irregular rather prolonged features'.

His chin is 'right over to the left', and his voice is harsh. He convinces Scrope that Brighton-Pomfrey's treatment of neurasthenia is quite inadequate and provides him with a drug which he warns will open his mind but also relieve his present condition. The result is the two visions which lead to the Bishop's resignation. When Scrope returns to obtain a further prescription from Brighton-Pomfrey he discovers that Dale has been killed (presumably in the war, although this is not actually stated) and that his formula for the drug has died with him. *The Soul of a Bishop*, 1917

DAVIDSON, SIDNEY : The eponymous character who experiences 'real vision at a distance' in 'The Remarkable Case of Davidson's Eyes'. What appears to be simply a sustained series of hallucinations is eventually revealed as a paranormal experience involving a shipwreck in the South Seas half the world away from the observer. 'The Remarkable Case of Davidson's Eyes', 1895

DAVIS, JOSEPH : A popular historical novelist who becomes obsessed with the idea that his expected child may be affected genetically by cosmic rays. The suggestion that such radiations might emanate from Mars is first mooted by a fellow club-member, 'a rufous man', during an argument on their possible source. Davis is infected with the notion, assuming that Mars, having cooled much earlier than Earth, would now have an ancient civilization far in advance of Man. In such circumstances, the argument runs, the Martians may be attempting to change Man by long-distance genetic engineering to mould him closer to the Martian personality and intelligence.

Davis confides these views to his wife's obstetrician, Dr. Holdman Stedding, who at first rejects the idea outright and entertains doubts regarding the writer's sanity. In retrospect, however, he, too, is intrigued by the theory and in his turn consults the philosopher and psychotherapist, Ernest Keppel, who professes interest. Davis in the meantime has largely abandoned his writing in favour of research into the supposed phenomenon. He is particularly interested in studying the schoolboys to whom he occasionally lectures, watchful for any signs of unusual intelligence and of a compulsion to contest accepted teaching. To him it seems clear that more highly intelligent and inventive people are being born than formerly—evidence that the Martians are increasing their psychological invasion.

75

In due course the theory is taken up by the Press, but it proves of short-lived news value. Nevertheless, convinced by his findings, Davis destroys the manuscript of his current book, a romanticized version of all human history, and comes to the realization that both he and his wife have themselves been 'Martianized'. Thus, in the course of the story, he has turned from the fear of radiation-bred monstrosities to a vision of a saner, more creative world encouraged by the intelligence of Mars. The novel is dedicated to Winston Churchill. *Star Begotten*, 1937

DAVIS, MRS. MARY : The dark-haired, grey-eyed, wife of the author. An independent spirit hailing from the Outer Hebrides, she is fifteen years her husband's junior, and from the first he finds her enigmatical. She becomes rapidly tired of any fresh experience and appears to have detached herself from Davis in a way he is at a loss to explain. It is when she insists on having a child that his preoccupation with cosmic rays begins. When their son is born he is convinced that he is under the genetic influence of Mars, and finally that both Mary and himself are similarly infected. *Star Begotten*, 1937

DELIA : The servant girl who works in the vicarage where the Angel is an unwanted guest. Initially, she sympathizes with him because he appears to be a hunchback and her own sister is also a cripple. She finds him strangely appealing and is later overwhelmed by his exquisite violin playing. Realizing his unhappiness at his rejection by the world of men, she endeavours to comfort him. During the vicarage fire she attempts to retrieve his instrument and is joined by him in the consuming flames : 'For a moment the Angel stood staring. Then in a flash he saw it all, saw this grim little world of battle and cruelty, transfigured in a splendour that outshone the Angelic Land, suffused suddenly and insupportably glorious with the wonderful light of Love and Self-Sacrifice. He gave a strange cry, and before anyone could stop him, was running towards the burning building.' They die together in the blaze. *The Wonderful Visit*, 1895

DENTON : An air landing-stage attendant in London at the end of the twenty-first century. The lover and subsequent husband of Elizebe θ Mwres, he elopes with her to the countryside in the face of her father's determination that she should marry another, and older man. However, the couple are ill-prepared for a life in the wilds and, after Denton is attacked by Food Company dogs, they return to the assumed safety of the city. There his various efforts to secure lasting employment are foiled by Bindon, the prospective husband Mwres had in mind for his daughter. Reduced at last to grinding servitude in the ranks of the Labour Company, Denton learns to defend himself against the physical attacks of his brutalized fellow workers, to be reprieved only when a dying and egotistically contrite Bindon bequeaths a substantial legacy to Elizebe θ. 'A Story of the Days to Come', 1897

DEVIZES, WILFRED : An expert in the law relating to lunacy who helps Christina Alberta in her attempts to rescue Preemby. He is dark, good looking, and has a nose extraordinarily similar to Christina Alberta's. There is evidence to suggest that he is her real father, since he knew her mother briefly a few months before she married Preemby. However, he refutes Christina Alberta's suggestions to this effect, insisting they regard each other as cousins; but later during a long political discussion he admits : 'It isn't common for a man to get an unexpected daughter abruptly at the age of twenty-one.' He visits Preemby at Dymchurch after the latter's escape from the mental hospital and convinces him that he is not exclusively Sargon, King of Kings, but that he shares that ruler's blood with all other men. *Christina Alberta's Father*, 1925

DIAMOND MAKER, THE : No name is given for this character, who encounters the narrator one evening on the Thames Embankment. His tale is one of woe, for although he has discovered the secret of making large diamonds artificially, he dare not sell them. The device he used has been mistaken for a bomb, and he is consequently placed on the police wanted-list as an anarchist. Reduced to penury, he offers a huge jewel to the narrator for a mere hundred pounds, but the bargain is not taken up. By the end of the tale he has apparently disappeared into obscurity. 'The Diamond Maker', 1894

DIRECK, MR. : The secretary of a society of Massachusetts businessmen who comes to England in the hope of persuading Mr. Britling to deliver a lecture to its members. Described as a type of man commonly found in America, he is reminiscent of the kind of 'clean and pleasant-looking person one sees in the advertisements in American magazines'. His first encounter with Britling comes near to disaster as a result of the latter's appalling driving. He has much to say to his host, but experiences some difficulty in overriding Britling's volubility. Finding himself soon at home in the Britling's informal and highly-mixed household, he is entertained to an alarming and hazardous game of hockey, at which he finds himself unexpectedly adept.

Direck is strongly attracted to Cecily Corner whom he discovers could be a distant relative. He seeks out her company at every opportunity. Concerned by her condemnation of America's, then, isolationist attitude to the First World War, he joins the Canadian army and embarks for France. The act wins Cecily's approval and secures their continuing romance. He attempts to discover the fate of Teddy, the husband of Cecily's sister who has disappeared in the war and is erroneously presumed dead. *Mr. Britling Sees It Through*, 1916

DOOBER, MRS. : The London boarding-house keeper selected under the auspices of Messrs. Colebrook and Mahogany to provide a roof for the young Tewler during his period at the Imperial College of Commercial Studies. Graced with a receptive personality, she presides over an unusually cosmopolitan household which includes among its paying guests Belgian refugees from the First World War and the illegitimate son of an Indian Rajah. Many discussions, and a variety of minor intrigues, take place in her communal dining-room; it is there that Tewler first encounters his future wife, Evangeline Birkenhead. *You Can't Be Too Careful*, 1941

DOUGLAS, CAPTAIN : A guest of the Laxtons at Shonts, and the unwitting target of the Lord Chancellor's ire when the latter suspects he is making him look a fool. He is asked to leave, a request he regards as placing his honour as an officer in doubt. That does not prevent his rendezvous on a motor-bike with the actress Madeleine Philips, beside the caravan in which she is travelling with friends and which also houses, unbeknown to Douglas, the recalcitrant Bealby. At the story's close he discovers a remorseful and hunted Bealby on the road and returns him to his mother in the gardener's cottage at Shonts. *Bealby: A Holiday*, 1915

DUNKERLEY, MR. : An assistant master at Whortley Proprietary school and a colleague of Mr. Lewisham. A kindly young man, he finds working in the country irksome, dreaming of a career in London where he plans to register amazing inventions—'The Patent Square Top Bottle' among them. In reality he later takes a teaching position at a suburban school and frequently attends the meetings of The Friends of Progress, a socialist group organized by Lewisham. *Love and Mr. Lewisham*, 1900

E

EASTON, SIR PHILIP : The lover of Amanda Benham who seizes his opportunity while her husband is travelling abroad. About the same age as Benham, he is a dark-complexioned young man, brown-eyed and good-looking, with a touch of Spanish blood. Liberal in outlook, he first appeals to Amanda by virtue of his hobby of collecting the work of ascendant painters, an area of the arts which interests her but leaves Benham cold. She assures Benham that Easton is a paragon of integrity and honour and that she is perfectly safe in his company, even though it is evident that he is hopelessly in love with her.

Benham returns from a visit to Moscow to find Amanda calling Easton 'Pip'; he is later subjected to a sugary account of how wonderful Sir Philip thinks she is. Benham feels that if he hears much more in a similar vein he 'might be constrained to invert very gently but very firmly the bowl of chrysanthemums over Sir Philip's head, or kick him in an improving manner'. Back from another trip abroad, he surprises them embracing. When he suggests he divorce Amanda, Easton is quick to agree, but she is unwilling and hopes for a reconciliation. In the outcome, Benham continues his travels, leaving his wife to Easton's attentions. *The Research Magnificent*, 1915

EDEN, EDWARD GEORGE : The unlucky medical student who finds himself tricked into exchanging his young body for that of the aged philosopher Elvesham. He commits suicide shortly after discovering the change. 'The Story of the Late Mr. Elvesham', 1896

EGBERT, KING : The British monarch who advocates a World

79

Government at the end of the Last War. He attends the international peace conference at Brissago, in Italy, where he argues that the world must become a single republic. To demonstrate his conviction he abdicates, to the consternation of his chief adviser who has accompanied him. He also calls for the confiscation of all existing stocks of 'Carolinum', the radioactive material used in the manufacture of atomic bombs, so that they can be placed under international control. When King Ferdinand Charles of the Balkans attempts to assert his country's independence, Egbert is instrumental in having him killed. *The World Set Free*, 1914

ELOI, THE : The degenerate descendants of Man encountered by the Time Traveller in the year 802,701 A.D. They strike him as very beautiful and graceful beings, but also exceptionally frail. Their complexions give the impression almost of the flushed attraction of a particular kind of consumptive. The Eloi inhabit ruined palaces where they live communally.

They display little interest in the Time Traveller, and their lack of concern for their own kind is evidenced by their failure to go to the rescue of Weena, the girl whom the Time Traveller rescues from drowning. It becomes apparent later in the story that the Eloi are preyed upon by the subterranean Morlocks and used by them for food. They are identified as the remnants of the earlier élitist class of the Establishment, now fallen into helplessness. *The Time Machine*, 1895

ELPHINSTONE, MISS : Dark and slender, a young woman of quiet deliberation who fends off the attackers of her pony-chaise with a whip in *The War of the Worlds*. She then produces a revolver in support of the narrator's brother who is struggling with the men. When he joins her on the vehicle she continues to hold the reins, proving her worth in the face of the growing panic of the crowds through which they pass during the flight from the Martians. Her composure contrasts sharply with the hysteria of her brother's wife, who is her other passenger. All three reach the coast safely near Tillingham, where they embark for Ostend. *The War of the Worlds*, 1898

ELPHINSTONE, MRS. : One of the two women rescued by the narrator's brother in *The War of the Worlds*; he comes to their aid when their pony-chaise is attacked during the mass exodus from London. Unlike her sister-in-law, who accompanies her,

Mrs. Elphinstone yields to deepening despair, forever calling for her surgeon husband, George, who has remained at their home in Stanmore and whose fate is never revealed. Like her companion, she passes out of the tale on board the steamer for Ostend. *The War of the Worlds*, 1898

ELSTEAD : A prototype deep-sea explorer who descends to a depth of five miles in the Tropic of Capricorn—his diving sphere bears a considerable resemblance to present-day counterparts. In the deep he encounters strange, tailed, bi-ped creatures who drag his craft to a submarine city largely constructed of sunken ships and decorated with the skulls and bones of drowned men. There he is worshipped as a god for several hours before his sphere breaks loose and hurtles to the surface. Having carried out improvements, he makes a second descent, from which he fails to return. 'In the Abyss', 1896

ELVESHAM, EGBERT : The noted, and aged, philosopher who, by a ruse, exchanges his decrepit body for that of the young medical student, Eden. The swap is effected by means of a chemical formula combined with hypnotism, but it is to little avail— Elvesham is run down and killed by a cab shortly afterwards. 'The Story of the Late Mr. Elvesham', 1896

EVANS, SIRRIE : A rather scandalous woman who becomes the mistress of William Clissold until her early death. 'Athwart my memories of these little opium doses of love', he writes, 'there flits the tall, slender figure of Sirrie Evans, with her fever-touched cheeks, her strong profile, and her burning, deep-set eyes.' Those eyes are a very fine dark blue; among her other characteristics are an essentially brave disposition, an adventurous humour, and a powerful impulse to explore and travel. With Clissold she visits many unfamiliar places, he being the only one of her several lovers to stand by her when her husband divorces her and is consequently named as co-respondent. Thereafter he buys a house for her in Richmond, on the borders of London, and she remains faithful to him even during his long absences abroad. They become deeply attached, as much in friendship and companionship as in physical fulfilment. She dies of tuberculosis in 1905, in Switzerland, where he has taken her in the hope of improving her health. She is described by Dickon Clissold, in his postscript to his brother's book, as one of the two women whom

William really loved, the other being his final companion, Clementina Campbell. *The World of William Clissold*, 1926

EVESHAM : Leader of the Conservative party during Remington's period as a Member of Parliament—a tall, bent-bodied man with a small-featured almost elvish face. Gentle mannered, and possessed of a singular gift of oratory, he is described as being at one time 'the most powerful man in England under the throne'. Remington is impressed by Evesham's ability, and even by the sheer unscrupulousness with which he gains points in the game of party advantage. His major criticism of the man is the doubt whether he particularly cares much about politics at all; nevertheless, Evesham's ideas on the organized state contribute substantially to Remington's change of allegiance from the Liberals to the Tories.

The character, as Wells later admitted, is a 'caricature-portrait' of the one-time Conservative Prime Minister, Arthur Balfour, with whom Wells had a number of social discussions during the Edwardian period. Balfour's appearance under the guise of Evesham is only one among several such thinly-veiled characterizations of real-life figures in the story. The character is mentioned in several of Wells's other novels of the same period. *The New Machiavelli*, 1911

EWART, ROBERT : A friend of George Ponderevo whom he first meets during his schooldays in Kent. As a lad he is described as 'a long-limbed lout', very tall, with a round knobby face, a blob of a nose and busy hazel-brown eyes. On maturity he affects a black moustache. He is the bastard son of a well-known artist, partly following his father's leaning by eventually becoming a designer and sculptor of monuments. As a young man he lives over an oil-shop at Highgate Hill, in London, in the frequent company of a prostitute whom he also uses as a model. He is the first to discuss the nature of love and sex with Ponderevo, and it is to him that George often turns for advice as an adult. Ewart's views, however, are usually so abstruse as to be of little practical value.

If anything, Ewart is an Existentialist. After a Fabian Society meeting, he announces that socialists are lacking in a sense of proportion. The sum total of his advice is to have no regrets, to seek after whatever one determines as beautiful and not to mind the hangover in the morning : 'The real trouble of life .... isn't that we exist—that's a vulgar error; the real trouble is that we *don't* really exist and we want to.' His sense of humour is eccentric and extends to placing what, in effect, are mustard pots at the four corners of a tomb he has been commissioned to carve. He also designs some thoroughly unsuitable posters for 'Tono Bungay' and undertakes occasional sculpting work for Edward Ponderevo. *Tono Bungay*, 1909

F

FARNESS, CATHERINE : The mistress of Richard Bolaris, and a patient listener to his long dialogue with his identical twin Ratzel during the civil war in which the two brothers find themselves on opposing sides. Tall and dark in appearance, she remains very much in the background, coming to the fore only occasionally to establish the feminine point of view. She agrees to help Bolaris in his plan to secure Ratzel's escape and suggests a scheme whereby the brothers impersonate each other—it is rejected as being impractical. She is with Bolaris when he is accidentally killed by his aide Handon, and the story closes with her lament on the loss of the hope for the future which he and Ratzel had come to represent. *The Brothers*, 1938

FARR, JOSEPH : Head of the technical section at Woldingstanton School, he plays the rôle delegated to Zophar the Naamathite in the original Book of Job. His face is clean-shaven, round, white and shiny; he has difficulty in keeping his hands at rest. He joins two of the school governors, Sir Eliphaz Burrows and Mr. Dad, in a discussion of the school's future with the headmaster, Huss. Both governors are persuaded that Huss should resign and give way to Farr, so that the tuition may be directed more to the preparation for careers in commerce. Huss, for his part, has attempted unsuccessfully to dislodge Farr for some ten years, recognizing that his assistant has consistently used the school's facilities in the search for a patentable discovery which would enable him to give up his teaching career. He says as much during the conversation, a charge which Farr does nothing to refute. His oblique counter-attack is to suggest to the governors that Huss's views on the nature of God hardly suit him for his position of responsibility over young boys. *The Undying Fire*, 1919

FAT WOMAN, THE : The landlady of the Potwell Inn, with whom Mr. Polly eventually finds refuge and a platonic contentment once he has despatched her hooligan nephew, Uncle Jim. Her pink plumpness and innate kindliness prove a source of comfort to the former shopkeeper, and while she is much given to weeping while the feud with Jim is at its height, she is clearly moved by Polly's resolve to protect her against a formidable adversary. *The History of Mr. Polly*, 1910

FERDINAND CHARLES, KING : The Balkan monarch who attempts to resist the establishment of a World Government at the Conference of Brissago on the ending of the Last War. Better known as 'the Slavic Fox', he is of a pallid complexion, long-nosed, with a short thick moustache and small blue eyes which are 'a little too near together to be pleasant'. His attempt to intimidate the conference with his aircraft fails, and he is killed while trying to defend the câche of atomic bombs which he is reluctant to turn over to international control. *The World Set Free*, 1914

FERNDYKE, MR. : Arnold Blettsworthy's solicitor and senior partner in the firm of Ferndyke, Pantoufle, Hobson, Stark, Ferndyke & Ferndyke. An aged man, who was once a schoolfellow of his client's uncle and is related to the Blettsworthys on his mother's side. He advises Arnold in the establishment of his book business in Oxford and cautions him against advancing unnecessarily large sums to his partner, Lyulph Graves. He also recommends a sea voyage following Blettsworthy's broken engagement and is consequently partly responsible for the events that follow. Acting as guardian during Blettsworthy's long period of delusion, he visits him in New York once he has recovered. Recalling how many of the Blettsworthy family have given their lives for the cause of civilization, he is instrumental in Arnold's decision to return to England and enlist. *Mr. Blettsworthy on Rampole Island*, 1928

FILMER : The constructor of an ingenious flying machine in the short story of the same name. His contraption combines both the principles of the balloon and the (then still theoretical) aeroplane. He is backed in his endeavours by an unscrupulous newspaper magnate, Banghurst, and much play is made with a successful working model of the craft. When the full-scale version is completed, Banghurst insists that Filmer must naturally pilot its maiden flight. The inventor, however, is so fearful of the idea of flying that he shoots himself on the day of what was to be the great occasion. It is left to one of his assistants to demonstrate the machine's worth. The tale includes one of Wells's speculations on the possibilities of aerial warfare, and also includes a forecast of radio control. 'Filmer', 1901

FINCHATTON, DR.: A young general practitioner sent to Les Noupets to recuperate from a deep psychological disturbance. He encounters the croquet-playing Frobisher, to whom he speaks of his experience in the village of Cainsmarsh, in the Fens. The marshes he claims are haunted by the brutish presence of early cavemen whose remains have been found there. He has seen the almost perfect specimen of a prehistoric skull in the local museum, and it has followed him through his dreams. He argues that the presence is responsible for the outbreak of uncharacteristic violence among the villagers—the aged vicar has attacked his wife, and a dog has been beaten to death. It is later revealed by Finchatton's psychiatrist, Norbert, that there is no such place as Cainsmarsh, although the incidents he has described were real. He has invented the story in an attempt psychologically to reconcile himself, as a sensitive intellectual, to violence erupting in many parts of the world. *The Croquet Player*, 1936

FISON: A retired tea-dealer staying at Sidmouth, in Devon, who becomes the first human to survive an encounter with *Haploteuthis ferox*, the murderous cephalopods of 'The Sea Raiders'. Of giant proportions these octopus-like monsters are capable of overturning small pleasure boats and chasing their prey along the sea-shore. Fison encounters them a second time when, in company with three others, he goes to retrieve the half-eaten remains of some unfortunate victim. Their boat is attacked, and one of the party pulled under—the whole scene is a brilliant and gripping piece of narrative. After terrorizing parts of the South West coastline the cephalopods move on, probably returning to the ocean depths from where, it is suggested, they originally came. 'The Sea Raiders', 1896

FOSSINGDEAN, LADY CATHERINE: An attractive divorcée whose

charms produce a predictable effect on the writer Sempack when both are the guests of Cynthia Rylands at Casa Terragena. Tall, dusky-haired and with dark-blue eyes, she has an engaging smile which is at the same time impudent, friendly and disarming. She and Sempack pass an idyllic morning in the villa's garden where they discuss the other members of the house-party and indulge in some preliminary love-making. They are disturbed by their hostess who is already upset at the discovery of her husband in the throes of a similar indiscretion with Puppy Clarges.

Lady Catherine returns to England during Sempack's subsequent absence on a walking tour. She joins with a friend, Sir Harry Fearon-Owen, who is organizing volunteers to man the public services in the event of a General Strike. Philip Rylands later writes to his wife to tell her that Catherine has run down two young men outside Rugby, one of whom was killed, and has failed to stop after the accident. *Meanwhile*, 1927

FOTHERINGAY, GEORGE MCWHIRTER : Another of the author's archetypal 'little men', but one of unsuspected powers, who is the central figure in 'The Man Who Could Work Miracles'. From the first simple demonstration of an inverted lamp in the bar of the Long Dragon public house, he progresses rapidly to the act of making a walking-stick bloom, consigning a police constable to Hades and converting all beer and alcohol to water (the last at the instigation of the local chapel minister, Mr. Maydig). His *tour de force*, however, is to arrest the rotation of the Earth, a feat leading to consequences he had not foreseen—everything detachable is hurled through the air at several miles a second and humanity is destroyed. Commanding his own preservation, Fotheringay orders a return to the moment before he worked his first miracle and for himself to be relieved of his powers. While light-hearted in content, the tale is an early foretaste of Wells's preoccupation with the dangers of the misuse of science by those who do not properly understand it.

The story was later filmed as a Korda production directed by Lothar Mendes. In the same year, 1935, Wells's screenplay of the movie was published as a book. Generally, the same characters feature in the film, which begins and ends with an argument in Heaven between three archetypal figures—The Observer, The Player, and The Indifference—the essence of the debate being Man's probable behaviour were he to be granted miraculous powers.

86

Additional figures in the screenplay include Major Grigsby, the owner of the department store in which Fotheringay is employed, who is of the clear opinion that miracles are bad for business. Also Colonel Winstanley, whom Fotheringay spirits instantaneously to Bombay in a demonstration of his gift. To add to the cinematic effect of the story's climax, Winstanley's house is transformed into a palace, to which the world's notables are summoned for Fotheringay's final Earth-stopping performance. 'The Man Who Could Work Miracles', 1898, and *Man Who Could Work Miracles*, 1935

FOXFIELD : A biologist and scientist whose work is published by Stephen Wilbeck. He is described as 'a big red talkative mouth with a vast fuzz of brindled black and grey hair, he looks at you through his spectacles like the lamps of a big car coming at you fast and rather out of control'. In the vein of the Wellsian scientist, he is prone to lecturing Wilbeck on the future possibilities ahead for Man. He enthralls Dolores with his descriptions of marine reproductive systems when she and Wilbeck meet him at the marine laboratory at Roscoff in Brittany. He also appears briefly in *Star Begotten*. *Apropos of Dolores*, 1938

FRAPPS, THE : The family to whom George Ponderevo is sent at the age of fourteen when he has been banished from Bladesover House. A cousin of George's mother, Nicodemus Frapp is a back-street baker at Chatham, in Kent : 'a bent, slow-moving, unwilling dark man, with flour in his hair and eyelashes, in the lines of his face and the seams of his coat'. He is dominated by a 'young, plump, prolific, malingering wife', who bears him many children, most of whom die in infancy. George shares a bedroom with two of the elder survivors. The Frapp household is devoid of books or even newspapers, the only relief to the servile monotony being the weekly chapel-going. George shocks them with his professed atheism, and one entire chapel meeting is devoted to a combined assault on his disbelief. When he learns that the efforts are to be renewed the following Sunday, he runs back to his mother at Bladesover; and the Frapps are heard of no more. *Tono Bungay*, 1909

FROBISHER, MR. : The narrator of *The Croquet Player* who is holidaying with his aunt at Les Noupets. He reveals little of his own personality, save that he studied at Keble and is regarded by Americans as a sissy. He reads only the sports pages of newspapers and plays croquet for an hour each morning, also intermittently in the afternoons. The bulk of the story is his encounter with Dr. Finchatton on the hotel terrace where he hears of the latter's nightmarish experience as a general practitioner in the village of Cainsmarsh, in the English Fen country.

Finchatton is convinced that his local community is being influenced by a brooding and evil presence in the marshes—the spirits of cavemen who walked the region for thousands of years in the past. He recounts some of the brutal incidents that have recently occurred in the village and seeks the croquet player's reaction to his interpretation of their cause. Frobisher, in keeping with his character, is entirely non-committal; but he agrees to meet Finchatton again the following day when he has had an interval to consider his tale. In fact, it is not the doctor but his psychiatrist, Norbert, who appears next morning, to reveal that Cainsmarsh does not exist and that Finchatton is suffering from a form of hallucination. Frobisher fails to warm to Norbert, who proceeds to harangue him on the resurgence of the caveman presence throughout all modern society. Tired of the other's ranting, Frobisher takes his leave, stating that the Stone Age may well be returning, and the sunset of civilization be at hand, but that doesn't alter the fact that he has an engagment that morning to play croquet with his aunt.

The novel represents a further attempt of Wells to indulge in allegory. As such, it is of interest and critically important, although it is doubtful whether he succeeded in recreating the allegorical import of *The Island of Dr. Moreau* which he had achieved in his mid-thirties in 1896. *The Croquet Player*, 1936

G

GEEDGE, MRS. WINIFRED : The third member of the caravanning party encountered by Bealby during his flight from Shonts. An inconspicuous woman, but with a pretty, clear profile beneath black hair. She considers there is something elfin about Bealby's small face, a quality which manifests itself to the full when he sends their caravan careering down a hill. *Bealby: A Holiday*, 1915

GERILLEAU, CAPTAIN : The faintly ludicrous Creole commander of the gunboat *Benjamin Constant* whose endeavours are observed by the engineer, Holroyd. Sent to eradicate an unusually advanced strain of formicaries threatening an area of the Amazon, Gerilleau's least practical solution is to fire at them with a cannon. He also loses his lieutenant to their poisonous assault, by insisting that he boards a vessel they have overrun. 'The Empire of the Ants', 1905

GERSON, GENERAL : The 'genius for comprehensive war plans' who becomes Mr. Parham's Supreme Commander during the Lord Paramount's global war. Powerful, short and thickset, he has a small bomb-shaped head covered with a wiry furze, a large mouth and a glass eye. His eyebrows are 'the fierce little brothers of his moustache'. He is assiduous in his translation of Parham's dreams of conquest into action, with disastrous results. His dedicated belief that once a weapon has been invented it should be used, leads to his assault on Woodcock's fortress where the only supplies of the lethal Gas L are stored. His attempt to shoot his opponents once within the refinery causes the explosion which brings the fantasy to an end. *The Autocracy of Mr. Parham*, 1930

GIBBERNE, PROFESSOR : A leading physiologist who develops a drug capable of vastly accelerating an individual's metabolism. The effects give the impression that all other living things have been reduced to almost complete stasis. Under its influence, the professor and the narrator cavort through the sunny streets of Folkestone while the remainder of the population appears as no more than statues, the only danger to the pair being the likelihood of singeing their clothes if they run. 'The New Accelerator', 1901

GIDDING : Stephen Stratton's partner in the publishing venture by which they intend to propagate the need for a World State. A wealthy young American : 'He has to a peculiar degree that directness and simplicity which is the distinctive American quality.' They first meet on board ship when Stratton is en route to the East and Gidding lectures him on the vanished glories of the Ancient Greek civilization. It is on their reunion in New York after Stratton has married Rachel More that they begin

89

the discussions which eventually lead to their partnership. *The Passionate Friends*, 1913

GIP : The nickname of Wells's eldest son, born some two years before 'The Magic Shop' was written, but possibly still the intended hero of the tale. The narrator takes his young son into an apparent joke shop, only to discover that its wares are the product of genuine magic. The boy is enthralled, the father uncertain. On returning to pay the bill he finds the shop has disappeared. 'The Magic Shop', 1903

GLENDOWER, ADELINE : The fiancée of Harry Chatteris and a close friend of the Bunting family. Not overtly attractive, nor unduly plain, she is intensely loyal to Chatteris and works assiduously in support of his parliamentary candidature. Although it is she who first calls for help for the Sea Lady during her simulated act of drowning, she rapidly forms an intuitive dislike of her, well before Chatteris has come under her spell. *The Sea Lady*, 1902

GOD, ALMIGHTY : An unexpected visitor to Noah Lammock who at first takes Him for an escaped lunatic. He calls upon Lammock to draw up a list of passengers for a new ark to escape the deluge of the Second World War, at the same time admitting that He had been shabby in His treatment of the original Noah once the Flood had subsided. Finally accepting Him as the Almighty, Lammock regards Him as unstable but essentially human.

During His second visit a week later He accuses Lammock of having written several of Wells's books, notably *The Time Machine* and *The Work, Wealth and Happiness of Mankind*— a suggestion which is vigorously denied. His third appearance coincides with Lammock's awakening on board the ark, where He contents himself with playing the harmonium during the ship's services—an activity He has long hoped to perform. *All Aboard for Ararat*, 1940

GOD, THE LORD (I) : Inevitably the dominant figure in 'A Vision of Judgment', in which tyrant and saint alike are exposed by the Recording Angel and finally flee from the truth to take refuge up the Almighty's sleeve. The brief vision ends with the sleeve shaking out all humanity on to a new planet circling Sirius, with the instruction to try again. 'A Vision of Judgment', 1899

GOD, THE LORD (II) : Participant in a wrangle with Satan during the Prologue of *The Undying Fire*. He is reminded by Satan of a wager between them whether the original Job would lose faith in God and curse Him for the afflictions which beset him. Satan argues that the entire human race has now become Job and that he has grown weary of tormenting it. God agrees to a renewal of the wager, but He warns Satan that while he is free to try Man to the uttermost, he must not kill him, insisting that he is imbued with the Spirit of God. *The Undying Fire*, 1919

GOGGLES, JIMMY : Actually a diving-suit worn by the un-named central character in a tropical island tale. The only survivor of an illicit salvage team attacked by natives, he finds himself worshipped as a god when he emerges from the sea. But he is obliged to remain inside the suit, since it would be fatal to reveal himself as a mere man. After several months he succeeds in escaping, but not before venting his feelings on a visiting missionary. 'Jimmy Goggles the God', 1898

GOOD, MATILDA : A friend of Martha Smith and the tenant of a boarding-house in Pimlico, London. Matilda is large, as Sarnac/Smith is later to describe her : 'She was much larger than any lady I had hitherto been accustomed to; she had a breadth and variety of contour like scenery rather than a human being; the thought of her veins being varicose, indeed of all her anatomy being varicose and fantastic, seemed a right and proper one … Her attitude to Harry Smith is considerably more yielding than his mother's. She nurses Martha solicitously during her final illness, and after her friend's death she passes out of the story. *The Dream*, 1924

GOOPES, MR. : A mathematical tutor who conducts weekly progressive gatherings at his home, and to which Ann Veronica is conducted by Miss Minniver. A small, dark man, generally reserved, he professes a favourite attire of pyjama-shaped canvas suiting secured by brown ribbons. As a rigid vegetarian, he subjects his guests to 'fruitarian refreshments' which leave Ann Veronica, at least, in a continuing state of hunger. The discussions over which he presides are designed to elevate the participants to the higher levels of thought. When arguments appear to be descending to an earthy basis, he is inclined to adopt the 'Socratic method' to rectify the lapse. *Ann Veronica,* 1909

GOTCH, SIR JOHN : The irate local landowner who finds the Angel's activities in his village insupportable. A little man, with scrubby hair and a small, thin nose 'sticking out of a face crackled with wrinkles'. His attention is first drawn to the Angel when the visitant demolishes a section of his barbed-wire fence. Subsequently he becomes incensed by further acts of trespass and the Angel's attempts to undermine his authority. When he tries to horsewhip him he is overpowered and viciously assaulted. However, he has already used his influence on the vicar to ensure the Angel's departure. *The Wonderful Visit,* 1895

GRAHAM : A youngish man at the opening of his story in the 1890s, he has been married and divorced, been involved in the wilder fringes of politics and written inflammatory pamphlets. After a period of excessive overwork he falls into a trance while holidaying in Cornwall, from which his body resists all attempts at revival. Finally he awakes in A.D. 2100 to find himself, in name at least, master of the world—mostly by virtue of money left to him by his cousin Warming, and property acquired on his behalf during the past two centuries. His awakening, when he is greeted by the White Councillor Howard, is hardly peaceful, and even before he can begin to adjust himself to his new position and surroundings, he realizes that he is at the centre of civil disturbance.

He later learns that he has been deliberately revived by the Labour boss Ostrog, in a bid to wrest power from the White Council who rule the world as Graham's trustees. Rescued by Ostrog from an attempt by the Council to poison him, Graham is initially content to allow the boss to assume control once the Council is overthrown. He takes the opportunity to explore the extraordinary environment of twenty-second-century London, now one of the only five cities existing in Britain. He is astounded by the size of the architecture, the enormous wind vanes which provide power, the achievement of manned flight, the moving pavements and roadways.

He discovers that the family household no longer exists, that the majority of the population eat in communal halls surrounded by moving advertisements. Children are raised in crêches, where robot wet-nurses also carry advertising, 'of interest to mothers'. Pleasure cities provide temporary euphoria for an effete middle class; the people are lulled before the receiving screens of 'kineto-tele-photographs'; and euthanasia is available on request. Religion, also, has moved with the times—exhortations to 'Put your Money on your Maker' are blared from loudspeakers in the streets.

During this period of acclimatization Graham learns to fly, much against the will of his attendants who fear for his personal safety. But the idyll comes to an end when he is advised by Ostrog's niece, Helen Wotton, of the oppressed masses who are little more than slave workers for the Labour Companies, and for whom her uncle has no intention of providing relief. With Graham's awakening, the blue-overalled labour workers are anticipating freedom. To keep them subjugated Ostrog imports black police from Africa, ignoring Graham's orders for their return. In the ensuing battle Graham leads the workers against the boss, and is killed destroying the last of the aerial landing-stages from which the Africans could disembark.

The story depicts Wells's attempt to project what he saw as contemporary tendencies into a future where they would undergo extreme exaggeration. In short, he pictured the social and technological trends of the late 1890s in 'a state of inflamed distension'. Everything was to be bigger, faster, and, for the Labour Company worker—worse. Taken with his earlier work, 'A Story of the Days to Come' (1897), which was set in the same future and gave an intimate view of the worker's lot, the novel acted as a prototype for many later dystopian visions by other writers. In a revised edition in 1910, Wells retitled the story *The Sleeper Awakes*, which he judged to be better English, and added a further chapter while omitting some six thousand words of the original. He also explained in a preface that he had eliminated a 'sexual interest' between Graham and Helen Wotton. *When the Sleeper Wakes*, 1899

GRAMMONT, v. v. : A young American woman who captivates Sir Richmond Hardy during a chance encounter at the ancient monument of Stonehenge. In her early twenties, she has the type of facial features which impress Hardy as hinting at a touch of the Amerindian—dark hair, soft cheekbones and an added breadth of brow. By coincidence, her father turns out to be one of the particular oil magnates whom Hardy intends to challenge in his quest for an international policy on fuel; her mother died when she was a child.

She has been engaged to the unremarkable son of a banking family, whom she rejects in favour of a disreputable artist later to be shot for cowardice during the First World War. She herself was engaged in Red Cross activities behind the front and still expresses guilt at having persuaded her lover to enlist against his will. In spite of their age difference, V.V. (as she is addressed by her friends) quickly warms to Sir Richmond, and is content to let him guide her on a brief tour through the West of England. In the company of her discreet, but talkative companion, Belinda Seyffert, the couple visit a number of sites and buildings of historic interest, in the meantime discussing ideas for a new and more rewarding way of life. V.V.'s intelligence and enthusiasm are revealed in these talks and within a day or so both realize they are in love.

Quite independently each reaches the conclusion that they must part. V.V. confesses that she has allowed herself to become re-engaged to her original fiancé; but, more immediately, her domineering father is arriving shortly to take her to Paris—there is little doubt in her mind that he would strongly disapprove of Hardy. She also admits she actively dislikes the man she has once again agreed to marry, although there is no indication what her future actions will be in this respect. The leave-taking at Exeter railway station is short and unemotional, both promising a regular exchange of letters and unaware that Sir Richmond has only a few weeks to live. Her photograph is among the scattered papers on his desk in the room where he dies. *The Secret Places of the Heart*, 1922

GRAND LUNAR, THE : The head, in more ways than one, of the Selenite civilization in *The First Men in the Moon*. His braincase measures many yards in diameter and is sustained and patted by a variety of attendants, who also soothe it with cooling sprays. In a semi-circle below him stand 'his intellectual subordinates, his remembrancers and computators and searchers and servants, and all the distinguished insects of the court of the moon'. He questions Cavor closely regarding human society and its limitations, and even more precisely on the subject of cavorite. The inventor reveals his secret, but later in a final, interrupted radio message he regrets his foolhardiness. Armed with the knowledge of the anti-gravity material, and possessed of a high degree of skill, discipline and organization, the Selenites are ideally placed to cross space and begin the conquest of Earth. *The First Men in the Moon*, 1901

GRAVES, LYULPH : The erstwhile partner of Arnold Blettsworthy in a book business in Oxford when both are in their early twenties. Little is given by way of physical description save that he has brown hair and reddish brown eyes. Quick-witted and inventive, he enjoys far fewer capital assets than his partner and borrows some three thousand pounds from him in the brief course of their enterprise. It ends when he is discovered seducing Blettsworthy's fiancée, Olive Slaughter, and Graves is stunned by a furiously wielded Chianti bottle. He absconds immediately, leaving the debt unpaid.

Not until Blettsworthy is in hospital during the First World War, convalescing after the loss of a leg, is the acquaintanceship renewed. Graves has been wounded in the head in Italy, and for a while he remains unrecognized beneath his bandages. He seems to accept Blettsworthy's forgiveness as a matter of course, although he announces his intention of repaying the loan in full. On leaving Oxford he has apparently marketed sewing machines on the Gold Coast in West Africa; after the war he is given the marketing account for Blettsworthy's new wine company. Somewhat to his wife's disapproval, Blettsworthy resumes a close friendship with Graves, finding in him the only confidant with whom he can discuss his recurrent fears of a return of his delusion. *Mr. Blettsworthy on Rampole Island*, 1928

GREEDLE, MRS. : Housekeeper to Gemini Twain and Stella Kentlake during their stay in Mary Clarkson's cottage in Suffolk. Essentially a kindly soul—much given to the culinary pursuit of 'bubble and squeak'— she is also distinguished by her nosiness. Her bucolic wisdom is evoked when she overhears Gemini arguing with the Rev. Morton Richardson : 'But you can't say such things to a parson, you know ... They've an innocence ... Even babies 'ave a knowingness. Dirty little darlins. But *parsons* ... Oh *parsons*! Don't even wet themselves. It isn't as though they was natural white paper; it's as though they'd been washed out. Sort of bleached ...' When the couple return to the cottage during Gemini's convalescence in the early part of the war, Mrs. Greedle surprises them by appearing noticeably the worse for drink. *Babes in the Darkling Wood*, 1940

GREGORY : The erstwhile brother of Freda Lewis who blackmails her husband David (later to become Alfred Bunter). A cocaine addict, fishy-eyed, lumbering and generally sulky, he has travelled in the U.S.A. and in the East. As garrulous as his sister, particularly so when drinking, he has discovered the facts about Lewis's first marriage in Scotland and threatens him with exposure. Drunk one night in Lewis's company when Freda is away, he falls into a disused shaft on a dump in Cardiff and is left by his brother-in-law either already dead or dying. His body, when at last discovered, is first correctly identified by his sister, but she later claims it is her husband's, Lewis having disappeared on the same evening. *Brynhild*, 1937

GRIFFIN : A young physicist who discovers the secret of invisibility —at the eventual cost of his life. Some thirty years old, and a pure albino, he is a former student of University College where he won a medal in chemistry before transferring his interest to physics. He steals money from his father to pursue his scientific research and fires the house in Great Portland Street in London, where he has lodged, to obliterate his traces once he has made his discovery. He soon regrets his hastiness, for it is mid-winter, and his early exhilaration gives way to the fear of frostbite as he hurries naked through the city's West End. Small details which he had failed to anticipate threaten to disclose his presence— mud-splashes partially identify his feet; he leaves footprints in the snow; and the snowflakes themselves tend to reveal his outline, as does the perennial London fog. Jostling passers-by on the pavements bump into him, seeing nothing to avoid, and he comes close to being run down by a hansom cab.

He seeks refuge in a large store, hoping to acquire clothes there overnight; but he is disturbed early in the morning and is obliged to strip again to make good his escape. Finally he robs a theatrical costumier, leaving him bound in a sack, and makes for Iping in Sussex, the point at which the narrative opens. He stays until Whitsun at the local inn, arousing the suspicions of the landlady, Mrs Hall, first by his rudeness and bandaged appearance, secondly by his odd behaviour. In a futile search for an antidote for his invisibility he becomes increasingly irate, smashing glass apparatus and taking less care to conceal his condition, particularly in the presence of the local doctor, Cuss. Short of money, he burgles the nearby vicarage, much to the mystification of the Rev. and Mrs. Bunting; however, he has aroused too much curiosity for his protests of innocence to be believed. After a desperate fight, during which he unveils, he flees the inn, leaving behind his notebooks, chemicals and clothes.

Later he prevails on the tramp Marvel to help him retrieve his property from Iping; and he terrorizes the village in the process. There follows the indiscriminate robbery of shops in nearby Port Stowe, until Marvel evades him and finds sanctuary in the coastal town of Burdock. Griffin is wounded by gun-shot in the pursuit, later stumbling into the home of Dr. Kemp, by coincidence a former student colleague. His callous attitude, as he relates his experiences, and the accounts Kemp reads in the press convince the doctor that he is harbouring a potential killer. Humouring Griffin, he secretly sends for the police, and while waiting for their arrival he hears of Griffin's plans to let loose a reign of terror. The trap fails and the Invisible Man remains at large for a further night and day, during which he beats to death an inoffensive steward. He returns to avenge himself on Kemp, shooting the local police chief, Adye, in the attempt, and chasing the doctor through the town. There, finally, he is cornered and killed by a crowd who cannot see how badly they are injuring him.

With death, the effect of invisibility ceases also : 'And so, slowly, beginning at his hands and feet and creeping along his limbs to the vital centres of his body, that strange change continued. It was like the slow spreading of a poison. First came the little white nerves, a hazy grey sketch of a limb, then the glassy bones and intricate arteries, then the flesh and skin, first a faint fogginess and then growing rapidly dense and opaque. Presently they could see his crushed chest and his shoulders, and the dim outline of his drawn and battered features.'

The message of the tale, in company with that of 'The Country of the Blind', is that what would appear at the outset to be a unique advantage is sometimes found to be the very reverse. It is also possible to view the story as an early Wellsian warning of the dangers of science when its benefits are placed in the wrong hands. It is not invisibility which drives Griffin to crime, for he had already stolen from his father before he found the formula, and, as he confesses to Kemp, he felt no remorse on his father's consequent suicide. In short, Griffin is a criminal who harnesses science to his own sinister ends. There is little sinister, however, about the sunny lanes of Sussex where he acts out his drama—a striking departure from the damp cellars of the Gothic genre and an inspired touch which makes his invisibility all the more strange.

For the first American edition Wells added an epilogue to the story, portraying Marvel as an innkeeper, and still in possession of Griffin's precious notebooks. *The Invisible Man*, 1897

GRISLY FOLK, THE : A tribe of Neanderthals who carry off two girl children of the competing species, Man. The leaders of the human group, Click and Waugh, organize a rescue attempt, and in the ensuing skirmish the latter dies. The tale is written in a documentary style, the events recounted being presented as mere possibilities, and not even as definite happenings in a fictional story-line. 'The Grisly Folk and their War with Men', 1921

GRUBB : Early partner and mentor of Bert Smallways in a bicycle hire and repair business. It does not prosper. They are considering the dubious prospect of forming a song-and-dance act, and performing a trial run-through at Dymchurch on the Kent coast, when Smallways is accidentally carried off in Butteridge's balloon. Thereafter, Grubb drops out of the tale. *The War in the Air*, 1908

H

HADDON : The surgeon whose patient in 'Under the Knife' dreams under chloroform that he has died during the operation. The patient's imagined journey from his body, out of the Solar System, and finally beyond the universe altogether, is told in a striking piece of sustained imaginative writing. In the event, the surgery proves a success. 'Under the Knife', 1896

HAGEN, CHANCELLOR : The chief minister of Clavery, the Central European state of which Paul Zelinka unexpectedly becomes King. Hagen proves loyal to the throne and helps to avert war with nearby Agravia by arranging a secret meeting between its president, Himbesket, and Paul. He also assists the new king in the arrest of prominent supporters of the rebellious Prince Michael, thereby forestalling an attempted *coup d'état*. *The King Who Was A King*, 1929

HALL, MRS. : Landlady of the Coach and Horses inn at Iping, in Sussex, and the first character in the tale to encounter the Invisible Man. She disregards his strange appearance, counting her good fortune in securing a guest in the depths of winter. However, she is taken aback by his persistent rudeness and becomes progressively less obliging to his whims. Initially she dismisses her husband's suspicions that the stranger may be a criminal in disguise, although her doubts are subsequently aroused over the non-payment of his bill. She has just begun to refuse him meals, and to demand an explanation of other irregularities, when circumstances force him to unveil. *The Invisible Man*, 1897

HAMMERGALLOW, LADY : The aged resident of Siddermorton House, who lives chiefly upon Burgundy and the little scandals of the village—'a dear old lady with a ropy neck, a ruddled countenance and spasmodic gusts of odd temper, whose three remedies for all human trouble among her dependants are, a bottle of gin, a pair of charity blankets, or a new crown piece'. When assured by the local vicar that the Angel whom he is harbouring has great musical ability, she arranges for him to perform in her home. The recital proves a disaster, for the player is incapable of reading music and reveals a lack of social etiquette which offends her guests and shames the vicar accordingly. *The Wonderful Visit*, 1895

HAPLEY : The famous entomologist who is haunted by an unusual hallucination in 'The Moth'. For many years Hapley conducted a vociferous feud with a fellow member of the Royal Entomological Society, Pawkins, frequently reducing that Society's meetings to 'nothing so much as the Chamber of Deputies'. On Pawkins's death, much of Hapley's *raison d'être* dies with him; and when he discovers what he believes is a new species of moth in his room, his main regret is that he cannot use it to humiliate his rival. It is, however, a specimen which only he can see; and after generally creating havoc in his attempts to catch it, he ends his days in a padded cell claiming it is the ghost of Pawkins. 'The Moth', 1895

HARDY, LADY : The long-suffering wife of Sir Richmond who reluctantly condones his extra-marital relationships. Although her husband talks of her in his discussions with Dr. Martineau, she makes only two brief appearances in the story. A small, frail middle-aged woman, she has a 'delicate sweet' profile, blue eyes and uneven shoulders. Her face is the type which even under 'the most pleasant and luxurious circumstances still looks bravely and patiently enduring'. She is distressed that she has not been called to Sir Richmond's deathbed from her family home in Wales, but Martineau refrains from telling her that it was her husband's wish. She agrees to allow Hardy's mistress, Martin Leeds, to see the body, prevailing on Martineau to make the necessary arrangements, so that the two women need not meet. *The Secret Places of the Heart*, 1922

HARDY, SIR RICHMOND : A man of affairs, arms manufacturer and leading member of the Fuel Commission, whose investigation into his own motivations forms the basis of the plot. Little physical description is recorded, save a height of 5′11″, but he is clearly an imposing personality, gaunt and dark. He is also a person of extensive reservations; his private life is 'in some respects exceptionally private'. He is first depicted in consultation with the leading nerve specialist, Dr. Martineau, whom he consults to discuss his fears of an impending breakdown, having allowed himself to become grossly overworked in his dealings with the Commission. Hardy is convinced of the necessity for an international agreement on the use and conservation of energy and has been engaged in an exhausting attempt to win over other members of the Commission to his persuasion. He is obsessed with the idea that he may become too ill to achieve this end : 'Friction! I'm grinding to death . . . And it's so *damned* important I *shouldn't* break down. It's *vitally* important.'

Martineau is drawn to his prospective patient and suggests that Hardy adopt a psychological approach to his inner compulsions. The two discuss Sir Richmond's attitudes to his work and the doctor agrees to a joint motor tour of the West of England during which 'Secret Places of the Heart' may be examined. The novel is basically an account of that excursion.

Lady Hardy is duly informed of her husband's intention, accepting it meekly in the knowledge of long experience that anything she might say would be unlikely to influence his decision. The tour begins unpropitiously when Hardy throws a violent tantrum in reaction to the breakdown of his car outside Maidenhead. A replacement is sent for while the pair pass the night in an hotel by the river. Martineau, who has been concerned at the ferocity of Hardy's outbursts, realizes that the other is very probably more ill than he had originally thought. In a boating trip along the Thames Sir Richmond confesses that he had spent other nights in the hotel with a mistress. He talks also of his three grown-up children and of his relationship with his wife, whom he describes as a 'wonderfully intelligent and understanding woman'. He admits that he has no excuse so far as she is concerned for his misbehaviour. Nevertheless, he feels compelled to seek out the company of other women. Chief among these at the present time is the illustrator, Martin Leeds, who has borne him a child.

With the arrival of another car, the tour continues and many ancient landmarks are visited, including the early monuments around Avebury. While investigating Stonehenge, on Salisbury Plain, Sir Richmond encounters the young American woman, V. V. Grammont, and her companion Belinda Seyffert. An immediate mutual attraction is apparent, and Hardy invites V. V. to accompany him. Martineau, disconcerted by this development, and exasperated by Miss Seyffert's continuous chatter, decides to take his leave. The incident reinforces his distaste of Hardy's pursuit of the opposite sex.

Sir Richmond conducts Miss Grammont through many of the churches and historic buildings of the western counties while Belinda Seyffert remains discreetly in the background. On the occasions when they are left alone the couple become very close and confess their love for each other. Hardy is torn by the realization that he is not only being disloyal to his wife, but also to Martin Leeds, and he resolves that he and V.V. must part. She, in turn, has reached the same conclusion, already being engaged to the son of a leading American banker although she is less than enamoured of him. Hardy takes his leave of her en route for Falmouth where she is to join her father's ship prior to a stay in Paris. He returns to London with renewed vigour to continue his work on the Fuel Commission.

The improvement in his health proves temporary, and although the Commission's report is completed, he leading a dissenting minority, the effort proves fatal. Martineau is hastily summoned and recommends a specialist, but the pneumonia cannot be arrested. At Lady Hardy's request, Martineau agrees to conduct Martin Leeds when she wishes to see the body. When she breaks down over the coffin he is appalled by the injustices and cruelty of love.

The novel falls into the 'discussion' category and is, by the author's admission, a further attempt to consider sexual activity as a waste of energy. Sir Richmond is seen as a man of great ability and altruistic ideals, but with a streak of coarseness which mars his personality. His disregard of those most close to him must be balanced against his public work, a judgment which Wells was conscious might be applied to his own career. *The Secret Places of the Heart*, 1922

HARMAN, LADY ELLEN : A woman whose struggle to break free from the strictures of a jealous and pathologically possessive husband forms the basis of her story. The daughter of a solicitor who was killed in a train crash, she has been educated at a boarding-school in Wimbledon and is only seventeen when she is first courted by Sir Isaac, a man more than twenty years her senior. At the opening of the narrative, when she visits the author, George Brumley, with a view to buying his house, she is twenty-six, but already has four young children. Tall and beautiful, she has a 'big soft mouth, great masses of blue-black hair on either side of a broad, low forehead, and eyes of so dark a brown you might have thought them black'. Introspective as a young girl, she marries Sir Isaac within a year of meeting him, the wedding being slightly delayed until he has received his knighthood. The match requires three proposals on his part, and she finally consents more out of pity for him than any real affection.

After a honeymoon in the Isle of Skye, they return to a house he has purchased on Putney Hill, in London, where a full retinue of servants awaits them. There Ellen is afforded every luxury, but entirely at her husband's dictation. He has decided the furnishings and entire arrangements of the household, and in much the same fashion he organizes the preparations for her pregnancies. She soon learns that he intends to allow her practically no freedom at all. He is not adept at meeting people, other than for business purposes, and shuns any involvement in social life. His attempts to hide in the garden, to avoid an encounter with Lady Beach-Mandarin when she calls on Ellen, verge on the comic.

Lady Beach-Mandarin is determined that Ellen shall become more active socially and invites her to a Shakespearian luncheon which Harman forbids her to attend. Defying him, she goes. At the luncheon she renews her acquaintance with Brumley and meets, among others, Agatha Alimony, an ardent advocate of women's rights. Later Brumley takes her to Hampton Court Palace and fails to return her home at the expected time, an oversight on his part which precipitates a violent row between Ellen and Sir Isaac. Her mother, who is staying with them, locks herself in her room.

Furious at her insistence that she will accept further invitations, Harman is even more disconcerted when Ellen attacks his company's policy while he is entertaining some business friends. He attributes her rebelliousness to the influence of her sister, Georgina Sawbridge, who makes no secret of her suffragette inclinations. In fact, Lady Harman's view of her husband's commercial pursuits is more the result of her talks with Susan Burnet, a young woman who renovates the household's furnishings and whose father has drowned himself after being bankrupted by Sir Isaac. With no allowance of her own, Ellen asks Miss Burnet to pawn a ring for her; but before the transaction can be completed, Harman has bought Brumley's house, 'Black Strand', and moved his family from London.

Kept a virtual prisoner in the country, Ellen is unaware that Lady Beach-Mandarin has attempted to visit her and has been turned away by the butler. Brumley himself is more successful and manages to talk to her alone for a few minutes, during which he declares his love. He returns later the same day, hoping romantically to carry her off, only to fail ignominiously.

Eventually Ellen effects her own liberation, helped by the money which Susan Burnet has finally been able to pass to her. Returning to London, she calls on Agatha Alimony in the hope that she will hide her for the time being. To the contrary, Miss Alimony advises Ellen to go back to Harman, arguing that if she is to win her rights then flight is no solution. In desperation Lady Harman smashes a post office window and, despite Sir Isaac's efforts to obtain her release, is sentenced to a month's imprisonment. On her release she finds her husband more amenable to her aspirations. He agrees to finance a chain of hostels which she wants to provide for his hitherto ill-treated shop-girls.

The store assistants warm to Ellen, whom they see as their champion; and the first 'International Hostel' is opened in Bloomsbury amid appropriate ceremony. However, although the refuges are ostensibly his wife's project, Harman is determined to have his way with their management. He appoints the officious Mrs. Pembrose as overall supervisor, a woman whose concept of discipline is entirely the reverse of Ellen's liberal intentions. Hostility ensues and many girls are ejected from the hostels, among them Alice Burnet, the sister of Susan. Nevertheless, Sir Isaac is adamant that Mrs. Pembrose must remain.

Three years pass, during which Ellen suffers a miscarriage and Harman's health declines. She continues to meet Brumley, whose passion for her remains undiminished, although he has largely accepted the prevailing situation. Much of the final part of the story is taken up with their discussions and Brumley's ruminations. After Sir Isaac's death in Italy, hastened by the knowledge that the writer is in love with Ellen, Brumley is convinced she will marry him. But she is disinclined to sacrifice her new-found freedom; moreover, the conditions of Harman's will deter any thoughts of further marriage. During Harman's last illness she has experienced a moment of revelation in St. Paul's Cathedral : 'Her spirit clung to this mood of refuge. It seemed as though the disorderly, pugnacious, misunderstanding universe had opened and shown her luminous mysteries. She had a sense of penetration. All that conflict, that jar of purposes and motives, was merely superficial; she had left it behind her. For a time she had no sense of effort in keeping hold of this, only of attainment, she drifted happily upon the sweet sustaining sounds, and then— then the music ceased. She came back into herself. Close to her a seated man stirred and sighed. She tried to get back her hold upon that revelation, but it had gone. Inexorably, opaque, impenetrable doors closed softly on her moment of vision . . .'

Basically the novel is a study in jealousy; and in this context it can be compared with *The Passionate Friends*, which had appeared in the previous year. In Ellen Harman, Wells had also created a further example of a young woman struggling to reach self-fulfilment, a theme he had already explored in *Ann Veronica* and on which he was to dwell in several future stories. He knew the Putney area of London well, having lived there with an aunt as a young man and renting a house in adjoining Wandsworth during his first marriage. *The Wife of Sir Isaac Harman*, 1914

HARMAN, SIR ISAAC : A wealthy caterer whose International Bread and Cake Stores have put many a small baker into the bankruptcy court. He has 'bought' his knighthood by contributing substantial funds to the Liberal Party organ, *Old Country Gazette*, but his general views are more reactionary than liberal. The only son of a failed steam-miller, he is in his mid-forties at the opening of the tale, a shortish man with greying brown hair and clean-shaven features of 'thin irregularity'. He has a habit of blowing out the flesh around his mouth and producing an odd whistling sound through his teeth. His nationwide business is entirely self-made, for he first began work as a clerk in a tea-office. In effect, he is 'one of those men whom modern England delights to honour, a man of unpretentious acquisitiveness, devoted to business, and distracted by no aesthetic or intellectual interests.'

A complete martinet in the conduct of his marriage, Harman attempts to prevent his wife from indulging in any form of social life, growing increasingly annoyed by her efforts to attain some degree of autonomy. He relents ungraciously after her month in prison and allows her some freedom in the planning of a number of hostels for his staff; but he remains obsessed with rules and rigid organization, the same qualities which he has brought to the development of his business. During the following three years his health, never very good, deterioriates rapidly. His immature emotional behaviour, which alternates between violent rages and tearful attempts at reconciliation, continues—but less forcefully. He takes an active dislike to his wife's regular consultations with the writer Brumley and forbids her to see him again. As a final act of spite, he inserts a clause in his will which dictates that, should she remarry, the management of the hostels will pass to a committee on which she will have no place.

The condition of his lungs and hardening arteries necessitates his removal abroad, and he shifts his household to Santa Margherita, in Italy, after transferring authority in his business to several trusted subordinates. He suffers a relapse on opening a letter addressed to Lady Harman in which Brumley declares his love. He resolves to disinherit her entirely, but dies before that can be accomplished. His body is brought back for burial at Kensal Green cemetery in London. *The Wife of Sir Isaac Harman*, 1914

HARRINGAY, R. M.: A second-rate artist whose portrait of an Italian organ-grinder assumes an increasingly diabolic expression each time he endeavours to improve it. Eventually the painting begins to speak to him, tempting him with the promise that he will produce a masterpiece if he sells his soul, and suggesting that he will never be capable of inspired work by any other method. Exasperated as much as offended, Harringay begins to obliterate the portrait with red paint, whereupon he is offered two master-pieces . . . then three, and more. Switching to blue enamel, he succeeds after a lively struggle in painting the tempter out. 'The Temptation of Harringay', 1895

HARROWDEAN, MRS. : The illicit lady-friend of Mr. Britling whose romance is interrupted by an irrational quarrel shortly before the outbreak of the First World War. She can summon tears and delights as one summons servants, being unable to control her jealousy of Mrs. Britling. Britling finally accepts that he must end the relationship, allowing her the freedom to marry another suitor. *Mr. Britling Sees It Through*, 1916

HARTING, DR. : A noted humanist and authority on international relations, he is lean and tall, but infirm with age. His lectures in America are a source of inspiration to Paul Zelinka, and his advocacy of a world authority to control the supplies of the vitally-needed mineral, calcomite, determines the young man's course of action when he becomes King of Clavery. Having won the Nobel Peace Prize, Harting travels to Clavery to congratulate Paul on the final achievement of their aims. *The King Who Was A King*, 1929

HARTING, MARGARET : A friend of Paul Zelinka while he is working in a factory in the U.S.A. Daughter of the distinguished doctor and lecturer, she is pretty, obviously fond of Paul, but shy of physical demonstrations. She helps to persuade him to accept the crown of Clavery, to which he has suddenly become heir, but she resists his pleas for her to accompany him to Central Europe, even in the rôle of his queen. She argues that she would probably prove unacceptable to his people, and that in any case her ailing father must be her first concern. However, she does visit Paul with the professor after peace has been declared between Clavery, Sævia and Agravia, and is clearly reconciled to his marriage to Princess Helen. *The King Who Was A King*, 1929

HEINRICH, HERR : The German tutor to Mr. Britling's younger children and a student of philology who is engaged on an appraisal of the dialects of East Anglia. A plump young man, with a pink face, sedulous eyes, glasses, and compact gestures. His formal Germanic manners endear him to the Britling family who regard him with tolerant amusement. He returns to his native land to fight in the First World War and dies in Russia. Britling subsequently corresponds with his father, expressing his condolence and admitting that his own son Hugh is also among the casualties of the conflict. *Mr. Britling Sees It Through*, 1916

HELEN : A mistress of William Clissold who fills a gap in his life left by the death of Sirrie Evans. Many people see her as beautiful, though none call her pretty. To them she appears a strong personality, an ambitious actress, hot-tempered, but with a charming smile and an adorable voice—and also an 'ungracious way with obtrusive admirers'. For Clissold himself she is more besides : 'For me she was wonderful and mystical; she was beautiful and lovely for me as no human being has ever been; she had in my perception of her a distinctive personal splendour that was as entirely and inseparably her own as the line of her neck or the timbre of her voice ... She not only evoked and satisfied my sense of beauty in herself, but she had the faculty of creating a kind of victorious beauty in the scene about her. She had a vision that transformed things, annexed them, and made them tributary to her magic ensemble.'

The affair, however, is stormy. Neither cares much for the other's work, and Helen cannot understand why Clissold will not marry her once his wife has died. They part in bitterness after several years when she embarks on a theatrical tour of South Africa. *The World of William Clissold*, 1926

HENDERSON, ETHEL : See 'Lewisham, Ethel'.

HEYDINGER, ALICE : A student at the Normal School of Science, and a lover of poetry, whom Lewisham comes to know when he joins the committee of the college Debating Society. In appearance she is hardly memorable to Lewisham when he endeavours to recall her during his first vacation. To the best of his memory she wears glasses and is often troubled by the unruliness of her light brown hair. Her dress is 'an amorphous dinginess', which she succeeds somewhat in improving when he shows an interest in her. His plans to form a socialist movement, seeing himself in the rôle of a Luther, fire her enthusiasm, and she wishes nothing better than to help him in his cause as a 'True Friend'.

Her discovery that Lewisham is escorting Ethel Henderson home each night leads Miss Heydinger to revise her estimation of him, thinking that he has been beguiled by a pretty face. She corresponds with him after his marriage, and her erudite letters are a cause of heartache on the part of Ethel. In a final meeting, she comes close to pleading with Lewisham to allow their friendship to continue, only to realize that he is beyond persuasion. *Love and Mr. Lewisham,* 1900

HILL, MR.: Son of a cobbler, and unfortunate protagonist in a story based very much on Wells's own experience as a biology student. Hill cheats in a vital exam by moving a microscope slide, thereby enabling him more easily to identify the specimen it contains. In so doing, he achieves final marks above those of Wedderburn, his rival for the admiration of a girl student. But he is torn by the dishonesty of his act, having always argued for righteousness. Finally he confesses and, on being told the rules oblige him to be failed, leaves the college ignominiously. 'A Slip Under the Microscope', 1893

HILLYER, THE REVEREND K.: The ornithologically-minded Vicar of Siddermorton who unwittingly shoots down the visiting Angel, only to find his enforced guest more of a burden than a wonder. He is a short, rubicund, red-haired man, with bright ruddy brown eyes. He is astonished to learn that the land of the Angel is inhabited by all the strange beasts of mythology, and that the visitant has no experience of eating, pain, or even death. Consequently, he endeavours to educate him in human ways, but with no degree of success. He becomes increasingly alarmed at the Angel's disagreeable encounters with the local residents, who refuse to accept him for what he is. The vicar himself remains convinced of his guest's authenticity but is rapidly persuaded by the doctor and the squire that the Angel is a threat to the community. Reluctantly he arranges for him to leave, an act which becomes unnecessary when the Angel dies in the vicarage fire. *The Wonderful Visit,* 1895

HIMBESKET, PRESIDENT: The elected head of the Central European state of Agravia, who meets King Paul of Clavery in secret in an attempt to avert war between their two countries. He is a middle-aged, substantial, good-looking man, with the politician's acquired habit of addressing invisible audiences. At first wary of Paul's intentions, he warms to him as their discussion progresses and a bond of mutual trust is established. Later, when the union of Clavery, Agravia and Sævia has been achieved, he welcomes the visit of Dr. Harting, a major advocate of supra-national controls, to the new Federation. *The King Who Was A King*, 1929

HINCHCLIFFE, MR. : The incredulous recipient of the Apple of the Tree of Knowledge, in the unlikely surroundings of a third-class rail compartment on a journey through Sussex. The un-named donor recounts how it came into his hands from an Armenian whom he had saved from starvation. The foreigner, in his turn, had been found grasping it in his hand after stumbling into a strange valley while escaping from an attack by Kurds. The fruit has a curious golden-yellow sheen, and shows no sign of wrinkling or drying in the three months the donor has possessed it. But he dare not eat it, fearing the burden of omni-science. He gives the apple to Hinchcliffe as the latter leaves the train; but the young man finds it an encumbrance and throws it over a wall. He returns to hunt for it later, but to no avail. 'The Apple', 1896

HOLDMAN STEDDING, DR. : Obstetrician in charge of Mrs. Mary Davis, whose husband consults him when he suspects that her forthcoming child may be damaged by cosmic rays. Initially the doctor is sceptical about the theory of radiations emanating from Mars, but he later becomes intrigued by the notion and follows Davis's research with interest. He also discusses the theory with his philosopher friend, Professor Keppel, who is similarly pre-pared to accept that it could be feasible. *Star Begotten*, 1937

HOLROYD : The amused Lancashire engineer who accompanies Captain Gerilleau on his expedition against a species of fighting ants discovered up the Amazon. Holroyd's rôle is confined to that of spectator and long-suffering recipient of the Captain's frequent outbursts of exasperation. The ants themselves prove a formidable adversary. Well-drilled, they advance in a way 'oddly suggestive of the rushes of modern infantry under fire'. Some two inches in length, they carry poison-dispensing weapons strapped to their bodies and appear to have developed a miniature tech-nology of their own. Already advancing down the Amazon and rapidly increasing their numbers, their progress, the narrator sug-gests, should see 1950 or '60 as the date for their discovery of Europe. 'The Empire of the Ants', 1905

HOLROYD, JAMES : The supervisor of the dynamo shed at Camber-well, in London, where power is generated for the electric rail-way. Overpartial to whisky, he is not above maltreating his native assistant, Azuma-zi, whom he finally forbids to service the biggest of the machines which the latter has come to worship. It proves the trigger-mechanism for the act of sacrifice Azuma-zi had been planning, and Holroyd is hurled to his death against the ter-minals. 'The Lord of the Dynamos', 1894

HOLSTEN : The physicist responsible for the release of atomic energy which precipitates a world financial crisis and leads to a global war. In 1933 he succeeds in forcing atomic disintegration in a particle of bismuth, causing a violent explosion and the production of a radioactive gas which in turn disintegrates after a week's interval. He is astonished to find that the end product of this reaction is gold. Holsten's subsequent development of an atomic motor creates havoc in the international money market and disrupts the economies of countries geared to energy pro-grammes hitherto dependent on fossil fuels. Widespread un-employment and the financial crash of 1956 are to follow. In the subsequent war, atomic bombs derived from the Holsten process are dropped on many major cities. *The World Set Free*, 1914

HOOKER : One of the two living characters—if not for long—in 'The Treasure in the Forest', who with his colleague, Evans, is searching for a hidden cache on a desert island. When they come across the precise location, they find the hoard already un-covered and a corpse lying beside it. Ignoring its significance, they begin to lift the gold ingots, only to find they have been spiked with poisoned thorns. Both die rapidly, in terrible convul-sions. 'The Treasure in the Forest', 1894

HOOPDRIVER, J. E. : A young draper's apprentice in Putney, Lon-don, who decides to spend his annual fortnight's holiday on a cycling tour of the South Coast. A newcomer to the mysteries of the bicycle, his efforts to accommodate himself to his machine are recorded by 'the Remarkable Condition of this Young Man's Legs'—a multi-coloured display of abrasions. The remainder of his appearance is less remarkable : a pallid expression, fairish hair, grey eyes and a wispy moustache beneath a 'peaked, in-determinate nose'. His education has been poor and he reads little else but popular novels. His parentage is not described.

Despite his bruises he makes good, if unsteady, progress in the early stages of his tour, enheartened by a passing altercation with a workman on Putney Heath who accuses him of taking on airs : ' "Don't you make no remarks to *'im*," said the keeper as the carter came up broadside to them. " 'E's a bloomin' dook, 'e is. 'E don't converse with no one under a earl. 'E's off to Windsor, 'e is; that's why 'e's stickin' his be'ind out so haughty." '

On the road Hoopdriver encounters a 'Young Lady in Grey', at first unaccompanied but later escorted by a man in a brown cycling suit similar to his own. The companion seems ill at ease, becoming openly hostile to the apprentice after several chance meetings. During an overnight stay in Midhurst he assumes Hoopdriver to be a private detective hired by either his wife or the girl's stepmother to spy on them. The couple, who have been passing as brother and sister under the name of Beaumont, are later revealed as the writer Bechamel and Jessica Milton, who has fled from her home in Surbiton to join him.

Hoopdriver has already elevated Jessica to a pedestal in his reveries, and finding her on one occasion in tears, he suspects that Bechamel is exerting some hold on her. Eventually he discovers that the writer has lured her with a promise of help in her career, only to distress her by more personal advances. Hoopdriver helps her to escape, taking Bechamel's cycle in place of his own second-hand machine. During the next few days he proves his gallantry by fighting a local youth who has made a coarse remark in her presence and by generally acting the rôle of knight errant. However, he is embarrassed by his lowly social standing and allows her to believe that he has been an ostrich farmer in South Africa. Passing as a colonial understandably ignorant of English social *mores*, he regales her with invented tales of lion-hunts and the unearthing of priceless diamonds.

Frequent relapses into the manners of his trade convince him that he cannot maintain the subterfuge indefinitely and on their last day, with their money all but exhausted, he confesses the deception. To his surprise she appears unconcerned and urges him to attempt to improve his education. They are finally overtaken at the Rufus Stone in the New Forest by Mrs. Milton, aided by her friends, Widgery, Dangle and Phipps, together with Jessie's old schoolmistress, Mrs. Mergle. When they part it is obvious to Hoopdriver that they are unlikely to meet again, but he is encouraged by Jessie's offer to lend him such books as may help his self-advancement. He rides back alone to London, his mind stirred by memories and the awakening of genuine ambition.

The novel marks Wells's initial attempt at sustained comedy and is also noted for its introduction of the first of his several draper's apprentice heroes. In the portrayal of Hoopdriver lie the prototypes of the fuller-rounded characters of Kipps and Mr. Polly. The descriptions of the passing countryside and of the tribulations of a cycling novice are given with the authenticity of one well acquainted with both. 'I learnt', he later said, 'to ride my bicycle upon sandy tracks with none but God to help me; he chastened me considerably in the process, and after a fall one day I wrote down a description of the state of my legs which became the opening chapter of *The Wheels of Chance*. I rode wherever Mr. Hoopdriver rode in that story.' The first edition was adorned with forty illustrations by J. Ashton Symington. *The Wheels of Chance*, 1896

HOOPLER, ALICE : The first wife of Stephen Wilbeck whom he meets when on leave during the First World War and while she is working in his father's publishing house. At the time she is a bright-coloured girl, slender and lovely, with alert brown eyes; later she runs to plumpness. They marry while Wilbeck is still on leave, and a daughter, Lettice, is born after he has returned to the front. On his demobilization, however, she has already developed an affection for Hoopler which leads fairly rapidly to a divorce. When Wilbeck renews acquaintanceship after an interval of some fifteen years, she insists that he pass himself off as Lettice's godfather. *Apropos of Dolores*, 1938

HOOPLER, GEORGE : The husband of Alice, and a shipping-office employee in Southampton. Tall, stooping and bespectacled, he initially lacks assurance at the time of Alice's desertion of Stephen Wilbeck, but he later becomes more self-possessed. He talks incessantly in a stilted manner, and is given to the construction of dreadful puns, as when his son enthuses over his model aeroplane :

' "Icarus", said Hoopler and then with a fatuous smile :

"And I am his Dad-alas !" ' '

Wilbeck is convinced that Hoopler exerts a deadening influence over his family. *Apropos of Dolores*, 1938

HOOPLER, LETTICE : Daughter of Alice and Stephen Wilbeck, she is sixteen when her father first comes to know her at all. Her face is attractive and appears fairly intelligent, but her manner is noted for its reserve and she generally converses in monosyllables. She warms to Wilbeck when he offers to pay for her education at college, and subsequently she tours Brittany in his company after the death of Dolores. To Wilbeck's disappointment she proves an uninteresting companion whose main concern is to return prematurely to England where a young man awaits her. *Apropos of Dolores*, 1938

HOPKINSHIRE, MAJOR HUBERT POLYDORE : The uncle of Stella Kentlake, who writes menacingly to Gemini Twain when he discovers the young couple are living together in a cottage in Suffolk. A squat unpleasant looking man, with an 'extraordinarily pseudo-equestrian' air, most of whose face has been 'sacrificed to an immense moustache and an oblique expression of scrutinizing determination . . .' He descends on Stella and Gemini, bringing the latter's father with him. In the subsequent confrontation his disagreeable personality is revealed in both his demeanour and his stilted speech. Nevertheless, he is successful in his insistence that his niece should return to her mother immediately. *Babes in the Darkling Wood*, 1940

HORROCKS : The jealous husband who by the pretence of escorting his rival, Raut, around an Iron Works hurls him to an incinerating death on the cone of the title. The tale is a fragment of what Wells had originally planned to be a novel, but it is the only part of the manuscript which still survives. 'The Cone', 1895

HOWARD : A member of the White Council, the ruling body of the world of 2100 A.D. into which Graham awakes. The first high official whom Graham encounters, he is described as very short, thickset, fat and beardless. He explains something of the two centuries of history that have passed during the course of Graham's catatonic trance but insists that the Sleeper must wait before meeting the people, hinting at civil unrest. He also prevents Graham from addressing the Council while they deliberate on his awakening. In the outcome, they decide to poison him, fearing his possible influence over the masses. Howard is assigned to the task but is overpowered, and Graham escapes through the agency of Ostrog, the powerful Labour Boss. *When the Sleeper Wakes*, 1899

HUMBLEDAY, MRS.: A large woman, 'extremely fine', who befriends Edward Albert Tewler's mother after meeting her at a Baptist Social Afternoon in Camden Town. The only small things about her are her accommodation and her voice, the latter being infinitesimal, 'a whisper at the best of times, and an inaudible wheeze, in which facial expression had to come to its assistance'. In fact, she has little facial expression, 'beyond a certain astonishment at the things she was saying'. Formerly in service, she alarms Mrs. Tewler with her accounts of sexual escapades and with her liberal attitude towards the lustful nature of the male. She dies of a heart attack during an air-raid on London in 1940. *You Can't Be Too Careful,* 1941

HUSS, JOB: The headmaster of the progressive public school, Woldingstanton, where he has adopted new approaches to education during the past twenty-five years. His story is told as a modern interpretation of the testing of Job of Uz, and at its opening Huss is indeed sorely afflicted. Within the space of a term disaster has overtaken Woldingstanton. Two boys have died in an epidemic of measles, another two in a fire which has destroyed the main School House, and a science master has been killed in a laboratory accident. Huss's personal affairs are also a cause for profound despondency: his life-savings have been lost in a foolhardy speculation in Russian roubles by his solicitor; his only son is presumed dead (the First World War is in its final year); and a growth in his side has been diagnosed as suspected cancer.

Before his operation at Sundering on Sea, where he has stayed since the fire put paid to his school accommodation, he is visited by two Woldingstanton governors, Sir Eliphaz Burrows and Mr. Dad, and by Farr, the head of the school's technical section. These three, with the addition of Dr. Barrack, his general practitioner, act the parts of latter-day 'Job's comforters', and the main body of the novel is a discussion of educational and religious viewpoints.

It is clear to Huss that while the governors concede the great service he has given the school, they are opposed to his determined concentration on world history and consider that Farr would be better suited to direct the syllabus more towards the preparation for careers in commerce. Huss is horrified. He denounces Farr as an opportunist and launches into a justification of his teaching philosophy which includes dissertations on the inherent cruelty of Nature, on his disbelief in personal immortality and on the horrors of submarine warfare. The debate goes to and fro, with Huss maintaining that some part of the Spirit of God exists as an undying fire in every man, to be brought to fruition by an enlightened mind : 'The end and substance of all real education is to teach men and women of the Battle of God, to teach them of the beginning of life upon this lonely little planet amidst the endless stars, and how those beginnings have unfolded; to show them how man has arisen through the long ages from amidst the beasts, and the nature of the struggle God wages through him, and to draw all men together out of themselves into one common life and effort with God. The nature of God's struggle is the essence of our dispute. It is a struggle, with a hope of victory but with no assurance.'

During the operation, under the surgeon Sir Alpheus Mengo, Huss experiences a vision of himself as the original Job, confronted by both God and Satan who urge him respectively, the one to hold fast, the other to abandon his faith. To the end, no consolation is given—Job will conquer only so long as his courage endures; should that fail, the sacred fire will die. God and Satan are repeating, in effect, the opposing philosophies they advanced in the Prologue to the novel. Huss awakens still asking the unanswered question : 'But will my courage endure?' However, a reply of sorts is provided : the operation is successful and the growth proves non-malignant. A distant cousin dies, bequeathing Huss a substantial legacy which does much to alleviate his wife's distress. His former scholars rally in his support, and the continuation of his headmastership is assured. Finally, with the collapse of the German armies and the end of the War in sight, he hears that his son, though a prisoner, is alive and well.

Many commentators have regarded *The Undying Fire* as the most important of Wells's discussion novels. In the arguments of Huss he had begun to crystallize the ideas on education and the teaching of universal history (followed up in the same year by an article, 'History is One', in the American *Saturday Evening Post*) which culminated in his three encyclopaedic volumes: *The Outline of History* (1920), *The Science of Life* (1930) and *The Work, Wealth and Happiness of Mankind* (1931). It is also the most noted product of the brief and uncharacteristic 'religious period' which he passed through towards the end of the Great War, the other books of the phase being *The Soul of a Bishop* and the non-fictional work *God The Invisible King* (1917). This last he was later to repudiate in both *The World of William Clissold* and his *Experiment in Autobiography* (1934). *The Undying Fire*, 1919

HUSS, MRS. : Wife of Job Huss who accompanies him to Sundering on Sea where he falls ill. Little is said of her, other than that she is dark and graceful, a little untidy, and that she blames Huss for the presumed death of their only son who has been shot down over German lines while serving in the Royal Flying Corps. She becomes ruthless in her anguish, accusing her husband of little less than murder. Her inept attempts to make her own mourning clothes anger the couple's landlady, and the persistent squabbling of the two women add to Job's depression. She breaks down on learning at the story's close that their son has survived. *The Undying Fire*, 1919

I

INDIAN PRINCE, THE : The distraught widower of 'The Pearl of Love', whose grief at the death of his young wife motivates him to the building of a mausoleum of exquisite beauty. As the years progress he makes continuous alterations, now elaborating the design, now simplifying it. Finally, when the vast edifice seems to him the epitome of perfection, he finds only one remaining aspect to mar it—the sarcophagus. He orders it to be taken away. 'The Pearl of Love', 1924

INFANTRY LIEUTENANT, THE : The Flying Man of the title of another exotic short story, recounting a skirmish between the Sepoys and the Chins. His conversion of a tent into a parachute, which enables him to glide from a cliff-top to the river valley below, earns him a reputation among the superstitious natives which extends far beyond his original achievement. 'The Flying Man', 1893

J

JANE : The central character in the short story 'The Jilting of Jane', a servant of the narrator who recounts her unfortunate romantic disappointments when she entertains the idea of marrying above her station. 'The Jilting of Jane', 1897

JESUS OF NAZARETH : The companion whom Wells finds 'most congenial in the Beyond' and who discusses his career on Earth in *The Happy Turning*—a suite of 'barbed fantasies' written towards the end of the author's life. Basically the work is a penultimate attempt by Wells to relieve his feelings in a number of directions. Jesus takes the central rôle in two chapters : 'Jesus of Nazareth discusses his failure' and 'Miracles, Devils and the Gadarene Swine'. He confesses that he survived the ordeal on Golgotha, being no more than unconscious from exhaustion when he was taken from the Cross. He is concerned at how badly he managed his mission, allowing his aphorisms to be misinterpreted even while he was alive and failing both his disciples and the mass of mankind. He recalls shouting this despairing realization before he passed out :

' "Eli, Eli, lama sabachthani?" I said.
"Did someone get that down?" he replied.
"Don't you read the Gospels?"
"Good God, *No* !" he said. "How *can* I? I was crucified before all that."
"But you seem to know how things have gone?"
"It was plain enough how they were going."
"Don't you," I asked rather stupidly, forgetting where we were, "keep yourself informed about terrestrial affairs?"
"They crucify me daily," he said. "I know that. Yes." '
The Happy Turning, 1945

JIM, UNCLE : The singularly unlovely nephew of the fat proprietress of the riverside Potwell Inn. Recently discharged from a Reformatory Home, he is squat, shorter even than Mr. Polly, foul-mouthed, and with barely a tooth through which to swear. Finding Polly on what he regards as his own personal territory at the Inn, he threatens him with a series of progressively more grisly fates. In all, they engage in three separate battles, the first ending in the successful propulsion of Jim into the river with the aid of a broom. On the second such encounter he appears drunk, in a state of 'ferocious decolletage', and brandishing a dead eel. But he has reckoned without the willingness of several picnicking customers to assist Polly in the affray, and in the face of overwhelming resistance and the threat of a further ducking, he retreats.

The final assault, and the most dangerous, occurs three months later, when Uncle Jim breaks into Polly's room to steal some of his clothes and a rook rifle. He also ransacks the bar and breaks open the till. The dawn sees him shooting at Mr. Polly, who has taken refuge in the Potwell churchyard. At the third shot, the rifle explodes and Jim abandons the siege. He is heard of no more until, some time later, his body is found in an unrecognizable state in the river, to be identified by Miriam, Polly's deserted wife, as her husband's on the evidence of his clothing. *The History of Mr. Polly*, 1910

JOHNSON, HAROLD : A cousin of Mr. Polly who, with his wife, cares for Polly's father until his death. The funeral wake takes places at the Johnsons' home, where for the first time Mr. Polly meets his female cousins, including Miriam who will become his wife. On receipt of his inheritance, Polly stays with the Johnsons for some months until he finds a suitable shop to rent at Fishbourne. *The History of Mr. Polly*, 1910

JULIP, JOHN : Uncle of Harry Mortimer Smith and a gardener who is dismissed for dishonesty. He is the brother of Harry's mother, a cynical and opinionated man—short and fat, with a 'smooth white face and a wise self-satisfied smile'. He provides his brother-in-law with vegetables and fruit stolen from his employer's estate, and these are subsequently sold in Mortimer Smith's shop. The young Harry is often used as a go-between for these transactions, to be stopped on one occasion and quizzed by Lord Bramble's butler. As a result, Julip loses his employment and attempts thereafter to work as a jobbing gardener. Unsuccessful, he turns to gambling and drink, leading Mortimer into the same pursuits. His own wife, Adelaide, is a chronic invalid, confined to hospital where she is not expected to survive long. To Julip, therefore, it seems natural that he should live with his sister after Mortimer's accidental death; but her eldest son Ernest, seeing him as a potential parasite, throws him out of the house. Adelaide dies soon after the Smith family move to London, while Julip's eventual fate is not recorded. *The Dream*, 1924

JUSTIN : The wealthy financier who is prepared to accept Lady Mary Christian as his wife on her own terms. However, he threatens divorce when he finds she is in love with Stratton and resolves to ruin the latter unless he exiles himself abroad. When the two lovers are briefly re-united in Switzerland, he is told of their meeting by Stella Summersley Satchel and actually files a divorce suit. He suffers considerable remorse over his wife's subsequent suicide and suggests to Stratton that they are both equally responsible for her death. *The Passionate Friends*, 1913

JUSTIN, LADY MARY : A young girl of nineteen when Stephen Stratton first meets her with her two brothers (*see under* Christian) during his visits to Burnmore House in Surrey. Slim and graceful, she has reddish hair, a low broad forehead and bright blue eyes—indeed a brightness suffuses her entire face. Her appearance, intelligence and voice—with its delicately clear intonation and a hint of a lisp—entrance Stratton, and he is soon in love with her. Although she reciprocates, she refuses to marry him, insisting that he hasn't the means to provide her with the opportunities she seeks of life. Instead, she enters into an initially sexless marriage with Justin, who only enforces his conjugal rights after he learns of her affair with Stratton. She bears him two children, but her obsession with her former lover remains. She begins to correspond with him and they meet accidentally in the Swiss Alps some years after their original parting. When her husband institutes divorce proceedings she kills herself.

Essentially her character is a further depiction of the type of young woman whom Wells showed as struggling for the right to fulfil herself as an individual. But she appears lacking in central purpose—a failure highlighted in a pungent piece of criticism levelled at the book by Rebecca West, with whom Wells himself had enjoyed a stormy relationship. In his autobiography he admitted, a little ruefully, that her polemic was of much the same order as his own earlier critical attack on Grant Allen's *The Woman Who Did*. *The Passionate Friends*, 1913

K

KARENIN, MARCUS : A prominent member of the education committee appointed by the World Council following the Last War. By birth a Russian, and a congenital cripple, he has a strong face of yellowish complexion, small deep-sunken brown eyes, a thin mouth and iron-grey hair. Since he is almost continuously in pain, he tends to be impatient and is quickly moved to anger.

Karenin is the most fully sketched character in a scientific romance which begins in 1933 with the discovery of nuclear fission by the physicist Holsten, a by-product of the process being gold. Twenty years later the Holsten-Roberts atomic engine is perfected, disrupting existing technology and throwing millions out of work with the advent of the financial crash of 1956. The crisis leads to war, initiated by the German invasion of France by way of Belgium. The conflict rapidly becomes global, and atomic bombs, derived from Holsten's discovery, devastate the world's major cities. Civilization lies in ruins : 'The old tendencies of human nature, suspicion, jealousy, particularism, and belligerency, were incompatible with the monstrous destructive power of the new appliances the inhuman logic of science had produced. The equilibrium could be restored only by civilization destroying itself down to a level at which modern apparatus could no longer be produced, or by human nature adapting itself in its institutions to the new conditions.'

The bombs differ from what was to become reality by continuing to explode over a long period and only gradually decreasing in intensity. (Their effect, and the suffering resulting from the pre-war slump, are graphically described by Frederick Barnet in his autobiography, *Wander Jahre*, on which sections of the narrative are allegedly based.) With no side victorious, peace is finally signed at Brissago, in Italy, where the Balkan King, Ferdinand Charles, endeavours to sabotage the peace conference and is killed defending his secret hoard of atomic weapons.

Largely at the instigation of the British monarch, King Egbert, who abdicates as a gesture of sincerity, the conference agrees to the foundation of a World Republic and selects a governing council. Reconstruction ensues and such Wellsian ideas as the compiling of a great central index of knowledge are begun.

The final section of the novel is set in the 1980s and introduces Karenin, who has himself worked on the index in its early stages. He has flown to a research clinic in the Himalayas to undergo an operation which may well prove fatal. He spends what he regards as his final hours in a discussion on life with his nurses and other well-wishers. Much of the talk is taken up with his attitude to sex, which, perhaps because of his own deformity, has reached the point of open disapproval. He regards it as an unnecessary pre-occupation which has hampered and held back the progress of civilization. His more healthy companions disagree.

His remaining thoughts dwell on the advancement of science and education, and their contribution to what he sees as Man's limitless potential. He looks ahead to the possibilities of space travel and when left alone, and speaking for the race, he addresses himself to the sun : 'You think I die—and indeed I am only taking off one more coat to get at you. I have threatened you for ten thousand years, and soon I warn you I shall be coming . . . One step I shall take to the moon, and then I shall leap at you . . . Old Sun, I gather myself together out of the pools of the individual that have held me dispersed so long. I gather my billion thoughts into science and my million wills into a common purpose. Well may you slink down behind the mountains from me, well may you cower . . .'

The operation is successful but a week later a blood clot from the healing scar passes to his heart and Karenin dies in his sleep.

As a future history with a minimum of characterization, the story can be considered as an early blueprint for the culminating effort which Wells achieved nineteen years later in *The Shape of Things to Come*. The prediction of atomic bombs half a decade before Rutherford actually discovered the atomic nucleus is a notable example of the writer's ability to extrapolate from existing knowledge. A further prediction, of a more personal nature, can be found among Karenin's final words and might appropriately be applied to Wells as his powers failed during his last illness : 'I do not see why life should be judged by its last trailing thread of vitality . . . if presently my heart fails me and I despair, and if I go through a little phase of pain and ingratitude, and dark forgetfulness before the end . . . Don't believe what I may say at the last . . . If the fabric is good enough the selvage doesn't matter.' *The World Set Free*, 1914

KEMP, DR. : A medical researcher in whose house at Port Burdock, in Sussex, the Invisible Man seeks refuge. A tall, thin, fair-haired man with an almost white moustache, he has once known Griffin when they were contemporary students at University College. The Invisible Man's entry into his home, however, is purely coincidence; and Kemp is as incredulous as anyone else at their first encounter. While Griffin is asleep, the doctor discovers from the press accounts of his misdeeds that he is a dangerous and wanted man. Appearing willing to assist the fugitive, he secretly sends a note to the local police and hears out Griffin's extraordinary tale while awaiting their arrival.

Griffin succeeds in escaping the trap, but he has told Kemp so many of the disadvantages of his condition that the latter is able to advise the authorities how best he can be caught. Enraged at his betrayal, the Invisible Man later attempts to murder Kemp, but is interrupted by the arrival of police reinforcements. There follows a chase through the town until Griffin overtakes his quarry. He attempts to throttle Kemp, but is beaten to death by an angry crowd before he can succeed. *The Invisible Man*, 1897

KENTLAKE, MRS. LUCY : Mother of Stella whose husband deserted her to paint in Paris when their daughter was eight. Blue-eyed, and with an expression of generalized anxiety, she moves about in 'a world that she felt might pounce upon her at any moment'. In short, she has 'a mouse-like unobtrusiveness and a mouse-like tenacity for crumbs'. Her mother died giving her birth and she was brought up by a pair of aunts who ran a boarding school for girls. She is genuinely reduced to tears by Stella's indiscretion with Gemini and is adamant that the girl shall not resume her studies at Cambridge. However, as in so many other respects, she allows herself to be overruled by her brother-in-law, Robert Kentlake. *Babes in the Darkling Wood*, 1940

KENTLAKE, DR. ROBERT : A philosophical psychologist at Cambridge University and the uncle of Stella. A man of larger features than his brother (Stella's expatriate father), he has a high-riding prominent nose and a 'habit of delivering careful but inexplicable judgements at the slightest provocation'. In many respects he can be considered the central character of the novel, particularly in terms of the discussion content, and his multitude of observations reflect views which Wells had in general already expressed elsewhere.

He rescues Stella from her mother's distress on the discovery of her liaison with Gemini Twain, and arranges for her to continue her course at Newnham on the understanding that she will lodge with him. In Cambridge he delivers her of a variety of impromptu lectures, ranging from the unreality of a university education (repeating a philosophical argument first expressed by Wells in 1903—*see The Scepticism of the Instrument under the entry for* The Narrator, *A Modern Utopia*) to the theory of the original disorganization of personality contained in Cottenham C. Bower's *Expansion of Sex*, a book which Stella has asked Gemini to review unfavourably.

Bower's arguments, in fact, play a major rôle in the form of psychotherapy with which Kentlake later treats Gemini after his traumatic experience of the Nazi advance into Eastern Europe. The major contention is that, far from the Freudian assumption that the psyche starts out whole and fractures under stress to display the various symptoms of psychosis, it is more likely that the mind begins in disunity and the problems of mental illness stem from its failure to achieve oneness with itself.

Under Kentlake's treatment Gemini regains his will to live. The doctor is also responsible for some rigorous soul-searching on the part of Gemini's mother, a process she is anxious to continue with his help. Unfortunately he is run over by a lorry after missing his footing on a kerb; he dies a few days later with Stella by his side. *Babes in the Darkling Wood*, 1940

KENTLAKE, STELLA : A university student at Newnham College, Cambridge, who decides to live for a brief period with Gemini Twain during her summer vacation in 1939. Slight and lithe, she has fair hair and alert dark-blue eyes, finely modelled brows and a wide expressive mouth. Having known her father only as a child, she is deeply attached to her uncle, Robert Kentlake, whom she clearly sees as a surrogate parent. Her relationship with her mother is less positive and she tends to behave towards her with a certain degree of condescension, although not unlovingly. This becomes perhaps more pronounced after her affair with Gemini has been disclosed. She is forever feeding Lucy cocktails and paying her other small attentions, but she relies on Robert to provide the necessary authority which will allow her to do what she wants. Not that she is incapable of handling difficult situations on her own—she acquits herself effectively, and with some dignity, during the harrowing confrontation when her other uncle, Major Hopkinshire, and Gemini's father descend on the two lovers in their cottage.

Her love for Gemini is straight-forward and enduring, although tinged with jealousy when she suspects him of infidelity with Mary Clarkson—a correct intuitive judgement which causes her some troubled dreams and long bouts of introspection. She is patient during Gemini's rejection of her while he is ill and after their marriage she buys Mary Clarkson's Suffolk cottage, where they first lived together, in anticipation of his recovery.

Lively minded, she is less skilful in argument than her lover but equally as determined. Her own views on Cottenham Bower's *The Expansion of Sex* are coloured by her awareness of her own sensuality and she rejects the American professor's argument that sex is an obstacle to human progress. She matures over the course of the year which the novel covers, and at its conclusion she can accept with equanimity Gemini's decision to serve in a mine-sweeper. She herself becomes a nurse. *Babes in the Darkling Wood*, 1940

KEPPEL, PROFESSOR ERNEST : The philosopher turned psycho-therapist who becomes interested in the theory of Martian rays in *Star Begotten*. He assumes that if the Martians have indeed evolved a higher intelligence than Man's, then they are almost certainly benign. He sees their influence on humanity, propagated by their radiations, as pointing the way to a world peace and to the disappearance of such dictator figures as are then dominating the European scene. A new liberating future, he suggests, will be the outcome—a very typical Wellsian argument. However, the work can easily be regarded as a product of Wells's final period of pessimism; the fact that it is the Martians who are required to instigate the betterment of Man hints that the author saw *Homo sapiens* as incapable of improving itself by its own initiative. *Star Begotten*, 1937

KIMPTON, MILLY : The second wife of Harry Mortimer Smith whom he marries after his divorce from Hetty Marcus. Employed in the same publishing company as Harry, she is some eighteen months his senior—a well-built woman with a 'broad, candid face' that never looks either angry or miserable. Fair-haired, she holds 'her countenance high, smiling towards heaven with a pleasant confidence and self-satisfaction'. She is intelligent, but without much sense of humour. Attracted to Harry when he first enters the firm, she indicates her interest in him by the loan of books and other small attentions. He does not realize how hurt she is when he marries Hetty.

Milly proves a capable wife, a good manager, and tender but without passion. She has two thousand pounds of her own, out of which she furnishes the house Smith buys close to London's Regent's Park. She meets his sister Fanny, but with none of the warmth which Hetty showed for the other. In due course she bears Harry a son. She seems to suspect that her husband is still in love with Hetty and senses that something is amiss when his former wife eventually turns to him for help. However, although Harry fails to find the companionship with her that he enjoyed with Hetty, he resolves not to desert her when the temptation occurs. *The Dream*, 1924

KIPPS, ARTIE : A draper's apprentice whose mixed fortunes in the areas of love, money and the class strata of late Victorian society are recorded in a subtle blend of comedy and pathos. Kipps never knows his parents; he has the vaguest memory of a maternal figure and a faded photograph exists which he realizes must be her portrait. Of his father he knows nothing. At an early age he is sent to live with his uncle and aunt who keep a shop in New Romney, on the South-East Coast. Providing limited funds for his education, his mother insists that he attends the Cavendish Academy, a boarding-school in Hastings and a supposedly middle-class establishment. In fact, its standards are abysmally low. During his vacations, Kipps develops a lasting friendship with Sid Pornick, the son of a neighbour, and also with Sid's younger sister Ann. Together, Artie and Sid indulge in the usual boyhood fantasies, imagining themselves Red Indians or castaways, scrambling over a real wreck which is washed up on the beach.

At the age of fourteen, Kipps is apprenticed to a draper in Folkestone, some miles to the east along the coast. By this time he has attained the physical appearance which he will carry into adulthood : 'thin, with whimsical drakes'-tails at the pole of his head, smallish features, and eyes that were sometimes very light and sometimes very dark, gifts those of his birth'. Because of the nature of his training, he is 'indistinct in his speech, confused in his mind, and retreating in his manners'. Before he leaves New Romney, Ann Pornick has agreed to become 'his girl', but she refuses to indulge in what she regards as the silly pursuit of kissing. Instead, they divide a sixpence between them, each keeping a half as a 'lover's token'.

Kipps undergoes the rigours of the Folkestone Drapery Bazaar with an air of resignation. His clumsiness and lack of organization make him an obvious target for the ill temper of the proprietor Shalford. ' "You make my tooth ache, Kipps," Mr. Shalford would say. "You gimme n'ralgia. You got no more System in you than a bad potato." ' He comes to detest Shalford, while further irritation is provided by the constant nagging of the window dresser, Carshot. The seemingly interminable working hours, the squalid dormitory and meagre food—all serve to conjure an atmosphere of imprisonment rather than a prelude to a career. Only the friendship of two young former apprentices, Buggins and Pierce, helps to alleviate the oppression, and then but spasmodically. To add to his isolation, Kipps finds on his return home for Christmas that Ann has left to go into service, and that Sid, too, has departed—to become errand boy for a bicycle shop.

With time he settles more to life at the Bazaar. Pierce advises him on the choice of more suitable clothes; and with the improvement in his appearance he is able to excite the interest of several of the girls who work in the store. Brief flirtations follow, as far as the rules of the establishment and the short leisure hours permit. In the last year of his apprenticeship Kipps joins the Folkestone Young Men's Association, where he is prompted to ask the presiding Mr. Chester Coote how he should set about bettering himself. When Shalford appoints him an 'Improver', at twenty pounds a year, he attends the local Science and Art classes, first practising freehand and later woodcarving.

The woodcarving sessions are conducted by Helen Walsingham, an attractive young woman some two years older than Kipps and who rapidly earns his devotion. When he inadvertently breaks a window and cuts his wrist, her solicitude leaves him all but tongue-tied. When the class disbands for the summer vacation Kipps despairs of occupying his time constructively on the weekly early-closing day. He resorts to the library and on his return from one such visit is knocked down by a bicyclist, the ebullient Chitterlow. Taken back to the latter's lodgings, he is liberally treated with Old Methusaleh whisky and enthralled by the budding playwright's account of his experiences in the theatrical world. He stays out beyond the Bazaar's curfew hour, returning in the morning to discover himself dismissed, or 'swapped'.

While working out his period of notice, he is shown an advertisement by Chitterlow through which a solicitor is attempting to trace him. Against Buggins's advice he replies, learning to his astonishment that his paternal grandfather, as recompense for his son's misdeeds, has left him twenty-four thousand pounds. Also part of the legacy is a house, fortuitously in Folkestone, where Kipps establishes himself and entertains his friends. He is subsequently cultivated by Chester Coote, a pretentious dilettante in his twenties who moves in 'polite' society and enjoys semi-independent means. At tea with Coote, he again meets Helen Walshingham, who appears more attentive to him than hitherto. Later he calls on her family, to be formally introduced to her widowed mother and to her brother, Young Walshingham, a freshly-qualified solicitor to whom Kipps transfers the management of his affairs.

An agreeable warmth develops between Kipps and Mrs. Walshingham, who is clearly assessing him as a prospective son-in-law. The family have been forced to live in what they regard as reduced circumstances, and Kipps's wealth is an obvious attraction. He spends much time in their company and during an outing to nearby Lympne raises himself in Helen's estimation during a confrontation with a bull:

'Helen was frightened, without any loss of dignity, and Kipps went extremely white. But he was perfectly calm, and he seemed to her to have lost the last vestiges of his accent and his social shakiness. He directed her to walk quietly towards the stile, and made an oblique advance towards the bull. "You be orf!" he said . . .'

Later the same afternoon, Kipps proposes and is accepted.

Hiring a car, he drives to New Romney to break the news to his relatives. While there he is reunited with Sid Pornick, who now manufactures bicycles and has a workshop of his own in London. Sid's reaction to Kipps's inheritance is mixed, for he has become a committed socialist under the influence of his lodger, Masterman. Kipps returns to Folkestone, realizing too late that he has neglected to tell his uncle of his engagement.

The following months are a time of agony, as both Helen and Coote endeavour to educate Kipps in the *mores* of upper-class society. He has a horror of receiving 'genteel' visitors, and of calling on them in return. He studies books of etiquette but learns little from them, and efforts to correct his pronunciation prove fruitless. On a further visit to his uncle, when he again forgets to impart his news, he meets Ann whom he has not seen for some seven years. She remarks on his newly-grown moustache and assures him that she still has her half of the sixpence. Kipps is vaguely troubled that he should now be consorting with a servant; but after an evening with Chitterlow, when the playwright talks of his conquests and of how women should be handled, he seeks out Ann again and they embrace passionately.

Finally, he writes to his family, only to be horrified by a reply from his uncle to say they will call on Helen that very day. Unable to face the inevitable embarrassment, he flees to London, booking himself into a smart hotel. Hungry, he lacks the confidence to enter any of the numerous restaurants he passes, and he wanders aimlessly until by chance he encounters Sid. Taken back for a meal, he is impressed by a socialist diatribe from the consumptive Masterman. He returns to the hotel to make an utter fool of himself in the dining-room, attempting to mitigate his social ineptitude with large and inappropriate tips. The following day brings another series of disasters, including the selection of a raucous tune on a harmonicon (a forerunner of the juke-box) which disturbs the entire drawing-room at afternoon tea. Completely demoralized, he returns to Folkestone.

Kipps's next social ordeal takes the form of an 'at Home', where a game of anagrams is to be played. Unable to make sense of the jumble of letters he is given, he imagines they may be reassembled as 'Cuyps'—an alternative spelling of his own surname which Chester Coote is recommending he adopt. But his perturbation is heightened by the discovery that Ann is working in the house as a maid. On an impulse he tells her that Helen is his fiancée. As the function progresses it is borne in on him how out of place he is and how much he hates the uselessness of the people with whom he is being obliged to mix. This conclusion is reinforced a few days later at a dinner party, where Helen shocks him by wearing a particularly revealing gown. On the same evening he pleads with Ann to marry him, and after some hesitation she agrees.

The couple seek refuge at Sid's home and spend their honeymoon in London. Kipps is relieved that Helen has waived any idea of suing him for breach of promise. On their return to Kent they begin to look for the 'little house' which Ann would prefer, but without success. Kipps decides to have one built, allowing his architect to persuade him—to Ann's disapproval—of the necessity for eleven bedrooms. During the early stages of construction he is dumbfounded to learn from Helen that her brother has misappropriated his fortune and absconded after losing it in foolhardy speculation. Happily there remains about a thousand pounds which Young Walshingham was unable to touch, and with this Kipps sets up a bookshop.

Initially the marriage passes through a difficult period in which Kipps struggles to preserve some of the social graces he has half acquired; consequently Ann feels she is beneath him. Such problems seem to pass with the birth of their son. Kipps has renewed his friendship with Buggins and Pearce (a relationship temporarily severed at the instigation of Coote), and Chitterlow's play, in which he had bought a large share, proves a money-spinner. In the event, Kipps becomes as wealthy as he was formerly; but he decides to retain the bookshop and follow an undemanding life. The close of the story finds husband and wife on an evening row on the Hythe canal:

' "Artie," said Ann.

He woke up and pulled a stroke. "What?" he said.

"Penny for your thoughts, Artie."

He considered.

"I reely don't think I was thinking of anything," he said at last, with a smile. "No."

He still rested on his oars.

"I expect," he said, "I was jest thinking what a Rum Go everything is. I expect it was something like that."

"Queer old Artie!"

"Ain't I? I don't suppose there was ever a chap quite like me before."

He reflected for just another minute.

"Oo!—I dunno," he said at last, and roused himself to pull.'

Much of the background of the novel was drawn from Wells's own experience as a draper's apprentice, first in Windsor and later at Southsea, near Portsmouth on the South Coast. The central character was inspired by a real-life apprentice, junior even to Wells: 'He had by the bye an amusing simplicity of mind, a carelessness of manner, a way of saying "Oo'er", and a feather at the back of his head that stuck in my memory, and formed the nucleus which grew into *Kipps* . . .' The story is also an indictment of the educational system of the period and a further example, after *The Time Machine* and *The Wonderful*

Visit, of the author's deep-seated hatred of the upper classes in British society. 'Kipps was invented in a mood of indignation', he wrote, 'he is an undernourished creature mentally and bodily, slightly ricketty and ungrammatical and weakly snobbish. I shall show, I said, what the greatest and richest and proudest Empire the world has ever seen can do for one of its sons.' A stage adaptation by Rudolph Besier was produced at the Vaudeville Theatre, London, in 1912. *Kipps*, 1905

KIPPS, OLD : The uncle of Artie who, with his wife, has looked after the boy since his infancy at their shop in New Romney, Kent. A type who prefers his own company, he is permanently annoyed by his hymn-singing Methodist neighbour, Pornick, whom he dismisses as 'a blaring jackass'. As a result of his uncle's preference for isolation, young Kipps has few friends in New Romney, with the exception of the Pornick son, Sid, an alliance which must needs be clandestine. On hearing of Kipps's good fortune, his uncle and aunt are dubious of the reality of his inheritance; but, when finally convinced, old Kipps fulfills a deep-seated longing by frequenting local auction-rooms and purchasing much imperfect bric-à-brac on his nephew's behalf. *Kipps*, 1905

KNOWLES, SIR TITUS : A noted and forbidding man of medicine whom Mr. Parham has actively disliked for some five years before the fateful séance which precipitates the arrival of the Lord Paramount. For Parham, Sir Titus combines 'all that is fearful in the medical man, who at any moment may tell you to take off everything and be punched about anywhere, and all that is detestable in the scientist'. A hostile critic of everything that smacks of the psychic, he nevertheless becomes the Lord Paramount's personal physician, preparing his diets and designing elaborate exercise programmes for him. *The Autocracy of Mr. Parham*, 1930

KURT, LUFT-LIEUTENANT : The English-educated, youthful German officer who is appointed to attend on Bert Smallways when it is still believed he is Butteridge. His manner is decidedly cooler when he learns of Smallways's true identity, but he preserves some vestiges of friendship. His task aboard the airship is to supervise the plugging of holes made by enemy bullets. He dies when the flagship is destroyed by the Asian fleet above the Niagara Falls. *The War in the Air*, 1908

L

LABEL, LADY CYTHERA : An attractive young woman in her early twenties whose charms are not lost on the author Rowland Palace. She espouses an interest in things literary, into which category she deems Palace himself to fall. She appears in a state of near nudity as the goddess Venus in a charade at a country-house party, overtowering Rowland's Paris, and later disappears briefly into the night with him, to the tolerant amusement of Mrs. Palace. *Brynhild*, 1937

LAGUNE, MR. : An ardent spiritualist who pursues his researches, a little incongruously, amid Lewisham's biology class at the Normal School of Science. A small, grizzled old man with a tiny face and very large grey eyes, he is allowed into the school's laboratories when they are not completely full. Taunted by the student, Smithers, who attacks his beliefs, he challenges him to attend a séance to see the spirit manifestations for himself. Smithers and Lewisham go together, and, by turning up the gas-light, reveal the medium's props. By the following day, however, Lagune appears to have recovered his composure and his faith in the medium, Chaffery. While he admits that the manifestations they had witnessed were a fraud, he argues that it had been necessary for Chaffery to stage the effects as a prelude to genuine contact with the Beyond—an explanation which convinces no one but Lagune himself.

To his surprise, Lewisham discovers that Lagune, reputedly wealthy, employs Ethel Henderson as his amanuensis. Although it is more than two years since he has seen the girl, Lewisham experiences a rapid reawakening of his feelings for her. He is all the more shocked, therefore, to learn that the bogus medium is her step-father. Towards the close of the story, Chaffery absconds, having duped Lagune by hypnotism into signing his name on a blank cheque. *Love and Mr. Lewisham*, 1900

LAMBONE, PAUL : A writer of short stories and novels who helps

Christina Alberta in her search for Preemby and in her later efforts to secure his release from the mental hospital where he is detained. A very fat and white-faced man in his forties, he describes himself as a kind of bachelor uncle to everyone, who has married a hundred times in theory but never in practice. His reputation is high in both Britain and America, but it is suggested he is far wiser in his thoughts and counsel than in his acts. He contributes to the philosophical discussion at the novel's close, arguing that what a person achieves is less important than what he contributes : '... even if Sargon had died unrescued in his asylum and all the world had thought him mad, all the same he would have escaped, his imagination would have touched the imagination of the greater life.' *Christina Alberta's Father*, 1925

LAMMOCK, NOAH : A modern counterpart of the biblical ark-builder who joins in a Voltarian dialogue with Almighty God during the opening stages of the Second World War. Lammock is a middle-aged writer, separated from his wife and childless when he is first confronted by his celestial visitant. Initially he mistakes God for an absconder from a nearby mental institution but is later convinced of His true identity. He accuses the Almighty of breaking faith with the first Noah by disrupting the growth of a universal language originally represented by the Tower of Babel and established by the generations of Noah's offspring.

He rejects God's offer to return his wife in a more amenable form, but agrees to prepare a memorandum listing what in his own view should be salvaged from modern civilization and taken aboard the new ark. There follows an argument whether 'the best of the old' or 'something new' would hold out greater promise for the future. In the end Lammock concludes that what is required is 'something quintessential for the élite and something very strong and clear and simple for the masses of mankind'.

After a second visitation he falls into a dissertation on Marx and Communism. He represents the élite in society as 'our necessity and our menace', reflecting how readily in the past the élite have allowed themselves to be absorbed into any prevailing governing system. An advocacy of Behaviourism is then advanced (along much the same lines as those set out in *Babes in the Darkling Wood—see under* Kentlake, Robert). All this Lammock imagines he has been addressing to the captive audience of one innocuous water-vole on a river bank. However, he is suddenly disconcerted to find himself aboard the ark, some thirty days out, and is informed by God that his words were in fact a sermon addressed to the ship's company.

Under Lammock's captaincy the voyage proceeds, and although the Almighty accompanies him, He confines himself to playing the harmonium during the service. A stowaway, Jonah, is discovered and promptly thrown over the side, to be swallowed by a whale which regurgitates him after three days. Taken back on board, he proves incapable of work and complains about the food. His shooting of an albatross precipitates a stagnant calm and he is again cast out—only to return with an olive branch. In exasperation Lammock finally shoots him; but his inflated corpse continues to float close to the ark, resisting attempts to sink it with lead weights. God admits that the original Jonah proved entirely as troublesome; and the parable ends with He and Lammock agreeing that there will be no place for such nuisances in the New World. Their first task of reconstruction must be the overcoming of the problems which began with the Tower of Babel.

The book is one of several of Wells's excursions into fantasy designed to present his criticisms of the existing order of human affairs. Both witty and pointed, the quality of its dialogue can be compared with the conversations between the author and Jesus of Nazareth in *The Happy Turning* which appeared five years later. *All Aboard for Ararat*, 1940

LARKINS, ANNIE : Sister of Miriam Polly, a high-spirited girl who, like both of her siblings, has designs on Mr. Polly. As a child she earned the enduring displeasure of Uncle Pentstemon by creating havoc in his mushroom bed. After her brother-in-law's presumed death, she joins Miriam in the management of tea-rooms at Fishbourne, where she 'fills out' noticeably and loses her hilarity. She fails to recognize a bearded Mr. Polly when he returns for a fleeting visit. *The History of Mr. Polly*, 1910

LARKINS, MINNIE : Miriam Polly's other sister, affectionate and given to frequent touching of hands and other endearments. She, too, lives in expectation of a proposal from Mr. Polly, and treats even his most casual remarks as a possible prelude to his seeking her hand. She disappears from the tale after her sister's marriage. *The History of Mr. Polly*, 1910

LARKINS, MIRIAM : See 'Polly, Miriam'.

LARKINS, MRS. : The mother of Annie, Minnie and Miriam, Mr. Polly's cousins. Stout and of an effusive disposition, she entertains an optimistic view of her daughters' prospects, both in work and matrimony. She insists on referring to them as dress-makers, whereas in reality they are simple machinists. No Mr. Larkins is apparent. *The History of Mr. Polly*, 1910

LAVEROCK, STEPHEN : The post-war fiancé of Margaret Broxted and, by coincidence, the doctor who examines Theodore Bulpington when he is feigning shell-shock in France. He threatens Bulpington with violence unless the latter refrains from pestering Margaret with letters on his return to London. A scuffle ensues in Theodore's flat, of which Laverock, having easily got the better of his rival, subsequently confesses himself ashamed. *The Bulpington of Blup*, 1932

LAXTON, LADY : The mistress of Shonts, a trifle fragile and indecisive. She has trouble in entertaining. Her first knowledge of Bealby is the news of his disappearance. In the absence of her husband, she decides for once to embark on determined action, ordering the house to be scoured, the panelling torn out, and the lawns dug up in a search for secret passages where the boy may have been trapped. Only later does it occur to her that she should first have satisfied herself that Bealby had not simply run away; but by then the damage has been done. Finally she offers a reward of five pounds for his safe return, and the posting of this notice in the locality results in the hue and cry to which Bealby is subjected. *Bealby: A Holiday*, 1915

LEADFORD, MRS. : The mother of William, widowed early when her husband was killed in a train accident; she has been reduced to taking in lodgers, among them the curate of Clayton, the Rev. Gabbitas. In common with the mothers of a number of Wells's leading characters, her character, demeanour and circumstances are a reflection of the author's observations of his own mother. She dresses in black, fears God and the Devil, and is perplexed and distressed by her son's progressive views. After the comet's passing she lives with several other old ladies in the commune organized by Leadford in Clayton, finally to be nursed by Anna Reeves who is later to become William's wife. Even after the 'Change' which the comet has wrought, she still retains her belief in Hell, but rejects the idea that anyone will actually go there. *In the Days of the Comet*, 1906

LEADFORD, WILLIAM : The narrator of *In the Days of the Comet* and a young clerk in the office at Rawdon's pot-bank at Clayton, in the Potteries. He lives with his mother but spends much of his leisure time in the company of Parload, a scientifically minded star-gazer with whom he shares an enthusiasm for socialism. From an early age he has been fond of a distant relative, Nettie Stuart, to the extent that they could be called childhood sweethearts. The story's opening finds him distressed by their growing estrangement and by her evident interest in Verrall, the son of a wealthy local landowner. A further cause of dissatisfaction is his employer's parsimony and he discusses with Parload the prospects of finding work elsewhere. It is not a propitious time—war with Germany is imminent, the Labour movement in Britain is in a state of unrest, whilst above it all hangs the potential threat of an approaching unknown comet.

Parload becomes pre-occupied with the astronomical phenomenon and expresses only a doubtful interest in Leadford's plans to organize a series of Socialist meetings. Leadford himself grows progressively more tormented by Verrall's pursuit of Nettie and buys a revolver with the intent of killing him; but he fails to use it during a riot at a miners' strike when he assaults Verrall who is accompanying the mine-owner, Lord Redcar. The elopement of Nettie and Verrall to Shaphambury on the East Coast coincides with the outbreak of war. Leadford pursues the lovers, overtaking them within sight of a battle between British and German dreadnoughts in the North Sea. He attempts to shoot them both, only to be overcome by a green gas trailed by the comet across the Earth.

On awakening he experiences an unprecedented metamorphosis—his senses of perception have been heightened in a manner very similar to the effects produced by hallucinogens : 'I did not awaken with a start, but opened my eyes, and lay very comfortably looking at a line of extraordinary scarlet poppies that glowed against a glowing sky. It was the sky of a magnificent sunrise, and an archipelago of gold-beached purple islands floated in a sea of golden green. The poppies too, swan-necked buds, blazing corollas, translucent stout seed-vessels, stoutly upheld, had a luminous quality, seemed wrought only from some more solid kind of light.

'. . . I held up my left hand and arm before me, a grubby hand,

135

a frayed cuff; but with a quality of painted unreality, transfigured as a beggar might have been by Botticelli. I looked for a
time steadfastly at a beautiful pearl sleeve-link'.

Still wrapt in contemplation, he encounters the British Prime
Minister, Melmount, who has a country retreat nearby. The
politician, incapacitated by a sprained ankle, enlists Leadford's
aid in summoning his Cabinet. In addition to worldwide
euphoria, the comet's tail has brought a new state of altruism
into the affairs of men—peace is declared and the foundations
laid for a World State. On a personal level, Leadford is able to
reconcile himself to the love between Nettie and Verrall and to
insist that she remains with the latter, even though she declares
an equal affection for both men. He helps to found a commune
in Clayton (a social way of life adopted more or less universally)
where his ailing mother is nursed by Anna Reeves. She dies
during the first great May-day festival at Beltane, at which much
of the obsolete bric-à-brac of the recent past is ritually burned.

Distraught at his mother's death and the loss of Nettie, he
finds solace with Anna and they are soon married. After the birth
of a son he realizes that Anna is prepared to accept his reunion
with Nettie, with whom he has continued to correspond; Verrall
also offers no objection. The four become close friends in the
enlightened spirit of the new world—the 'Change' wrought by
the comet's passing endures.

The story is Wells's first novel of jealousy, centred on Leadford's murderous impulse to kill Verrall and, *in extremis*, to
destroy Nettie, too. The characters' final acquiescence in what is
virtually a *ménage à quatre* led to attacks by the Press suggesting that in a Wellsian Socialist Utopia wives were to be regarded
as so much common property; but the hostility aroused fell well
below the level of the furore which *Ann Veronica* was to create
three years later. The portrayal of the Potteries towns earned
Arnold Bennett's respect and led to a long friendship between
the two writers. *In the Days of the Comet*, 1906

LEDBETTER, MR.: An unfortunate school-teaching parson who
yields to the temptation to emulate a burglar, but paradoxically
enters the house of an embezzler about to flee the country. The
defaulting bank manager, Bingham, refuses to believe Ledbetter's real profession and regards the clerical collar merely as a
disguise. Since the parson has witnessed the counting of the
spoils, he is kidnapped and imprisoned on a boat, to be aban-

doned on a desert isle some twenty days later. Eventually he succeeds in returning to England, where he has some difficulty in explaining his absence to his aunt. 'Mr. Ledbetter's Vacation', 1898

LEEDS, MARTIN: The young mistress of Sir Richmond Hardy whom he describes as 'emotionally adhesive'. An artist specializing in humorous illustrations, she is possessed of a sad and handsome face, 'the face of a sensitive youth rather than the face of a woman', fine grey eyes and a wide forehead. In build she is short and broad. She has known Sir Richmond for a number of years and has a daughter by him. The opening of the story sees her retreated temporarily to her cottage in Cornwall, suffering from a carbuncle. Hardy joins her there briefly after his episode with V. V. Grammont and before his final bout with the Fuel Commission.

Returned to her London flat, she learns of her lover's death and obtains Lady Hardy's permission to let her view the body, being received by Dr. Martineau on the widow's behalf. After confessing how much she loved him, she breaks down completely over the coffin, lamenting that for the sake of his work he has sacrificed both his own happiness and hers. *The Secret Places of the Heart*, 1922

LETTY: The wife of Teddy, Mr. Britling's secretary at the opening of the story. She is the sister of Cecily Corner, as pretty, but darker haired. Originally it was feared in the village that she and Teddy were living in an unmarried state. Their child is born shortly before her husband embarks for France during the First World War. Subsequently she is distraught at the news that he is reported missing, and assumes after an interval that he must be dead. This belief is only reinforced by the death of Mr. Britling's son Hugh. In the event Teddy finally returns minus an arm. Her relief is so great after the long period of doubting his survival that she seems not to mind his injury. *Mr. Britling Sees It Through*, 1916

LETZLINGEN, THE FÜRSTIN: The widowed cousin of Stephen Stratton who engineers his reacquaintance with Rachel More during his visit to her villa on the Rhine. Much given to matchmaking, she upbraids Stephen for his continuing preoccupation with Lady Mary Justin and urges him to consider the affection which Rachel so evidently holds for him. Her designs are eventually fulfilled. *The Passionate Friends*, 1913

LEWIS, DAVID : See 'Bunter, Alfred'.

LEWIS, MRS. FREDA : The deserted wife of the man who is later to become the writer Alfred Bunter. A highly-talkative woman who over-dramatizes both herself and her husband; she first meets him through a number of business connections who are also her relatives. They indulge in a brief affair until, claiming falsely that she is pregnant, she traps him into marriage. After his disappearance on the night of her brother's death, she seems on occasions to be shielding him; but her nature is too volatile for Lewis to risk communicating with her. He only does so when the investigations of Immanuel Cloote reveal his true identity. *Brynhild*, 1937

LEWISHAM, ETHEL : Wife of Mr. Lewisham and step-daughter of the fake medium Chaffery. She first meets Lewisham when she is staying with her aunt at Whortley, in Sussex. His dalliance with her one afternoon and evening results in his dismissal from Whortley Proprietary School. She returns to live with her mother and step-father in Clapham, an area of London which Lewisham later searches in the vain hope of finding her. More than two years pass before they meet again, at a séance of Chaffery's which she knows to be faked. Since leaving school, she has been working as an amanuensis for the psychic researcher, Lagune, an occasional visitor to Lewisham's science college.

Of sturdy build, with a well-shaped head, curly black hair and hazel eyes, she reawakens Lewisham's interest immediately but is distressed by his inflexible attitude towards her stepfather's trickery. She allows him to walk her home each evening from Lagune's house in Chelsea, a time-consuming ritual which drastically affects Lewisham's studies. Under pressure from Chaffery, she begins to reattend his séances and allows herself to be persuaded to participate in mind-reading experiments, a lapse largely due to Lewisham's insistence that he cannot afford the time to escort her daily. Learning of the situation from Lagune, Lewisham decides to marry Ethel, an act which subsequently compels him to leave the college and seek employment.

Now Mrs. Lewisham, and no longer assistant to Lagune, Ethel attempts to supplement her husband's meagre income by typing authors' manuscripts, but with little success. She is swindled by her first potential customer and secures scant work other than the occasional verses of Edwin Peak Baynes, a young man whose name rouses Lewisham to furious jealousy when he mistakenly assumes there is some involvement between the poet and Ethel. In turn, Ethel's own doubts of her husband's loyalty have been sown by his regular receipt of letters from Alice Heydinger, a former student friend; and her suspicions, together with her intellectual inability to understand much of Lewisham's studies and interests, lead to a deterioration in their relationship. Fresh hope, however, comes with the discovery that she is pregnant, and the story ends in an atmosphere of renewed affection. *Love and Mr. Lewisham*, 1900

LEWISHAM, GEORGE EDGAR : An assistant master at Whortley Proprietary School when his story opens—a passable young man of eighteen, fair-haired, with an incipient moustache beneath a somewhat prominent nose, on which he wears unnecessary glasses to produce an appearance of greater age. He is taken to affixing exhortatory notices around the walls of his lodgings : 'Knowledge is Power' and the like; but the most important of such documents in his *Schema*, a forward projection of his progress year-by-year envisaging such future milestones as his B.A. degree with honours in all subjects, the award of a gold medal and the authorship of pamphlets 'in the Liberal interest'. His work at Whortley—under the headmastership of Bonover—is distracted by the arrival of Ethel Henderson for a stay with her aunt; and his neglect of school duties while he accompanies her on a long ramble leads to his dismissal. Their attempts to communicate by letter on her return to London are thwarted; they do not meet again for some two years.

After a period of uncertainty, during which he is advised by his colleague Dunkerly, Lewisham obtains his planned-for admission to the Normal School of Science at South Kensington and the award of a guinea-a-week grant. As an impoverished student in London he is obliged to wear a hideous waterproof collar as a necessary economy, but his embracing of the socialist dogma is indicated by his prominent red tie. At the college he becomes close friends with Alice Heydinger, a young woman for whom 'Friendship' appears of intense significance. She admires his contributions on socialism to the debating society, which lead to the formation of a group known as 'the Friends of Progress'. Her enthusiasm wanes somewhat on her discovery that Lewisham is escorting Ethel Henderson home each evening; he has re-encountered her during a faked séance conducted by her step-father, Chaffery, who is exposed by the sceptical student, Smithers.

Lewisham's thoughts of Ethel increasingly interrupt his studies during the day, and the hours he has allotted for evening work are greatly diminished while he pays her court. After a climactic session of the Friends of Progress, when the justification of marrying before one has sufficient means is discussed, he resolves to remove Ethel from the pernicious influence of her step-father and make her his wife. Almost from the beginning their marriage is strained by financial problems, and Lewisham is obliged to abandon his studies to take poorly-paid work as a teacher. Ethel's lack of interest in any of his own enthusiasms depresses him further, while she in turn is frequently disturbed by the letters he regularly receives from Alice Heydinger. Affairs come to a head when, quite irrationally, he suspects her of deceiving him; but he is soon contrite.

With the disappearance of Ethel's step-father, accompanied by the balance of his patron Lagune's bank account, the couple move into her mother's house in Clapham. In the knowledge that Ethel is pregnant, Lewisham resigns himself to the destruction of his adolescent dreams and, in the closing scene, tears up his precious *Schema*.

In describing Lewisham's efforts to acquire an education, Wells portrayed very largely his own experiences. He, too, had worn the sticky waterproof collar, studied in the same labora-tories in the same Normal School of Science, and taken part in after-hours socialist debates. In this respect, and in the matter of an early unsatisfying marriage he was, as he put it, 'on all fours' with Lewisham. The essential difference between the two was that Wells was fortunate enough during his first marriage not to become a father. Unlike Lewisham's, his own *Schema*—for that also is an autobiographical touch—remained intact though much amended. Although he was perhaps to draw upon his own personal relationships more directly in *Ann Veronica* (in emotional terms), the distress displayed in *Love and Mr. Lewisham* records the frustrations of a young man who loved well, but not particularly wisely. Such was the history of Wells's first marriage—to his cousin—a woman for whom he showed continuing devotion (well after it had become impossible for him to live with her) and to whom he displayed considerable generosity once he had achieved success. *Love and Mr. Lewisham*, 1900

LIKEMAN, BISHOP : An early mentor of Edward Scrope and the man to whom the latter turns for guidance following his First Vision. Scrope finds him older and 'more shrivelled on account of the war, but still as sweet and lucid and subtle as ever'. His voice resembles that of a kindly old woman. Earlier in Scrope's career, Likeman had been responsible for interceding on his behalf with Queen Victoria regarding his appointment as a Bishop, and he is now deeply concerned at the course which his former pupil is likely to adopt. He argues with Scrope on the nature of heresy, suggesting that it is a one-sided aspect of religious revelation :

'Your vision—if it was a vision—I put it to you was just some single aspect of divinity ... We make the mistake in supposing that Heresy has no truth in it. Most heresies are only a disproportionate apprehension of some essential truth. Most heretics are men who have suddenly caught a glimpse through the veil of some particular verity ... They are dazzled by that aspect.'

Likeman's conclusion is that, whatever doubts the Bishop may privately entertain, his duty to his flock demands his over-riding consideration. To announce his own doubts in public would be to distress them, to shake their confidence, and finally to convince them of nothing. He asks Scrope to take no action for three months, advising him in confidence that powerful influences are already at work for the liberalizing of the Church and the establishment of an ecumenical movement. When Scrope finally resigns Likeman upbraids him and suggests that his decision is a result of an essential weakness in his character and his craving for theatricality and personal excitement. *The Soul of a Bishop*, 1917

M

MCMANUS, MRS. : The Ulster nurse who appears in Italy to care for Cynthia Rylands in the closing stages of her pregnancy. She presents 'a decided profile, a healthy complexion and lightish hair just shot with grey'. She expresses strong views on the merits of Protestantism and on the character failings of the Italian Fascists. In view of Mrs. Rylands's condition, much of the mechanics of organizing Signor Vinciguerra's escape when he shelters in the villa from pursuing Blackshirts is left to Mrs. McManus. This is achieved by allowing him for part of the time to disguise himself in her clothes. *Meanwhile*, 1927

MAGNET, WILLIAM : The disappointed fiancé of Marjorie Pope whom she jilts in favour of Trafford. By profession a fairly successful humorous writer, he is in his forties, pale, grey-eyed, and with thinning fair hair which is a point of some concern to Marjorie. By nature he is unassuming, with little pretence to being 'beautiful'. Averse to public speaking, he claims that when rising to make an after-dinner speech 'all the ices he had ever eaten seemed to come out of the past, and sit on his back-bone'. After his rejection by Marjorie, he soon marries her elder sister, Daphne. *Marriage*, 1912

MAN IN THE BEAUTIFUL SUIT, THE : Another 'little man' whose mother, having laboured long to make him a beautiful suit of clothes, forbids him to wear it except for particularly important occasions—and even then with its buttons covered and a wealth of other protections. Finally one night he dons it as it should be worn and steals out into the moonlight in an ecstasy. He wades shoulder deep through a duckpond and runs deliriously, trailing duck-weed, until he falls into a stone-pit and breaks his neck. On his dead face, when he is found the next morning, there is an expression of supreme happiness. 'The Beautiful Suit', 1909

MAN IN THE RED ROOM, THE : The narrator of his own experience in the Red Room of Lorraine Castle. Sceptical of its reputation for being haunted he decides to spend the night there, but he soon loses his composure when one-by-one the candles are mysteriously snuffed out more rapidly than he can relight them. When even the fire dies instantaneously, he blunders about in the darkness until he knocks himself out. His conclusion next day is that the room is haunted by no individual ghost, but, more terribly, by the naked force of fear itself. 'The Red Room', 1896

MAN WITH A NOSE, THE : A character in one of Wells's earliest published stories, collected in *Select Conversations with an Uncle*. He is obsessed with his most striking facial characteristic and thoroughly miserable. 'The Man with a Nose', 1894

He attempts suicide by setting fire to his home, with the intention of cutting his throat during the blaze. But the alacrity with which the flames take hold distracts him, and he ends the day a hero by rescuing the deaf and aged mother-in-law of his neighbour. The acclaim which he is duly accorded does nothing to satisfy his fundamental dissatisfaction and, abandoning his wife, he follows a tramp-like existence until he comes to rest at the Potwell Inn, a riverside house where he acts as ferry man and general help to the plump and kindly landlady. After three comically-described but potentially lethal battles with her criminal nephew, Uncle Jim, he settles down to a peaceful and platonic existence with the 'fat woman', but not before paying a fleeting visit to Miriam about whom he suffers intermittent guilt. On discovering that he has been presumed dead, and that she has started a tea-shop on the proceeds of his insurance, he returns to the inn at peace.

One of the most felicitous of his author's creations—part cowardly, part brave—Mr. Polly is also distinguished by his marked appreciation of beauty. He loves sunsets, and it is in a sunset that the story ends, but with little sentimentality. His *raison d'être*, and the nature of his travail, have already been summarized by Wells on the occasion when Polly is debating whether to return to the inn and face the ferocity of Uncle Jim : 'Man comes into life to seek and find his sufficient beauty, to serve it, to win and increase it, to fight for it, to face anything and dare anything for it, counting death as nothing so long as the dying eyes still turn to it. And fear and dullness and indolence and appetite, which, indeed, are no more than fear's three crippled brothers, who make ambushes and creep by night, are against him, to delay him, to hold him off, to hamper and beguile him and kill him in that quest.' *The History of Mr. Polly*, 1910

POLLY, MIRIAM : The third of the Larkins sisters, quieter than the others and, according to her mother, the most industrious and house-proud of the three. In fact, she proves to be severely unpractical, and her culinary ineptitude contributes in no small measures to her husband's perpetual indigestion. She ceases to listen to his talk from the day of their marriage, developing a permanent furrow in her brow and accusing Polly of laziness. She drives him to retreat even more regularly to the local inn or to long and solitary bicycle rides.

No small part of the cause of his attempted suicide can

G

be attributed to her. When she finally believes him dead, she sets up a tea-shop in Fishbourne with her sister Annie. However, she recognizes Mr. Polly immediately on his return after some years to investigate her welfare, and is relieved to find that he is content to remain officially deceased. *The History of Mr. Polly*, 1910

PONDEREVO, EDWARD : The inventor of 'Tono Bungay', a patent medicine with which he founds a business empire that makes him a millionaire and finally brings him to ruin. He is twenty-six or so on his introduction in the novel, the proprietor of a small chemist's shop at Wimblehurst, in Sussex. Even at this age his body displays 'an equatorial laxity', and his movements a 'nimbleness without grace'. His face is fat, and behind gilt glasses his eyes are brown. His nose is irregularly shaped, although it has 'aquiline moments', and his hair sticks up and forwards above his forehead. There is something 'slipshod' about his mouth, so that he suffers a mild lisp. At times he draws in air through his teeth with a curious whispering sound which his nephew can only describe as 'Zzzz'.

He accepts George as an apprentice when the boy is banished from Bladesover House and makes himself responsible for his learning Latin. He also makes himself responsible for some six hundred pounds which his sister-in-law has saved for her son, money which he proceeds to lose—along with his own investments—in speculation on the Stock Exchange. With that, he moves to London, finding employment as the manager of a pharmacy, but he is reluctant to discuss George's purloined funds. By playing off one backer against another, he succeeds in raising sufficient capital to launch 'Tono Bungay', which he bottles and despatches in cramped premises in Holborn. The medicine is offered as a tonic for virtually all ills but, in fact, it contains little that could be beneficial, and one ingredient positively harmful to weak kidneys. It is also laced with a liberal measure of alcohol.

Ponderevo's real talent lies in his grasp of advertising techniques, and it is this which ensures 'Tono Bungay's' success. He devises all his own advertisements and posters, leaving George, whom he persuades to join him, to cover administration and distribution. He begins to diversify, first by handling the affairs of a soap manufacturer who has inherited a concern which he has no desire personally to run. Later he branches into 'Domestic Utilities' and 'Household Services', which he floats as public companies and on which he pays high dividends. He considers buying control of a newspaper, a plan that finds disfavour in the eyes of an antagonistic Press Lord who sets out to undermine confidence in Ponderevo's empire. The press campaign is all too effective, and after George's failure to deliver a rare radioactive mineral from Africa, which might have helped to avoid the threatening disaster, bankruptcy follows.

At this point Ponderevo reveals that he has forged certain documents and that a bankruptcy investigation is bound to lead to criminal proceedings. Now a sick and broken man, he agrees to let George fly him to France; but he suffers from exposure during the crossing and dies soon after landing. Throughout his meteoric career he has displayed a restlessness which was evident in his Wimblehurst days. Partly this personality trait has been reflected in his search for ever bigger and more luxurious accommodation, progressing from flats in London, a house in Beckenham and a mansion in Surrey, to the vast building at Crest Hill which remains unfinished at his death. His sense of insecurity is also shown in his passion for buying almost anything which catches his eye as his wealth increases. A brief love affair, soon ended by his wife, is a further indication. However, the overriding fault in his character is a singular moral failing. He rejects George's arguments that he is cheating the public with a quack medicine, and in much the same way—but on a larger scale—he cannot accept that he has done anything wrong by indulging in fraudulent financial deals. He can see himself only as the victim of persecution : ' "It's cruel ... They asked me questions. They *kep'* asking me questions, George ... They bait you—bait you, and bait you. It's torture. The strain of it. You can't remember what you said. You're bound to contradict yourself. It's like Russia, George ... It isn't fair play ..." ' *Tono Bungay*, 1909

PONDEREVO, GEORGE : The nephew of Edward and the narrator of an autobiography which also chronicles his uncle's rise and fall. He is the son of the housekeeper of Bladesover House, a large country mansion on the Kent Downs. Still an infant when his father left his mother, what little he learns of the paternal side of his family is gleaned from his father's brother, Edward. He imagines his father a sceptic, considering that he has inherited his own innate scepticism from him. As a child, and later as a man, he is reluctant to take anything for granted.

George offers vivid glimpses of life in the servants' quarters at Bladesover: how retired retainers are entertained annually—below stairs—and how the great of society come and go on the upper floors. With the connivance of a maid he would pay hasty visits to the House's library, so that his knowledge of the classics was appreciably better than that of other boys in a similar position; he was particularly drawn to the radical works of Tom Paine, Swift and Voltaire. Also at Bladesover he meets the Hon. Beatrice Normandy—four years his junior—with whom he indulges in some childish love-play. She is responsible for his banishment from the House when she lies about the cause of a fight he has with her half-brother.

His full-time education ends at the age of fourteen, soon after he has left Bladesover. Until then he has attended a private boarding-school where the teaching standards—of the headmaster, at least—are reasonably high. There he makes friends with Bob Ewart, a relationship which continues into adulthood. On parting with his mother he is sent for a brief period to her cousin, Nicodemus Frapp, a baker in the Kentish port of Chatham. The dingy and bookless household oppresses him, and his avowed atheism leads to his persecution in the local chapel. He runs back to Bladesover, only to be immediately conducted to his uncle's shop at Wimblehurst.

The next few years he passes in concentrated study. In addition to his apprenticeship as a chemist, he attends the Government Science and Art Department classes at the nearby Grammar School and is successful in his exams. He becomes very fond of his aunt, intrigued by her unusual sense of humour and her habit of throwing things at her husband. His uncle he finds perhaps more comical than endearing, nevertheless he listens seriously to his frequent complaints of the lack of opportunity in Wimblehurst and his advocacy of London as the only place where a man can get on. His apprenticeship at the shop continues when his relatives move to the capital, but he dislikes the new proprietor and resents the loss of his mother's money which his uncle has gambled away.

Winning a scholarship to the Consolidated Technical Schools, in London's South Kensington, George takes lodgings nearby and at first studies hard. He seeks out Ewart, who is leading a bohemian existence as a struggling sculptor; George spends regular, and variously unsober, evenings in his company. Drawn to socialism, he shares with Ewart some disappointment at the

178

seeming ineffectiveness of the Fabian Society when they attend a typical meeting of that body. At this time his chief interest lies in the exploration of London itself. He visits the street markets, museums and concert halls; and in the art galleries he discovers the beauty of nudity—not what he had earlier thought of as shameful, but something to be desired.

His studies begin to deteriorate on his acquaintance with Marion Ramboat, a young woman whom he has seen in the Art Museum and whom he helps when she has mislaid her fare during a bus journey. She awakens a powerful physical desire in him which he realizes can only be assuaged by marriage, although she—for her part—appears content to let their friendship continue as it is. A crisis is reached when George is reprimanded by the school registrar for his slackness and bad behaviour. He is made to see the paucity of his future once his scholarship has expired. At this point he is rescued by the fortuitous offer of his uncle to join him in the marketing of 'Tono Bungay' at the, then, generous salary of three hundred pounds a year.

George entertains some doubts about the moral propriety of his uncle's enterprise, recognizing that it is at best a placebo which he is foisting on the public. He consults Ewart but receives an unhelpful reply. Finally, his need for Marion overcomes his scruples; however, even this improvement in his finances is not enough to satisfy her. Not until he reaches an annual level of five hundred pounds does she agree to marry him, a mercenary attitude he finds distasteful. Against his own inclinations he submits to a church ceremony with the conventional trappings, and the couple settle in a house in Ealing. The marriage is not successful. Marion proves physically unresponsive, while on an intellectual plane there is little meeting of minds. In frustration George devotes the major part of his energies to his work, contributing greatly to the development of his uncle's business operations. These involve him in considerable travel within the British Isles, so that he is frequently away from home.

His urgent sexual needs are eventually relieved by an affair with Effie Rink, a typist from his office. He spends a week with her on the coast, where he is unfortunately seen by the brother of Marion's closest friend. A long series of hostile recriminations ensues, ending in divorce. The relationship with Effie is also relatively short-lived, since there was never any intention by either party that it should be more than a passionate *passade*. George grows increasingly interested in aeronautics (following the Wright Brothers' flight at Kitty Hawk) and persuades his uncle to release him from many of his duties so that he may experiment in that field. Initially his work is mainly theoretical; it earns him a Fellowship of the Royal Society when he is thirty-seven. Subsequently he builds models and full-scale machines in the grounds of his uncle's house in Surrey.

Almost entirely absorbed with flying, he loses track of Edward Ponderevo's financial activities which are becoming progressively risky. One of the latest speculations is the purchase of an electric light-bulb patent that stipulates a radioactively-coated filament. His uncle has heard from an explorer of a substantial source of 'Quap'—a suitable radioactive material—on Mordet Island, off the coast of West Africa, and plans an expedition for its illegal mining. George's attentions are further distracted by his reunion with Beatrice Normandy, who is staying near his uncle's home. Much of the time she is in the company of Lord Carnaby, a discreditable former politician some thirty years her senior. In the moments when they are alone together, George comes to love her; and when she nurses him after he has crashed in his machine, he proposes to her and is accepted. But Beatrice is tantalizingly vague about certain difficulties which she says will stand in their way.

With his recovery, he flies again, on one occasion narrowly missing Beatrice who has ridden over to see him. She seems reluctant to talk to him intimately following this incident, until his sudden departure abroad. Hounded by the newspapers of a business rival, his uncle has found his unsoundly-based organization on the point of crashing. He places his entire hopes in the acquisition of 'Quap' and the revolutionary light-bulb it would enable him to manufacture. In the absence of the explorer, who has broken a leg, George decides to lead the expedition.

The sea voyage out in a cramped wooden brig is uneventful, but George is dismayed at the captain's lack of co-operation once Mordet Island is reached. Trade is forbidden with the owner country, and the captain demands a ten-per-cent share of the profits before he will allow the crew to excavate the mineral. The loading is subject to constant delays, during which George impetuously murders a native who has unluckily strayed on to the scene. On the return passage the 'Quap' rots the ship's timbers and the vessel sinks in the Atlantic. All aboard are saved, but the vital cargo is lost. Back in Britain, George learns that his uncle has been bankrupted.

Visiting Edward at the hotel suite from which he has run his empire, George finds him ill and dispirited. He also discovers that criminal charges for fraud are likely to be brought. In an attempt to save his uncle from a prison sentence, he flies him to France, arranging for his aunt to join them by more conventional means. However his aircraft, which is more or less a dirigible with wings, is still in the prototype stage; and the two men are left exposed to the elements in a wire cradle suspended beneath it. Blown off course, they spend far longer in the air than anticipated—with fatal results. Edward contracts pneumonia and dies in a frontier village near Bayonne before his wife can reach him.

Beatrice comes to George while he is winding up his affairs in Surrey, and they pass two weeks as lovers before parting for good. She reveals that she is being kept by Carnaby and intends to go back to him, but insists that she has given her real love to George. Knowing that he cannot support her for the time being, he begs her to wait a year; but she is adamant. Emotionally shattered, he nevertheless embarks on a new career, as a supervisory engineer on the construction of warships. His story ends with a remarkable trial of a new destroyer down the Thames through London and out to the North Sea. On passage, he reviews his life, taking the destroyer as a symbol of the force which has driven him and his contemporaries—an entity at the same time so essential and so irrelevant to most human concerns :

'Sometimes I call this reality Science, sometimes I call it Truth. But it is something we draw by pain and effort out of the heart of life, that we disentangle and make clear. Other men serve it, I know, in art, in literature, in social invention, and see it in a thousand different figures, under a hundred names. I see it always as austerity, as beauty ... I do not know what it is, this something, except that it is supreme. It is a something, a quality, an element, one may find now in colours, now in forms, now in thoughts. It emerges from life with each year one lives and feels, and generation by generation and age by age, but the how and why of it are all beyond the compass of my mind ...'

Wells thought the book one of his most important efforts in the field of fiction. He saw it as a 'full-dress' novel and planned it as 'a social panorama in the vein of Balzac'. It does indeed review turn-of-the-century society in England through many levels, from the serving-hall to the boardroom; and its descriptions of London, notably the river passage in its closing pages, are particularly evocative. It also demonstrates the author's clear understanding of the persuasive use of advertising and propaganda techniques. While it takes the form of a fictional autobiography, it is—in its early chapters—genuinely autobiographical, many of the scenes at Bladesover, Wimblehurst and South Kensington being drawn from Wells's own experience. No brief synopsis of the plot can convey the wealth of social criticism and compassion with which the story is imbued. Wells's penetrating attacks on the social institutions and mores of the day struck a chord in many of the readers of his own generation, let alone the young. His questioning of the whole fabric of society, already much in evidence in his early works, rose to a crescendo in *Tono Bungay*; it was to occupy the major part of his attention for the remainder of his writing career. *Tono Bungay*, 1909

PONDEREVO, MARION : Wife of George, whose physical desire for her prompts him to join his uncle in marketing 'Tono Bungay'. The daughter of a clerk in a London gas-works, she is first noticed by Ponderevo in the environs of South Kensington, where he is studying science. He frequently observes her in the Art Museum, copying details from pictures which are later incorporated into designs for dress material. With brown hair and eyes, she has a certain duskiness of skin (although her complexion is not good), finely-modelled lips and brow, and a prettily rounded head. Her body is slender and she moves with noticeable grace; her voice is pleasantly soft. Nevertheless, her looks belie the quality of her mind, which is commonplace—her conversation rarely rises above the mundane.

It is evident from the opening stages of their relationship that Marion is sexually very inhibited, a fact which George chooses to overlook, but which eventually drives him into the arms of Effie Rink. Their engagement is broken off and renewed on several occasions; chief among the reasons for the breaks is her feeling that he will not be able to support her. Another cause for contention is his insistence on a registry-office wedding, a stipulation she will not accept; and eventually she has her way. All these difficulties she confides to her close friend 'Smithie', a dressmaker whose influence is hardly helpful.

Curiously for one intimately connected with clothes, Marion's own dress-sense is abysmal; she is quite incapable of appreciating what will suit her or of realizing her own grace of form. She irritates her husband by wearing hair curlers and old clothes in his presence at home, arguing that no one is likely to see her, thereby dismissing him as a 'no one'. From 'Smithie' she has been infected with a dread of maternity, and thus there are no children. In short, she remains fixed in the limited ideas of her class, displaying an 'immense unimaginative inflexibility' to change, while George expands his horizons and moves to a more challenging way of life.

Her reaction to his affair with Effie is perfectly in character—she says that she cannot bear him to touch her again. But when the final separation before divorce comes, she breaks down, declaring that she has failed to understand him and that consequently her life is a wreck. In due course she goes into partnership with 'Smithie' and is remarried to an agent for paper dress-patterns. There follows some argument about the continuance of her alimony and her continued use of Ponderevo's name for her business—matters which are duly resolved. *Tono Bungay*, 1909

PONDEREVO, MRS. : The mother of George, whom he claims did not love him because he resembled his father. A hard, severe woman, she was deserted by her husband before George was old enough to form any memory of him. In indignation, she has destroyed every vestige of his relationship with her, save only her wedding-ring and marriage lines. She refuses outright to discuss him with her son and is consistently upset by the mention of the word 'colonies', believing that Ponderevo is living—possibly bigamously—somewhere abroad. Her treatment of George is very much according to the dictates of her mistress, and she has no hesitation in sending him away from Bladesover House when he appears to have offended the prevailing social code. She dies suddenly, shortly after his departure. *Tono Bungay*, 1909

PONDEREVO, SUSAN : Wife of Edward and consequently the aunt of George, to whom she behaves half as a mother. When George first meets her she is in her early twenties, slender (she later broadens), pretty, with a delicate complexion, blue eyes and small quizzical features. A great humourist, and given to 'connubial badinage', she has woven an 'extensive net of nonsense' around her domestic relations until it has assumed the status of reality. She applies the epithet 'old' to a diverse collection of people and things, often employing it as a suffix. As the fortunes of 'Tono

Bungay' progress, she begins to dress with 'cheerfully extravagant abandon'.

Her early attempts to be friends with George's wife, Marion, give way to the irresistible impulse to make fun of her lack of taste, and her visits to her nephew's home become infrequent. She moves with enthusiasm into each new house her husband acquires, usually objecting to his choice of decor—'Pestilential old Splosher!' Increasing leisure time enables her to broaden her knowledge; she reads regularly and for a time attends afternoon lectures. However, she remains mystified by Edward's business affairs, being told very little of them, and is hurt when he stays in his hotel after his financial crash so that George has to bring her news of him. She follows him to France after his flight, but he has died before she arrives. Her last appearance in the tale sees her lamenting the knocks he received in life and referring to him as her only child. *Tono Bungay*, 1909

POPE, MARJORIE : See 'Trafford, Marjorie'.

POPE, MRS. : Marjorie's mother who helps her daughter to decide between Trafford and her fiancé, Magnet. She is a fine-featured, small anxious looking woman, all of whose children resemble her in physical appearance. Her clothes seem rather ill-chosen and her hair is arranged in 'a manifest compromise between duty and pleasure'. Highly observant, she quietly manoeuvres circumstances to facilitate Magnet's proposal to her daughter and she continues to visit her when Mr. Pope refuses to see Marjorie following her marriage to Trafford. In spite of her husband's convictions, she occasionally attends church and entertains some interest in Christian Science. A firm believer in tact, she has learnt early in life to be 'careful' with her thoughts. *Marriage*, 1912

POPE, PHILIP : The father of Marjorie, who is the second of his five children. 'Character is one of England's noblest and most deliberate products, but some Englishmen have it to excess.' Mr. Pope has. Born into a coach-building family and educated at City Merchant's School and Cambridge, he is 'one of that large and representative class which imparts a dignity to national commerce by inheriting big business from its ancestors'. Eventually the company fails as a result of his inflexibility and he is obliged to sell out to a competitor. Thereafter he devotes his time to a futile rearguard action against the onslaught of the motor car. He shares with his sister-in-law, Aunt Plessington, an abiding interest in the control of the lower social orders for their own good and hopes vainly to be adopted as a Liberal candidate for Parliament. An avowed anti-churchman, he is not above renting a vicarage for a family summer holiday. Pope attempts unsuccessfully to prevent Marjorie from marrying Trafford, and is estranged from her for a number of years when she goes against his wishes. *Marriage*, 1912

PORNICK, ANN : The recipient of Kipps's half-sixpence and the girl for whom he foresakes his fiancée, Helen Walshingham. Quick-coloured, with dark blue eyes and brown hair, she is something of a tomboy when in her teens, racing Kipps around New Romney and insisting that kissing is 'silly', although she agrees to be his girl. She is forthright and direct, and of a happy disposition— Kipps often hears her singing in the scullery next door. It is left to her to file the sixpence in two when Kipps is unable to break it. She retains her half into adulthood, as does he.

Ann goes into service at Ashford, in Kent, during Kipps's apprenticeship at the Folkestone Drapery Bazaar, and she does not meet him again until, by chance, both are visiting their relatives in New Romney on the same day. By then she has revised her ideas on intimate embraces. Kipps has heard she has changed her employment, but without knowing the details. He is therefore astounded to find her a servant in a Folkestone house where Helen and he have been invited to a party. He returns to propose to her in the kitchen, and after some persuasion she accepts. Following their marriage she hopes to settle in a 'little house', considering their architect's plans for eleven bedrooms as beyond her capabilities. In the event the building remains unfinished due to the loss of Kipps's fortune, an event which Ann accepts stoically after an initial bout of despair. She settles happily into his newly-acquired bookshop and bears him a son. The end of the tale sees her spending an idyllic evening with her husband in a boat on the Hythe canal. *Kipps*, 1905

PORNICK, SID : The son of old Kipps's neighbour at New Romney and the brother of Ann. When Kipps leaves for Folkestone to become a draper's apprentice, Sid is employed as errand boy in a bicycle shop and their friendship is not renewed until they meet at the time of the former's inheritance. By then, Pornick has a bicycle business of his own in London, has married and produced a son. He takes the news of Kipps's good fortune ambivalently, for he has developed into an ardent socialist under the influence of his ailing lodger Masterman. His reactions go some way to convincing Kipps that marriage with Helen Walshingham is ill-advised. When Kipps subsequently becomes the husband of Ann, no one could be more delighted than Sid. *Kipps*, 1905

POTTER : An Eurasian Jew, and owner of the birds which occupy the central stage in 'A Deal in Ostriches'. It is he who insists on auctioning them individually; but, since he is later seen in jovial company with the diamond's original owner, Padishah, the outcome suggests that the two have perpetrated an ingenious fraud. 'A Deal in Ostriches', 1894

PREEMBY, ALBERT EDWARD : The ex-laundryman who suffers the delusion that he is a reincarnation of the most noted of the ancient Chaldean monarchs, Sargon the First, King of Kings. He is plump and short, with blonde hair; in maturity he grows a large moustache. In both character and appearance he is very much a Wellsian 'little man' until his metamorphosis overtakes him. In his youth he was a member of the Y.M.C.A., although he was more interested in the literary pursuits of the movement than in its religious aspects.

He meets his future wife when he falls off his bicycle into the arms of one of her friends and allows himself very rapidly to be persuaded into marriage. His inpecunious state is rectified by the gift of his wife's family's laundry business in Woodford Wells, where they remain until her death. As a widower, Preemby decides to sell the laundry to Sam Widgery, a transaction which is never completed. Instead, Widgery manages the business and remits a share of the profits to Preemby.

After a brief stay in London with his daughter at the flat of the Crumbs, friends of Christina Alberta, he has an extraordinary experience in Tunbridge Wells. He attends a séance at which a series of messages are received from a spirit claiming to be Sargon and intimating that his reincarnation is present in the room. This is identified as Preemby, who is much disturbed by the revelation. He becomes obsessed with the idea and resolves that he must fulfil a grandiose mission through which Sargon will revolutionize the world. Back at the Crumbs' flat, he gives them the slip and finds lodgings in the same house as a young aspiring writer, Bobby Roothing. From there he launches his campaign to attract followers, going about the streets and accosting passers-by. Having recruited a group of motley hangers-on, he makes himself over-conspicuous in a restaurant, so that the police are called.

Preemby is held in custody for a while in London, Roothing denying all knowledge of him in a manner reminiscent of an earlier biblical denial. He is then certified insane and transferred to a mental asylum at Cummerdown Hill, in Kent. In due course he is visited by Roothing, who outlines a plan for his escape; but he has doubts whether Preemby/Sargon has grasped the nature of his plan, since he has had to describe it by innuendo. In the middle of the night Preemby experiences a period of lucidity when he realizes what Roothing has been trying to tell him (he regularly goes through such brief returns to reality during his delusion and frequently suffers crises of identity when he is uncertain who he really is).

He follows Roothing's instructions and meets him in the morning in the hospital grounds. He is taken by motorcycle to a boarding house in Dymchurch on the Kent coast; but he is still in his nightclothes and consequently arrives suffering from exposure. His health has already begun to fail while he was kept at the asylum; it now deteriorates rapidly. However, he has only to remain at liberty for fourteen days to make a new order recertifying him necessary.

Christina Alberta and Devizes, her lawyer and probable father, call on him at Dymchurch, Devizes endeavouring to convince him of his real connection with Sargon in terms of universal human heredity. Preemby finds the explanation a comfort. As he later tells Roothing: 'Talking to your friend Devizes has cleared my mind greatly. I *am* Sargon, but in a rather different sense from what I had imagined. Preemby was, as I had supposed, a mere accidental covering. But . . . I am not *exclusively* Sargon. You—you perhaps are still unawakened—but you are Sargon too. His blood is in our veins. We are co-heirs. It is fairly easy to understand. Sargon, regal position. Naturally many wives. Political—biological necessity. Offspring numerous. They again—positions of advantage—many children. Next generation, more. Like a vast expanding beam of intellectual and moral force . . . We are all descended from Sargon, just as . . . nearly all the English and Americans are descended from William the Conqueror. Few people realize this. A little arithmetic—it is perfectly plain. Long before the Christian era the blood of Sargon was diffused throughout all mankind. His traditions still more so. We all inherit ... All that rich wine from the past is in my veins. And I thought I was just Albert Edward Preemby!'

Although he is attended by a nurse, Preemby insists on getting up to read and consult books. Finally he is found outside at night, gazing at Sirius through a pair of field-glasses. There follows a relapse and he dies shortly afterwards. (The remaining developments in the story are summarized in the next entry.)

Christina Alberta's Father is Wells's first major work on the theme of self-delusion; he was to write several more before the end of his career, as has been noted elsewhere. The idea of modern men sharing the blood of the ancients was a concept which particularly intrigued him and he referred to it more than once. He gave it some prominence in his short philosophical work, *First and Last Things* (1908), a book which he subtitled 'A Confession of Faith'—although the 'faith' was naturally vested in Man and Wells himself, rather than in any deity. *Christina Alberta's Father*, 1925

PREEMBY, CHRISTINA ALBERTA: Apparent daughter of Albert Edward Preemby, and a headstrong independent girl of twenty-one. She has a penchant for bobbed hair and short skirts and is distinguished by a somewhat prominent nose. 'The magic forces of adolescence assembled her features into a handsome effect, but she was never really pretty.' She is expelled from her first school, but does well at the second, winning a scholarship to the London School of Economics. She is greatly attached to Preemby and shares his secret dreams about the lost continent of Atlantis.

On her mother's death she moves to London to stay with the Crumbs, Preemby accompanying her until they find him accommodation in Tunbridge Wells. In the meantime she has had a brief affair with Teddy Winterton, with whom she is infatuated but without particularly liking him. Suddenly summoned to Tunbridge Wells, she is deeply concerned to discover that Preemby now believes himself to be a reincarnation of Sargon. She takes him back to London, where he eludes her, and she elicits the help of Teddy Winterton and another friend, the writer Lambone, in an effort to find him. Both prove ineffectual.

On hearing from the police that Preemby has been certified, she consults the lawyer, Devizes. She is astonished to find they are facially very much alike, and having learned that he knew her mother before her marriage, she suspects him of being her real father—an allegation which Devizes at first dismisses but later tacitly admits. She is also summoned to the laundry at Woodford Wells, where the manager Sam Widgery suggests he need no longer hand over Preemby's share of the profits. An acrimonious quarrel ensues.

Receiving a telegram from Bobby Roothing at Dymchurch, Christina Alberta visits Preemby's retreat accompanied by Devizes, who succeeds in bringing Preemby back to a semblance of reality. After Preemby's death she eventually agrees to marry Roothing; but she changes her mind when Devizes announces his own engagement, although she insists she will continue to love Bobby. The close of the story sees her working at the Royal College of Science and joining in a discussion with Lambone, Roothing and Devizes, in which—among other vehement declarations—she confesses her fear of having children.

Wells himself thought Christina Alberta one of the most appealing and alive of his heroines—he ranked her much higher as a character than Ann Veronica Stanley. As a sign of changing attitudes, it is interesting to note that whereas the account of Ann Veronica's affair with her tutor caused a storm of public protest sixteen years earlier, not a voice was raised against Christina Alberta's behaviour which was morally less defensible. *Christina Alberta's Father*, 1925

PREEMBY, MRS. : Wife of Albert Edward, whom she first meets at Sheringham, in Norfolk, in 1899. Three years older than her husband, she is very much the senior partner in the marriage. She views Preemby's intellectual preoccupations with friendly sympathy but takes no part in them herself. She entertains doubts about her daughter, and is averse to her being educated 'above her parentage and station'. She forces her to leave the London School of Economics after only a year's study.

There is evidence that Chrissie Preemby has had an affair with the solicitor Devizes, but it is not explicitly stated. She dies early in the narrative. *Christina Alberta's Father*, 1925

PRENDICK, EDWARD : The narrator of *The Island of Dr. Moreau* and a student of natural history. He arrives at the Island via a shipwreck, after which he is befriended by Moreau's assistant, Montgomery. Prendick is horrified to find the tropical isle inhabited by a grotesque variety of misshapen creatures whom he takes to be men who have suffered at the hands of Moreau in the interests of research into vivisection. Escaping from the doctor's compound, he is chased through the jungle to the beach, where he threatens to commit suicide by drowning. To restore the peace Moreau offers to explain : the Beast Folk were never men, but animals on which he has imposed a humanoid form by grafting and other techniques. Although satisfied with none of his results to date, he is optimistic of success with his latest acquisition, a female puma. Prendick discovers that Montgomery, on the other hand, has some liking for the doctor's bizarre creations, although, imitating Moreau, he always carries a whip.

During the early part of Prendick's stay, he comes across a rabbit whose head has been torn off, a sign, which Moreau confirms, of the Beast Folk's gradual reversion to an animal state.

In an attempt to identify the culprit, a gathering of the Beast Folk is called, during which the doctor is attacked by the Leopard Man. The ensuing hunt culminates in Prendick's shooting of the quarry, to Moreau's chagrin.

Prendick himself experiences some close encounters with the Beast Folk, including a visit to the cave where the Sayer of the Law intones the rules Moreau has decreed for their observation. But once the taste for blood has infected the island, the degeneration is rapid. The half-flayed puma breaks its restraining chains and kills Moreau when he tries to recapture it. In a drunken stupor, Montgomery feeds liquor to several of the Beast Folk, including his servant, M'Ling, and in the ensuing struggle both he and several of their own number die. In his haste to go to the rescue Prendick overturns a lamp which sets fire to the doctor's residence, so that he eventually finds himself alone with the anthropomorphs, and devoid of protective shelter. In an effort to establish his authority he endeavours to persuade them that Moreau still lives and is watching them from the sky, but they remain unconvinced. Having no other choice, he is obliged to share their existence and live with them as an equal.

After some ten months of constant vigilance in fear of the more predatory of the now completely degenerate beasts, Prendick succeeds in boarding a drifting boat, later to be picked up by a brig en route to San Francisco. On his return to civilization, however, he finds little consolation : 'I could not persuade myself that the men and women I met were not also another, still passably human, Beast People, animals half-wrought into the outward image of human souls, and that they would presently begin to revert, to show first this bestial mark and then that ... I feel as though the animal was surging up through them; that presently the degradation of the Islanders will be played over again on a larger scale.'

On its initial reception the novel, one of Wells's most powerful essays into allegorical writing, was almost universally misunderstood by the critics. Ignoring the deliberate attempt at blasphemy, they chose to regard it as a straightforward horror story and professed themselves suitably shocked at its contents. Several decades were to pass before the underlying psychological, and physiological, implications of the work became fully appreciated. Commentators now recognize with disquiet Wells's vivid references to the 'beast within Man' and the novel is now accepted as a major literary achievement. *The Island of Dr. Moreau*, 1896

PROTHERO, WILLIAM : A Cambridge don and an early influence on his lifelong friend, William Benham. They first meet at school, when Prothero takes an interest in Benham after the latter has defied an angry bull. At the time Prothero is a sturdy boy, 'generously wanting in good looks', with coarse hair, a shapeless nose which he holds high with an air of the unconcerned. He professes, and practises, cowardice 'to the scandal of all his acquaintances'. His manner of attire is slovenly, becoming more so in adulthood, but he has a ready gift of pin-pointing the absurdities in other people. Unlike Benham, he is demonstrably fond of animals. A professed socialist, he enters into many discussions with his friend but fails to convert him entirely to his own persuasions. However, he stimulates Benham's thoughts in the direction of social reform and community service. His clever pencil sketches and caricatures of masters and others also open Benham's eyes to the sordid pettiness of so many of his fellows.

When both have gone up to Trinity College, Cambridge, Benham's mother, Lady Marayne, invites Prothero to stay for a few days at her home in Hertfordshire. She is concerned by her son's close friendship with the youth and tries, unsuccessfully, to belittle him in Benham's eyes. Prothero is obliged to reveal that his mother is a dressmaker and that he subsists entirely on his scholarship grant. After graduating, he stays on at Trinity while Benham moves to London.

He re-appears in the narrative when Benham suggests they visit Moscow together. Benham, in the meantime, has married

Amanda Morris; but Prothero himself is in a state of neurotic frustration brought about by his own celibacy. His physical needs are partially alleviated by an affair with a Russian prostitute, but he becomes emotionally involved and entertains the unrealistic hope of taking her back to Cambridge. Realizing the impossibility of the situation, she disappears and eludes his efforts to trace her. After a further interval he accompanies Benham to China, where he discovers the attractions of opium and is soon addicted. To counter Benham's disgust he attempts to justify his habit in philosophical terms, suggesting that even while he is destroying himself he is saying 'good things'. Finally he is murdered by an opium gang when Benham refuses to provide the money he owes them. *The Research Magnificent*, 1915

PYECRAFT : An overweight gourmandizing member of a London club who is obsessed with his fatness and seeks an effective slimming cure from the narrator. Subsequently an ancient Indian recipe for 'loss of weight' is procured, which is precisely the result it produces—Pyecraft becomes weightless and crawls about on his ceiling 'like some great, fat blow-fly'. After some comic adaptations to his room to take account of his new condition, lead underclothing is eventually prescribed, and he is free again to overeat at his club. 'The Truth About Pyecraft', 1903

R

RAJAH, THE : An Indian potentate whose secret treasure leads to intrigues against him by his heir and a number of his court, culminating in his murder. The treasure is subsequently revealed as a cache of whisky. Unpublished in any collection in the U.K., this brief tale appeared as the sixteenth item in *Thirty Strange Stories*, U.S.A. 1897. 'The Rajah's Treasure', 1896

RAMAGE, MR. : A successful businessman, on nodding terms with Ann Veronica's father, who occasionally travels in the same train as Stanley and his daughter from Morningside Park to the City of London. An 'iron-grey man of the world', in his fifties and possessed of slightly protruding eyes, he takes an instant interest in Ann Veronica for less than platonic ends. Discovering she has fled from her father's overbearing strictures to take a room of her own in town, he entertains her to intimate lunches and cajoles her into accepting a loan of forty pounds to enable her to continue her biological studies. However, his help is offered with the intention of exacting a price; he declares his love for her in an embarrassing scene during a performance of *Tristan and Isolde* at Covent Garden.

The next day he more than forces his attentions upon her in a private room at a restaurant. Shocked and disillusioned—she has always counted on him as a good friend—Ann Veronica sends him back the twenty pounds still unspent of his loan. These he promptly returns, to be burned by her in a fit of revulsion. She sees no more of him until shortly before her elopement with Capes, by which time the Ramages of this world have passed beyond her concern; but she later recalls her monetary debt to him and confesses it to her lover. *Ann Veronica*, 1909

RAMBOAT, MARION : See 'Ponderevo, Marion'.

RAMPOLE ISLANDERS, THE : The imaginary savages among whom Arnold Blettsworthy finds himself during the course of his long period of delusion. They live in squalor and degradation, worshipping the tree sloth and regularly practising cannibalism. They are governed by a small group of 'ancients' or 'sages' who are every bit as repulsive as their charges. Order is maintained by the threat of the 'Reproof' which is intended as physical chastisement but usually proves fatal, the victim then being eaten.

The only named islanders are Chit the soothsayer, a metamorphosis of Blettsworthy's doctor, Minchett; Ardam the warrior, who represents a combination of the entire real-life military establishment; and Wena, the girl rescued from drowning, who is actually Rowena and subsequently Blettsworthy's wife. *Mr. Blettsworthy on Rampole Island*, 1928

RATZEL, ROBERT : The identical twin of Richard Bolaris and son of an engineer on a Louisiana riverboat. After the flood in New Orleans which leads to Richard's disappearance at the age of eighteen months, Ratzel remains with his mother until her death when he is twelve. He comes to Bolaris's country as a young man to work in the mines, an experience which converts him to Communism and begins a chain of events which ends in his command of the forces fighting the right-wing régime during the civil war. He is captured by Bolaris, who is about to carry out a *coup d'état*, and the two brothers find that their aims are virtually the same, although they are on opposing sides. Allowed to escape, he is shot by Bolaris's aide Handon who is unaware of his leader's plans. *The Brothers*, 1938

RAUT : One of the two central characters of 'The Cone', a man literally cooked to death by the other protagonist of the tale, Horrocks, who suspects him of pursuing a liaison with his wife. 'The Cone', 1895

RAVEN, DR. PHILIP : The fictitious author of the future history, *The Shape of Things to Come*, the book being presented as Raven's manuscript assembled for publication by Wells. There is no real characterization in the work, and Raven himself is tentatively described as a member of the League of Nations Secretariat who died in 1931. His outline of the future extends to the first decade of the 22nd century, beginning with a broad factual review of political, economic and social trends during the early 1900s.

The prophetic section of the book opens in the 1930s and correctly identifies 1939 as the year of the outbreak of the Second World War. The period immediately preceding it has become noted for the growth in organized crime and most particularly in the incidence of hijackings. Britain remains neutral during the global conflict principally because of her economic exhaustion. The Axis powers of Germany and Italy attempt the conquest of Europe, while Japan, still fighting to subdue China, is finally defeated by the United States. In the meantime much of the East has fallen under the spell of Communism.

A peace treaty is signed in Prague in 1949, to be followed by famine and the outbreak of cholera and bubonic plague on an unprecedented scale in the wake of a collapsed civilization. By 1956 the world's population has been effectively halved. A global Air Dictatorship comes into being (such a supranational organization of aviators was first advocated in 1942, according to the history, in a book of Gustave De Windt, an intellectual worker who like Marx had spent much of his time in the British Museum and had died in Bloomsbury).

In 1965 the first Basra Conference is held, instituting international transport control and leading to the foundation of the Modern State Movement in 1975. Economic privation has seen a return to widescale debt serfdom; however, it is evident that many national powers have still found it possible to begin re-armament programmes. To curtail the move towards further warfare, the second Basra Conference of 1978 decrees the sur-render of all national decision-making to a Bureau of Transition. A Thirty Year Plan is established and the rule of the Air Dictatorship, later to be known as 'the Puritan Tyranny', con-tinues. It is to last until 2059.

Under the Dictatorship the traditional life-styles of humanity are transformed. All former religious practices are suppressed—the Pope is temporarily gassed when about to consecrate an Italian airfield. Many previous literary works are 'disinfected'; ecological improvement is vigorously encouraged; and the prevailing ascetic atmosphere of the times is described as 'the cold bath that braced up mankind after the awakening'. The Conference of Mégève in 2059 winds up the Air Dictatorship and establishes a permanent World Government. It is attended by, among others, the noted painter and designer Ariston Theotocopulos, who champions the cause of cultural, as opposed to purely material, progress.

The final fifty years of Raven's dream book chronicle the general harmonization of the World State and its effect on the individual. After some alarming examples, all genetic experi-ments are proscribed, although the science of Eugenics is widely adopted. Considerable advances are made in meteorology and much of the world is transformed into a universal garden. En-lightened methods of education become the chief means of controlling social behaviour; a standard world-language de-veloped from phonetically-spelt Basic English is introduced. Education also helps to foster a 'Sublimation of Interest'—crime and lawlessness are reduced to a minimum and 'sexual serious-ness' is encouraged, aided by the practice of birth control and informal marriage. The acquisition of personal property goes increasingly into the discard, whilst individual dwellings are systematically replaced by community housing developments. General standards of health are improved and by 2105 the average age at death has risen to 90. Finally, to support and further human intellectual progress, a vast Encyclopaedia organization employing seventeen million workers is founded—'The Memory of Mankind' (a fictional counterpart of the body which Wells was later to call for in his collection of lectures and articles under the title *World Brain* in 1938). Raven's vision concludes in a characteristic vein :

'The body of mankind is now one single organism of nearly two thousand five hundred million persons, and the individual differences of every one of these persons is like an exploring tentacle thrust out to test and learn, to savour life in its fullness and bring in new experiences for the common stock. We are all members of one body. Only in the dimmest analogy has anything of this sort happened in the universe as we knew it before. Our sense of individual difference makes our realization of our common being more acute. We work, we think, we explore, we dispute, we take risks and suffer—for there seems no end to the difficult and dangerous adventures individual men and women may attempt; and more and more plain does it become to us that it is not our little selves, but Man the Undying who achieves these things through us.'

The book was recognized at the time as Wells's most concentrated effort to portray the evolution of a world state. It points the way to the ideal society depicted in *A Modern Utopia* and *Men Like Gods*, although in those works he showed such a state as already in existence and offered but the briefest of explanations as to how it had come about. Again it is characteristic that a World Government is seen as a genuine possibility only as a consequence of a devastating war, echoing *The War in the Air* and *The World Set Free* and presaging *The Holy Terror*. Raven's history is a closely reasoned and detailed document, with convenient gaps in the manuscript where Wells found it propitious to jump through time. However, for the Alexander Korda film production which the book inspired, *Things To Come*, a much blunter and more emotive approach was taken.

The movie, directed by William Cameron Menzies and scripted by Wells, was made in 1935; Wells's screenplay appeared as a book in the same year. The production is still regarded as one of the most impressive undertakings in cinematic history, chiefly for its use of huge sets, archetypal images and futuristic designs. Many critics praised it for these particular qualities but otherwise found it a blatant, even vulgar, vehicle of Wellsian propaganda. The characterization, of necessity, is thin; the opening scene, set in Everytown, shows a Christmas Eve discussion between the friends Cabal, Passworthy and Harding on the imminence of war.

The world conflict duly ensues, an individual scene being devoted to a confrontation between Cabal and a crashed, and dying, enemy pilot. Views of London illustrate the extent of the devastation, whilst a superimposed calendar crawls to the year 1966 with no apparent end to the hostilities. Harding is revealed in his laboratory attempting to discover a cure for the plague which is spreading globally. Cabal, who has enlisted the help of the aeroplane mechanic, Gordon, visits Harding in 1970 and the three are detained and compelled by the Boss (a minor warlord and grotesque parody of Mussolini) to repair his diminutive airforce.

Gordon escapes and flees to Cabal's H.Q. in Basra, where the Air League (or 'Wings over the World') sends out a squadron which overcomes the Boss and his retinue with an anaesthetizing gas before the hostages can be harmed. The airmen become the virtual rulers of mankind.

There follows a rapid transition to 2054 A.D., by which time Oswald Cabal, the grandson of the earlier figure, is President of the World Council. A space-gun has been built to pave the way for manned exploration of the moon, the President's daughter and Passworthy's great-grandson being selected as the first astronauts. After a last-minute insurrection led by Theotocopulos (the only surviving character from the book), who objects to the preoccupation with technological progress and calls for fewer sacrifices and more leisure, the gun is successfully fired and the closing scene moves to the observatory from which the spacecraft's flight is viewed. The fathers of the two astronauts add a postscript to the peroration of Raven's original future history :

'*Passworthy* : "My God! Is there never to be an age of happiness? Is there never to be rest?"

Cabal: "Rest enough for the individual man. Too much of it and too soon. But for Man no rest and no ending. He must go on—conquest beyond conquest. This little planet and its winds and ways, and all the laws of mind and matter that restrain him. Then the planets about him, and at last across immensity to the stars. And when he has conquered all the deeps of space and all the mysteries of time—still he will be beginning." '

The Shape of Things to Come, 1933, and *Things to Come*, 1935

REDWOOD, PROFESSOR DANDY : A scientist, and joint-inventor with Bensington of the growth-stimulating drug later to become known as 'Boomfood'. When administered in infancy, it is found to induce an increase in final stature some six or seven times the norm. At first the chemical is tested at an experimental farm in Kent, where mishandling on the part of the manager, Skinner, results in an outbreak of giant wasps and rats, to which a number of unfortunates succumb. The huge vermin are hunted down and the farm razed with the help of Cossar, an engineer whose three sons are fed the drug. Redwood's own boy and several other children are similarly treated, in at least two cases by people who are unaware of what the final results will be (*see under* Caddles, Albert Edward).

The existence of 'Herakleophorbia' becomes public knowledge; and a hostile opposition to its use is led by the politician 'Jack the Giant-killer' Caterham. Fear of the giants, now approaching adulthood, is fostered for political ends, so that Caterham comes to power in a landslide election victory. Thereafter, he introduces a series of measures designed to constrain the giants, who in final exasperation launch an assault on London from the Cossar fortress. Their main weapon is the drug itself, which is fired in canisters that explode over the city.

Redwood is arrested and brought before Caterham, to be given the Prime Minister's terms for peace : the giants must undertake not to breed and agree to live apart from 'normal' society—a suitable reservation will be found for them—and the manufacture of 'Herakleophorbia' must cease. The story ends with the rejection of Caterham's offer, the forty-foot high youths being determined to fight, if necessary, to the death. Their attitude is given voice by a Cossar child : 'But that is what Caterham says ! He would have us live out our lives, one-by-one, until only one remains, and that one at last would die also, and they would cut down all the giant plants and weeds, kill all the giant under-life, burn out the traces of the food—make an end to us and the food for ever. Then the little pigmy world would be safe. They would go on—safe for ever, living their little pigmy lives, doing pigmy kindnesses and pigmy cruelties each to the other; they might even perhaps attain a sort of pigmy millennium, make an end to war, make an end to over-population, sit down in a world-wide city to practise pigmy arts, worshipping one another until the world begins to freeze . . .'

Ignoring the giant chicken, which are the first products of

'Herakleophorbia', along with the enormous insects and examples of vegetation, the novel concentrates on the reaction of ordinary sized men to the most formidable of the drug's results—giant human beings. In biological terms, it is a story of two strains of the same species each struggling to preserve its existence; for the giants, despite their size, are very obviously human. There is no evidence that they enjoy enhanced intelligence, and they have been incorrectly judged by some commentators as a Wellsian vision of the future superman. The purpose of the tale, rarely apprehended when it first appeared, but subsequently made clear by the author, was to symbolize the conflict between 'localized' and 'de-localized' types of mind in the area of human administration—a subject which Wells had raised in the Fabian Society at the time and with which he was making little headway. In effect, he was already envisaging a supranational type of administrator and thinker whose evolution was being stifled by the small-scale politics and government with which such a potential innovator was currently surrounded, e.g. the pigmy-like pettiness vehemently challenged in the giants' concluding diatribe. *The Food of the Gods*, 1904

REDWOOD, EDWARD MONSON : Son of the co-inventor of 'Herakleophorbia' and the first of the giant children. He is brought up with the Cossar boys at Chislehurst, and, within the confines of the tale, is the only male of his kind fortunate enough to secure a mate—she being the Princess of Weser Dreiburg, whom he meets accidentally during a walk in a royal park. The couple flee to the Cossar redoubt at the start of the war between men and giants, Redwood sustaining a slight injury before they reach safety. *The Food of the Gods*, 1904

REEDLY, MARSHAL : A 'disgruntled military genius and expert, with a gathering animus against all constituted authority, based on some personal grievance of his own against what he called the "privileged set" '. He is used by Rud Whitlow to disseminate propaganda for the Common-Sense Party among the British armed forces and is later appointed Liaison Officer to Whitlow's headquarters in Holland by the British Prime Minister. During the second global war he becomes Marshal of the Allied Armies once the sources of supply fall increasingly into the hands of Rud's movement. Despite his vaguely socialistic leanings, however, he has become conditioned to fundamentally military solutions for armed conflicts and connives with the enemy general staffs in an attempt to seize power. He disobeys Rud by independently negotiating the German surrender with that country's High Command, only to be killed in a bombing raid ordered when he has foolishly revealed his whereabouts. *The Holy Terror*, 1939

REEVES, ANNA : The young woman who nurses Leadford's mother during her last illness. A member of the Clayton commune set up after the comet's gas has transfigured the world, she is short, somewhat sturdy, with a ruddy complexion, brown eyes and reddish hair. At first Leadford is unmoved by her physical appearance, although he is impressed by the care she devotes to his dying mother. Anna comforts him when he is overcome by what he regards as a permanent separation from Nettie Stuart and the loss of his mother. They are married according to the customs of the commune and within a year she gives birth to a son. When the opening passion of the relationship has waned, she accepts her husband's renewed pre-occupation with Nettie, offering no objection to sharing his attentions with her. *In the Days of the Comet*, 1906

REID, MR. : A young widower who is subjected to a harrowing experience after his wife has died. He spends days in reminiscence of their past happiness, becoming engrossed in his morbid pre-occupation—until he believes he has briefly seen her ghost beside his fire-place. He waits months for a second visitation, but when it comes he realizes that the illusion is a mere trick of the light, providing all the suggestion that his longing for his wife had required. 'The Presence by the Fire', 1897

REINHART, HETTY : Briefly the mistress of Peter Stubland before his marriage to Joan. A pretty woman in her late twenties—some six years older than Peter—she is dark-haired, slender-necked, and displays a particular delight in the beauty of her body. She has an openness of manner and an easy familiarity which Joan finds detestable. Aunt Phoebe Stubland, on the other hand, is impressed by Hetty's courage in leaving her native Preston, in Lancashire, to manage for herself in a lonely flat in London. Peter and Hetty are holidaying in Italy at the outbreak of the First World War. She attempts to dissuade him from returning to England, where he plans to enlist, but is successful in delaying him by only a day or two. *Joan and Peter*, 1918

REMINGTON, MARGARET : Wife of the politician and editor, Richard, and a major factor in the early success of his career. She first meets her husband on her return from a recuperative period in Italy, having exhausted herself during her third year of study for the History Tripos at Newnham. Her thin and delicate face, beneath fair hair, appeals as readily to Remington as does her dedication to socialism. Their original encounter, in the company of his cousins, is followed by an interval of five years, precipitated by a political quarrel between Remington and his uncle. They resume acquaintance in London, through the agency of Oscar and Altiora Bailey, a leading organizational couple in the Liberal movement. Although inferior to Remington in intellectual ability, she is an eager listener and tireless helper in the further-ance of his political ambitions. Since she has a substantial private income, and he is relatively poor, their marriage provides him with the financial wherewithal to stand as a Liberal candidate for Parliament.

His election appears to substantiate her faith in him, for she refuses to see him in other than an idealistic light—even to the extent of rejecting his attempted admission of his various sexual escapades before their marriage. She is the more hard-hit, there-fore, when he abandons his Liberal seat to launch a weekly paper aimed at the Conservative and Imperialist Right—she turns the key of her bedroom-door against him. However, with the passage of time, she begins to read his publication and finds herself able to accept the rationale behind his change of direction. Her enthusiasm for his work revives, also her physical affection. Paradoxically, this renewal coincides with Remington's final commitment to a love affair with Isabel Rivers and he is unable to accept his wife's advances. Eventually, in the light of a grow-ing scandal, he is forced to confess his infidelity to her. But she remains loyal, prepared to support him against social opinion when she learns he is attempting to break off the liaison. Even after his elopement with his mistress, she writes to him, offering monetary aid to them both in their reduced circumstances.

In the relationship between Margaret and Remington, it could be construed that Wells was attempting to show how two part-ners, apparently well-suited, may experience a distance between each other which somehow cannot be bridged. There is a failure on Margaret's part to adjust herself to her husband's growing political awareness, but to balance that a lack of understanding is indicated in Remington's inability to convey to her his new way of reasoning. It is not that they have gradually drawn apart, but more that there has always existed a gulf between them—a gap, which, the story seems to imply, may be explained on a basis of sexuality, but not on so simple a concept as lack of mutual attraction. The novel is as much about the outcome of this relationship between a man and a woman as it is about the major political and social concerns of its day; and, while many of its political arguments are now probably only of interest to the historian, Margaret's loss of Remington to Isabel Rivers remains of continuing relevance. *The New Machiavelli*, 1911

REMINGTON, MR. : Father of the central character in *The New Machiavelli*—a science teacher at the Bromstead Institute and a lank-limbed man given to the wearing of dilapidated tweed clothes. Much of his personality is a portrait of Wells's own parent, and his books and his talks with his son prove an early influence in the later development of Remington's political thinking. He is particularly unsuccessful at gardening and prone to effecting havoc among his backward vegetables. He dies falling from a ladder while pruning a vine, an accident which also befell the senior Wells, although in his case the result was fortunately no more than a fractured thigh. *The New Machiavelli*, 1911

REMINGTON, MRS. : In the same way that her husband's character is largely based on Wells's father, so, too, does the wife resemble the author's mother : 'She never began to understand the mental processes of my play, she never interested herself in my school life and work, she could not understand things I said; and she came, I think, quite insensibly to regard me with something of the same hopeless perplexity she had felt towards my father.' A devout church-goer, she reads the monthly *Home Churchman* avidly, a habit to which her son subsequently ascribes much of her unenlightened attitude. Her other reading consists mainly of popular newspaper accounts of the daily events in the life of the Royal Family. However, that there is a more secret side to her nature is revealed in a quotation from the inscription on T. H. Huxley's tomb found among her papers after his death—an incident identical to one which Wells revealed regarding his own mother in his *Experiment in Autobiography*. He was to portray her again, rather more bitterly, in *The Betterave Papers* a year before he himself died. *The New Machiavelli*, 1911

REMINGTON, RICHARD : The disgraced politician whose auto-biography serves as the basis of Wells's first major attempt at a discussion novel—a departure from his earlier works by virtue of the ideas which it endeavours to convey taking precedence over the story-line. Remington's childhood bears a marked resemblance to Wells's own, from the portrayal of himself and his parents to the description of the town of his birth (the factual Bromley giving way to the fictional Bromstead).

The essence of his story is the development of his political reasoning and the emotional causes of his downfall. First educated at City Merchant's School, where he meets the future press baron, Cossington, he becomes a fellow of Trinity at the age of twenty-two (*see also under* Willersley), displaying such promise as a political writer that he is taken under the patronage of Oscar and Altiora Bailey, two leading Liberal intellectuals and planners. His marriage to one of their less gifted, but wealthy, protégées enables him to win a seat in Parliament representing a Midlands constituency. Idealistically a socialist, he rapidly becomes disillusioned with the personalities—rather than the ideologies—of each major party. He sees his own, the Liberals, as representing too random a conglomerate of interests. The Tories, on the other hand, under the leadership of Evesham, do not represent the existing establishment—they *are* it. The Socialists he regards as incapable of fulfilling their highest ideals because their rank and file lack the necessary education and training. Also he recognizes the innate objections to change : 'Every party stands essentially for the interests and mental usages of some definite class or group of classes in the existing com-munity, and every party has its scientific-minded and construc-tive leading section, with well-defined hinterlands formulating its social functions in a public-spirited form, and its superficial-minded following confessing its meannesses and vanities and prejudices. No class will abolish itself, materially alter its way of life, or drastically reconstruct itself, albeit no class is indisposed to co-operate in the unlimited socialization of any other class. In that capacity for aggression upon other classes lies the essential driving force of modern affairs.'

Remington's solution is to lift what his growing experi-ence suggests are the pertinent qualities in each ideology and to amalgamate them into a political doctrine of his own, with love and fine thinking as its foundation. Giving up his parliamentary seat, he founds a political paper designed to further his ideas, the *Blue Weekly* (edited with the assistance of his friend, Britten); but in developing his new concept of an organized and revitalized state, he is obliged to align himself with the more moderate advocates of a 'New Imperialism' on the Tory benches. His publication becomes widely read and he returns to the House of Commons for a London constituency as basically a Conservative supporter. Although many of his friends and colleagues sympathize with his action, others, including his wife, consider his defection a betrayal. His political career is terminated by his elopement to the Continent with Isabel Rivers, a young woman who has devoted much of her energy to his arguments since the time he first met her when she was still at school. His former school friend, Shoesmith, offers to marry Isabel, in order to avert a scandal—a gesture which is declined.

Because Remington is very much a projection of Wells himself, the novel is discursive throughout. Its opinions range from the beneficial aspects of the Boy Scout movement to the injustices of the British Raj in India. It contains many illuminating insights into the society and social conditions in Britain shortly before the First World War; and its intermittent scenic views of London, a city which the author loved, are often memorable. Many real-life leading figures are either portrayed, caricatured or lampooned; and a considerable array of minor characters appear as no more than brief contributors to Remington's discussion with himself—too brief, as in several of Wells's 'novels of ideas' to warrant here an entry to themselves.

Even a good many of the incidents are drawn from real life. The odd debating group, the 'Pentagram Club', of which Remington is a member, had its historical counterpart in the 'Coefficients', to which Wells himself belonged—among its limited membership were such diverse figures as Sidney Webb, Sir Edward Grey, Lord Milner, Bertrand Russell and the poet Henry Newbolt. The extraordinary account of a fire at a semi-political dinner, when the guests argue on as a shower of water descends on them through the ceiling, and during which Remington finally decides to elope, is a re-creation of an actual party given by the editor of the *Pall Mall Gazette*, Harry Cust.

Another important aspect of the novel is its account of the

failure of what should surely have been an enduring and success-ful marriage. Remington's telling of his rather distasteful sexual sorties during his young days parallels Wells's own, as given briefly in *Experiment in Autobiography*. In the event, it is the element of sexuality in his make-up, suppressed during the greater part of his marriage, which brings him down. In several passages Wells takes pains to indicate that in a conventional sense Remington and Isabel Rivers are not 'good' people, at the same time deftly hinting that, since they are in a class of their own in the intellectual and innovatory sense, they have his approval. In an allied area, Wells's championship of the woman's cause comes through in the words of Remington : 'I confess myself altogether feminist ... I want to see women come in, free and fearless, to a full participation in the collective purpose of mankind. Women, I am convinced, are as fine as men; they can be as wise as men; they are capable of far greater devotion than men. I want to see them citizens, with a marriage law framed primarily for them and for their protection and for the good of the race, and not for men's satisfactions ... I want to change the respective values of the family group altogether, and make the home indeed the women's kingdom and the mother the owner and responsible guardian of her children.'

In terms of publishing, the novel raised problems. Its first chapters appeared as a serial in *The English Review* before the reactionary reception to *Ann Veronica* had entirely subsided. Because of its criticisms of living people and prevailing political doctrines, together with its underlying motif of sexuality, the story of Remington was refused by three book publishers before it eventually found a list. When it did, further unsuccessful attempts were made to silence its author. In later years Wells re-ferred to it as one of his most confused books, but also as one of his most revealing. Remington's throwing away of his career and his voluntary exile in Italy, where he sat down to write a Machiavellian study of the power structure he had abandoned, was Wells's method of psychologically discharging his own inner compulsion at the time. *The New Machiavelli*, 1911

RICHARDSON, THE REV. MORTON : The Suffolk vicar who regards it as his duty to visit Gemini Twain and Stella Kentlake while they are living together at Mary Clarkson's cottage. A tall, thin man, distinguished by an ascetic aquiline face, he is visibly discon-certed by the couple's bald declaration of their unmarried state,

but endeavours to accept it with a qualified tolerance. He joins with Gemini in a discursive metaphysical conversation on the conflict between Christianity and science, during which it is inevitable (particularly in a late Wellsian discussion novel) that he should argue ineffectually. He meets them again in 1940, when it is clear that the strain of the wartime situation has driven his 'never very venturesome mind' back to 'High Anglicanism, and to fear and defensive hostility towards anything outside it'.
Babes in the Darkling Wood, 1940

RINK, EFFIE : A mistress of George Ponderevo and the cause of his separation from his wife, Marion. Her neat figure, chestnut hair and sidelong glances bring her to George's attention when she is working as a correspondence typist in the offices of 'Tono Bungay'. Their affair begins tumultuously when he finds her alone one day, and they immediately go off for a week together. Effie is passionate, hot-blooded, 'magnificently eupeptic' and infinitely kind-hearted—all qualities which her lover finds lacking in Marion. At the end of their relationship Ponderevo helps her to secure a new position which she has coveted, and she later demonstrates her business capacity by setting up a typewriting bureau. Eventually she marries a youth half her age—a wretched poet and drug-taker—because, as she says, he needs nursing.
Tono Bungay, 1909

RIVERS, ISABEL : A young political journalist whose affair with Remington eventually leads to the ruination of his career. Daughter of a military baronet resident in Remington's parliamentary constituency of Kinghamstead, she is a schoolgirl when she first begins her devoted support of her future lover, working enthusiastically for his election and attracting his interest with her lively movements and a vocabulary which indicates a breadth of reading. Black-haired and blue-eyed, she has a warm brown complexion which fluctuates in depth according to her changes of excitement.

Later she studies at Ridout College, Oxford, the only woman to take a 'first' in her final year; and her presence prompts Remington to accept speaking engagements in that city which he might otherwise have declined. On the completion of her education, she embarks on a writing career in London where the quality of her work earns her a rising reputation. She becomes a regular contributor to Remington's paper, *Blue Weekly*, and

MAN WITH THE WHITE FACE, THE : The experiencer of a continuing dream over a number of nights which he relates during a train journey from Rugby to Euston. A solicitor by profession, he changes in his nocturnal vision to the leader of a political party who has renounced his career in favour of a mistress with whom he has retired to Capri. The dream is set in the future when a floating pleasure city virtually surrounds the island. It also includes a preview of future warfare, including tanks and aircraft, which erupts when the dreamer's successor in power resorts to aggression. Although implored to return to prevent military action, the dreamer declines; and, caught between the two opposing armies, both he and his love are killed. 'A Dream of Armageddon', 1901

MANNING, HUBERT : A civil servant of the Upper Division and the nephew of Lady Palsworthy, the social leader of Morningside Park. Thirty-seven years old, tall, handsome, with a large black moustache, he is given to writing the most appalling verse and striking rhapsodic stances. He professes exquisite passion for Ann Veronica, who, in a moment of aberration, allows herself to become engaged to him. However, her attachment to her biology demonstrator, Capes, convinces her that she must cease the deception. Manning accepts the break with pronounced theatrical distress, and it is clear to Ann Veronica that he is merely acting out a rôle in keeping with his totally self-absorbing egotism. Any guilt she may have felt at raising his hopes insincerely is consequently diminished. *Ann Veronica*, 1909

MARAYNE, LADY : The mother of William Benham whose second husband is a noted London surgeon. She is a small woman, blue-eyed and delicately complexioned, quick of movement, witty, with an enthusiasm for things handsome, brave and successful. She expects, and usually receives, a good deal of respect and affection from all with whom she has dealings. She deserts the Reverend Harold Benham for the greater attraction of a wealthy young man who has come to Seagate to recuperate from snake-bite, malaria and a shooting mishap in Brazil. He dies in Wiesbaden only days before her husband's divorce is made absolute, but her concern for her lover has commended itself to Marayne who is treating him. Being a person of 'great spirit, enterprise and sweetness', she marries the surgeon and later sets up home at Chexington Manor, in Hertfordshire.

William visits her regularly and their relationship is affectionate; he is addressed by her fondly as 'Poff'. She attempts to guide him into a prominent career and to ensure he mixes in what she regards as an appropriate level of London society. But her son's obsession with a 'natural' aristocracy defeats her; she sees him as taking after his father and considers her efforts to influence him a failure. Suspicious of his amatory adventure with Milly Skelmersdale, she is even more alarmed when Benham announces his intention of marrying Amanda Morris, for she has discovered that the girl's father was a swindler who chose suicide rather than gaol. However, she is charmed by Amanda once they finally meet, although her attitude reverts to one of outright disapproval when her daughter-in-law takes Sir Philip Easton as a lover. *The Research Magnificent*, 1915

MARCUS, HETTY : The first wife of Harry Mortimer Smith whom he divorces when she conceives another man's child. He first meets her when he is about to embark for France during the First World War and is taking a final walk along the South Downs. In her turn, she is shortly to join the Women's Auxiliary Army Corps. Harry is drawn to her fine, tranquil face and her dark eyes; and in the space of a single afternoon they both fall in love. They are married when he returns to England to recover from a wound in the arm. Hetty is introduced to Harry's sister Fanny, and the two women get on well; there is no condemnation on Hetty's part of Fanny's way of life.

When Smith returns to the Front, she allows herself to be seduced by an officer, Sumner, becoming pregnant as a result. The child is born too late for it possibly to be Harry's and he refuses to forgive his wife for an evening's lapse when she was not entirely sober. After the divorce she feels obliged to marry Sumner, who proves to be a drunkard and a crook. Unhappy and almost destitute, she turns again to Harry several years later, asking him to help her escape to Canada. This he does, realizing how harsh he had been in rejecting her. She appeals to him to go with her, but he is unwilling to abandon his second wife. They spend her last day together on the Downs. Shortly after she has left the country Harry is shot by the jealous Sumner. *The Dream*, 1924

MARSHALL, MR. : The drunken reveller whose unsober state is witnessed by both the vicar and curate of Sussexville one Christmas Eve. However, when certain evidence is produced, suggesting that Marshall was elsewhere at the time, the somewhat gullible vicar assumes that they have been confronted by a doppelganger. His curate is less convinced, and comes to a different conclusion. The tale is related by a member of the Society for the Rehabilitation of Abnormal Phenomena. 'Mr. Marshall's Doppelganger', 1897

MARTIANS, THE : The ruthless alien invaders of *The War of the Worlds*. Their first space cylinder, one of seven, falls on Horsell Common, near Woking and close to the narrator's home. In appearance they generally resemble an octopus, having a head some four feet in diameter and sixteen whiplike tentacles growing from around a fleshy, beak-shaped mouth. Their eyes are large and dark, but there is no evidence of a nose and it seems they are devoid of a sense of smell. They hear by means of a taut tympanic membrane situated at the back of the head. Of a body there is no evidence; the Martians do not eat, but sustain themselves by injections of blood from other living creatures. They bring with them a slender biped being, presumably as nourishment during their long journey, but they rapidly turn to humans as a more plentiful source of supply.

While their movements prove sluggish and laboured under a denser atmosphere and a more powerful gravity than those of their native planet, they swiftly assemble a host of machines which they either operate in person or handle by remote control. The most formidable of these is the Fighting Machine, a tripedal structure a hundred feet high and topped by a cabin housing a single Martian. Its three legs carry it forward at alarming speed, and over the roughest terrain. Because of its height, it can negotiate the deepest rivers and venture some way out to sea. A much smaller artefact is the Handling Machine, also controlled from within, equipped with extendable hose-like arms and other manipulative devices.

On their arrival, a reception party and a body of troops, ostensibly to protect the visitors, approach the cylinder—only to be ruthlessly wiped out by the Martians' heat-ray, a terrifying weapon carried on an arm of the fighting machines and capable of incinerating almost anything in its path. The most advanced of Man's artillery and explosives prove powerless against the invaders, who swiftly devastate the Surrey towns and country-side before approaching London. On the way, they reveal another horrendous weapon—a lethal black smoke which they shoot in cannisters. Heavier than air, it spreads along the ground, killing entire urban populations, finally to be washed away by sprays applied from the fighting machines. It is with this gas that the Martians attack the capital, clearly intending to preserve the major part of its architecture intact. Nor are they bent on destroying the inhabitants to a man, thereby removing their food supply. They capture many unfortunates, whom they sling into great baskets suspended from the rear of their cabins. Towards the end of their campaign of terror and demoralization, they send a flying machine aloft to distribute more of the deadly gas.

But the Martians are not invincible. They succumb to earthly bacteria to which their bodies have no resistance. Coming across Primrose Hill, where the last cylinder has landed, the narrator finds them rotting amongst their mechanical marvels '—dead, slain by the putrefactive and disease bacteria against which their systems were unprepared ... slain, after all man's devices had failed, by the humblest things that God, in his wisdom, has put upon this earth ... By the toll of a billion deaths, man has bought his birthright of the earth, and it is his against all comers; it would still be his were the Martians ten times as mighty as they are. For neither do men live nor fight in vain.'

By presenting his extraterrestrial beings as physically repulsive and inexorably hostile to man, Wells created an archetype which was to be emulated in countless science fiction stories for several decades before it occurred to writers that such aliens could equally well be attractive and benign. *The War of the Worlds*, 1898

MARTINEAU, DR. : A leading nerve specialist consulted by Sir Richmond Hardy when the latter is suffering from the effects of overwork. Martineau is short, 'humanly plump', with a round 'cheerfully wistful' face reminiscent of a full moon. He dresses untidily. His initial manner to Hardy is matter-of-fact—an attempt to dispel the reservations and doubts which he can detect in his patient. He agrees to spend a few days touring the West of England with Sir Richmond in the hope that the change of scene will prove beneficial.

As the journey progresses he falls under his companion's spell, at the same time inwardly horrified by the other's naked egotism and sexual proclivities. He finds a common meeting-point in Hardy's concern for the future, taking the opportunity to discuss his ideas for his own *magnum opus, Psychology of a New Age*. Disconcerted by Hardy's manifest interest in V. V. Grammont, whom they meet by chance at Stonehenge, and more particularly by the overbearing conversational habits of her companion, Belinda Seyffert, he excuses himself from the party and returns prematurely to London.

He is called to Sir Richmond's bedside some weeks later when it becomes clear that the man is dying. Subsequently he receives Hardy's mistress, Martin Leeds, who has obtained Lady Hardy's permission to view the body. When she breaks down in a paroxysm of grief, Martineau closes the story with a reflection on the cruelty of love. *The Secret Places of the Heart*, 1922

MARVEL, THOMAS : A richly-described South Country tramp who becomes the unwilling, and very temporary, assistant of the Invisible Man. Marvel is 'a person of copious, flexible visage, a nose of cylindrical protrusion, a liquorish, ample, fluctuating mouth, and a beard of bristling eccentricity'. He is accosted by Griffin, in the form of a disembodied voice, while trying on a pair of over-sized boots. At the outset he is ill-disposed to accept the reality of an invisible being, until he is persuaded to feel the other's body :

'"I'm dashed!" he said. "If this don't beat cock-fighting! Most remarkable!—And there I can see a rabbit clean through you, 'arf a mile away! Not a bit of you visible—except—" He scrutinized the apparently empty space keenly. "You 'aven't been eatin' bread and cheese?" he asked, holding the invisible arm.'

Impelled by threats of violence, he helps Griffin to recover the notebooks which the latter has left at an inn in Iping and attempts twice to escape from him—on the second occasion successfully. He is locked, at his own insistence, in the police station at Burdock, where he remains until after the Invisible Man's death. But he fails to disclose the whereabouts of the books which he was carrying for Griffin—at least in the original version of the tale. For the first American edition Wells added an epilogue in which Marvel appears as the proprietor of an inn near Port Stowe named 'The Invisible Man'. He has been allowed to keep the money which Griffin stole, since there was no way of identifying to whom it belonged, and has earned more by telling of his escapade for a guinea a night at the Empire Music Hall. When the bar is closed and he is alone, he regularly fetches out the books, to browse over the meaningless hieroglyphs in which the secret of invisibility is preserved. *The Invisible Man*, 1897

MASTERMAN : The consumptive lodger who occupies a room above Sid Pornick's bicycle shop in London. A man of about forty, he shows signs of his illness by his emaciated appearance : hollow-eyed, with a spot of red in his cheeks and a wiry black moustache beneath a short red nose. His teeth are 'darkened ruins'. Introduced to Kipps by Sid, he launches into a virtual monologue on the benefits of socialism, and it is evident that his influence has played a significant part in Pornick's conversion. He misses few opportunities to express his hatred of the Establishment, to whose strictures he ascribes his own condition. Accusing them of barring university scholarships to anyone over the age of nineteen out of fear of such men as he, Masterman laments the fact that he has eschewed the company of women and ruined his health in the quest for knowledge, only to be trampled by 'a drove of hogs'. *Kipps*, 1905

MASTER MATHEMATICIAN, THE : The only identifiable human character in the noted short story 'The Star'—although the central figure is the Star itself. It is the mathematician who calculates that the foreign body from space which has collided with the planet Neptune, and is now hurtling sunwards, will be deflected as it passes Jupiter and probably scorch the Earth. In a sustained piece of graphic writing, the reactions of mankind and the subsequent cataclysm are described; but complete destruction is averted by the shield provided by the moon. Beyond Earth, the intruder plunges into the sun. 'The Star', 1897

MEDICAL STUDENT, THE : The brother of the narrator of *The War of the Worlds*. He lives in rooms near Regents Park, in London; and it is through his experiences that the poisoning of the capital and the hurried exodus of its inhabitants are reported. Because of the Martians' destruction of the communications network, little news of the invasion reaches the city during the first few days. The first real signs of the gravity of the situation are seen at the railway termini, where trains are commandeered for troops and equipment. When the invaders reach the outskirts, spreading

the lethal black smoke which they have adopted in favour
of their heat-ray, mass hysteria overwhelms the population.
Stampeding crowds fight for standing room on the few trains
still running and every possible method of transport is put to use
in the rush to escape. Many are killed in the melée.

The student steals a bicycle which carries him north as far as
Edgware before its front wheel breaks. Continuing on foot, he
rescues two women in a pony-chaise who are being attacked for
possession of their vehicle (*see under* Elphinstone, *page 80*).
Thereafter he travels with them, and witnesses a series of shocking scenes as the roads become increasingly congested and the
refugees more desperate. Turning away from the main flow, the
trio pass through Tillingham to find at the coast a huge flotilla
of ships assembled for the evacuation. Safely aboard a steamer
headed for Ostend, they watch a bitter engagement between the
naval ram *Thunder Child* and two Martian fighting machines
which have waded deep into the sea. Both are toppled by the
ironclad, even as it explodes under the onslaught of the heat-ray.
In his last view of England, the student is astonished to see an
alien craft in the sky, raining down black smoke on the land.
While he appears no more in the story, he must clearly be
reunited at last with his brother, who includes his eye-witness
accounts in the narrative. *The War of the Worlds,* 1898

MEDINA-SAROTÉ : The blind girl with whom Nunez falls in love in
'The Country of the Blind'. She has no local suitor, being 'little
esteemed in the world of the blind, because she had a clear-cut
face, and lacked the satisfying, glossy smoothness that is the
blind man's ideal of feminine beauty . . .' Finally faced with the
choice between her love and the retention of his sight, Nunez
chooses the latter. 'The Country of the Blind', 1904

MELMOUNT : The British Prime Minister whom Leadford finds
slightly injured at Shaphambury on the East Coast in the dawn
of the comet's passing—he has sprained his ankle when overcome by the green gas while descending from the cliffs to the
beach. A large impressive looking man with reddish fair hair, a
domed head, a well-modelled nose and 'a sensitive, clumsy, big
lip, known to every caricaturist in the world'. He invites Leadford
to his nearby bungalow where he reviews the stupidity and
narrow views of those statesmen—including himself—who have
allowed war to break out with Germany. He asks Leadford to

despatch a series of telegrams convening the Cabinet which, in the new spirit of enlightenment, meets to set out the guidelines for a World State. *In the Days of the Comet*, 1906

MELVILLE, MR.: Cousin of the narrator of *The Sea Lady*, who provides him with the substance of the tale. To some extent he is the confidant of the mermaid, and also of Harry Chatteris, on whom she has designs. Principally, he is a close friend of the Bunting family, with whom the Sea Lady resides at Folkestone when she first leaves the sea. His attempt, in a London club, to bring Chatteris to his senses fails. *The Sea Lady*, 1902

MENGO, SIR ALPHEUS: The surgeon who operates on Job Huss for suspected cancer. A small man, firm-jawed and active-eyed, he arrives heatedly at Huss's boarding-house incensed that no one has met him at the station. He is also astonished to find Job in the midst of the long discussion with his 'comforters' and orders him immediately to bed. The operation, nevertheless, is a success, and a non-malignant growth is removed. *The Undying Fire*, 1919

MERGLE, MISS: Jessica Milton's former schoolmistress, to whom the girl appeals after her escape from Bechamel and who, unbeknown to Jessie, 'by means of a coruscation of sixpenny telegrams had precipitated the pursuit upon her'. She joins in the chase through the New Forest and is quick to upbraid her pupil when she is eventually caught. Following a lecture on 'Ideals, True Womanliness, Necessary Class Distinctions, Healthy Literature and the like,' she has a ready response to Jessie's query as to how she should behave if she wishes to be fearless and honest: 'If you really want to live fearlessly and honestly, you should avoid doing such extravagant things.' *The Wheels of Chance*, 1896

MERGLESON, MR.: The head butler at Shonts, where Arthur Bealby is sent as a serving-boy. An ample man, large-nosed, with mutton-chop whiskers and a protruding lower lip—his voice resembles that of 'a succulent parrot'. He seems hardly impressed with Bealby, but displays some concern on the boy's disappearance. His notable action in the tale is an unanticipated struggle with the Lord Chancellor of England which precipitates both parties from the head to the foot of the grand staircase. Later he is set upon by the Lord Chancellor at lunch, from which he emerges with a black eye. *Bealby: A Holiday*, 1915

MILTON, MRS. HETTY : The stepmother of Jessica and a mere ten years her senior. A widow, she is also the successful authoress—under the pen-name 'Thomas Plantagenet'—of the witty and 'daring' book, *A Soul Untrammelled*. In her private life she is the epitomé of charm and respectability—dressing correctly, furnishing correctly, and entertaining 'severe notions of whom she might meet'. On discovering Jessie's disappearance she organizes a pursuit with the redoubtable aid of her acquaintances, Widgery, Dangle and Phipps. Her opinion of Hoopdriver, when she overtakes the couple in the New Forest, is low; she finds it hard to believe that he has acquitted himself with chivalry. *The Wheels of Chance*, 1896

MILTON, JESSICA : First introduced into the narrative as 'The Young Lady in Grey' when she comes to Hoopdriver's aid after one of his many bicycling mishaps. The daughter of a deceased proprietor of a popular lotion, she is in her early twenties, slender, dark-haired, with 'a bright colour and bright eyes'. She dresses in uncomplicated 'rational' clothes. Determined to make her own way in life, she has fled from her stepmother's house in Surbiton to accompany the married writer, Bechamel, on a cycling tour through Surrey and Sussex. Deceived by his promise to launch her on a literary career, she allows him to pass her off as his sister during their overnight stays but rapidly becomes disenchanted when he begins a protracted attempt at seduction. A crisis is reached in Bognor, where he books her into an hotel as his wife, and she enlists the help of Hoopdriver whom she has seen several times on the road since their original encounter.

With Hoopdriver she escapes to Chichester, spending several days with him as they head into Hampshire where she is finally retrieved by Mrs. Milton. Her feelings towards her rescuer are at first mixed. She trusts him, but is nevertheless aware of his ungainly manners. She imagines him to be a colonial and he is happy to concur with that assumption. Her growing respect remains undiminished when he confesses his true identity; she defends him vigorously against the deprecations of her stepmother and her old schoolmistress, Miss Mergle. However, she realizes that it is not a friendship which can survive her return to Surbiton. She promises on parting to lend him books which might help him in his efforts at self-improvement. *The Wheels of Chance*, 1896

MINCHETT, DR. ALOYSIUS G. : The mental specialist who treats Arnold Blettsworthy during his five years in New York when he actually believes he is a prisoner on Rampole Island. Physically he resembles the imaginary islander Chit—squat, broad-shouldered with a large head and very bright dark eyes. He explains to Blettsworthy the theory of double personalities and the nature of the profound reverie in which he has passed the last half-decade. He also reveals that Rampole Island does exist and that the rescue ship put in there briefly; but the place is a barren wilderness with none of the high vegetation which his patient thought he saw. Later he offers to provide certificates which will prove Blettsworthy unfit for active service in the First World War; however, the latter decides to return to England and enlist. *Mr. Blettsworthy on Rampole Island*, 1928

MINNIVER, NETTIE : A slim spinster in her early thirties who first meets Ann Veronica at the home of the Widgetts and later exerts some influence on her when she lives in London. Of dingy appearance, with petulant mouth and wide emotional blue eyes magnified by glasses, Miss Minniver is a compulsive talker whose arguments are characteristically nebulous, but persuasive by dint of constant repetition. A dedicated propagator of the feminist cause, she considers the male sex generally abhorrent and can scarcely bring herself to imagine something more than a platonic relationship with any of its representatives. An avid vegetarian, she attributes carnal desire to the eating of meat; for her the spirit is all, a concept which Ann Veronica—who is not without spirit of her own—finds as short-sighted as its advocate. *Ann Veronica*, 1909

MISUNDERSTOOD ARTIST, A : Another character from one of Wells's first literary endeavours. The story was collected in *Select Conversations With An Uncle*. The artist in question is a cook, and the action of the tale takes place during a short train journey. The misunderstanding of the title arises because of the character's inability to please a particular client for whom he has to prepare a special diet. 'A Misunderstood Artist', 1894

MITZINKA, BARON : War Minister of Clavery, a close colleague of the Foreign Secretary, Monza, and a member of the plot to over-throw King Paul. Thick-set and spectacled, he presents a squat, reptilian figure in his dark military uniform. He hints at new, terrifying weapons provided by an unnamed super-power in his summary of Clavery's offensive advantage over adjoining Agravia. Among these is a more annihilating gas than any employed during the First World War. His arguments in Council, however, only harden the King's resolve to avoid armed conflict, and the baron is arrested, in company with Monza, before their projected invasion can begin. *The King Who Was A King*, 1929

M'LING : The Beast Folk servant of Montgomery and the most human-looking of all Moreau's creations. Fashioned from a bear, with a taint of dog and ox, it displays a devotion to its master uncharacteristic of the other animal hybrids which inhabit Moreau's island. M'Ling joins avidly in the hunt for the escaped Leopard Man and is sufficiently trusted to carry simple weapons, but it, too, has been corrupted by the taste of blood. Finally it dies with Montgomery at the end of a drunken debacle follow-ing Moreau's own death. *The Island of Dr. Moreau*, 1896

MOGGERIDGE, LORD CHANCELLOR OF ENGLAND : One of the most irate of Wells's creations, and verging on the psychotic. Less than enthusiastic at being invited for a weekend at Shonts, he assumes that some trick is being played when he is butted from behind by Bealby after he has stolen down in the night to appropriate his host's whisky. He connects this occurrence with the tales of poltergeists recounted over the dinner table by Captain Douglas, and suspects him as being the instigator of a plot. When the butler Mergleson attempts to come to his aid, he loses his temper and struggles, with the result that both men fall the length of the grand staircase locked in each other's arms. The following day Mergleson receives orders to keep his Lordship away from drink, an act of deprivation which so incenses that worthy at lunch that he blacks the butler's eye. He leaves in the evening in no better frame of mind. *Bealby: A Holiday*, 1915

MONSON : The constructor of *Monson's Flying Machine* in 'The Argonauts of the Air', another of several aeronautic stories written by Wells some years in advance of the reality of manned flight. Monson and his friend, Woodhouse, make a maiden flight in the machine over Wimbledon Common and other parts of

South West London before finally falling out of the contraption to their deaths in the exact locality where Wells had studied science. 'The Argonauts of the Air', 1895

MONTGOMERY : Drunken assistant to Dr. Moreau, who befriends Prendick after he has been rescued from a drifting open boat and takes him to Moreau's island; later he comes to regret that he has exposed Prendick to the horrors of the doctor's experiments. Unwittingly allowing his beast-people servant to skin a rabbit, and in so doing to taste blood, Montgomery sets loose a chain reaction which engulfs the island in a welter of carnage. Following Moreau's violent death, he, too, meets his fate at the hands of the Grey Beast Man, leaving Prendick to survive as best he can. *The Island of Dr. Moreau*, 1896

MONZA, GENERAL : The Foreign Minister of Clavery, a tall evil-looking diplomat who is the personification of 'Man, the Destroyer', as established at the opening of the scenario. He is deeply in league with Prince Michael in the latter's plot to overthrow King Paul and to declare war on Agravia. At a meeting of the King's advisers he reveals himself content to drag all nations into a second global war provided Clavery survives. He is arrested with other followers of the prince when Paul acts against Michael's abortive *coup d'état*. *The King Who Was A King*, 1929

MORE, RACHEL : The future Mrs. Stephen Stratton. She is seventeen when they first meet—tall and slim, with brown hair and 'very still deep dark eyes'. Stratton has recently returned from the Boer War and seeks to relieve some of his unhappiness about Lady Mary Justin's marriage in Rachel's company. She falls deeply in love with him but his preoccupations lie elsewhere. They are eventually married some years later after a reunion in Germany under the auspices of his widowed cousin, the Fürstin Letzlingen. They have three children, and it is to his son that Stratton addresses himself in the narration of his autobiography. Rachel is perturbed by the resumption of correspondence between her husband and Lady Mary, but stands by him during the opening stages of Justin's divorce proceedings. *The Passionate Friends*, 1913

MOREAU, DR. : A noted physiologist, hounded from Britain for his

154

experiments in the vivisection of animals. He resorts to a tropical island where, with his assistant Montgomery, he is free to carry out his research without interference. Moreau is obsessed with the possibility of creating new beings from existing animal forms. Having experimented, often disastrously, with early prototypes, he turns ultimately to the human shape as the ideal for which he should aim. Grafting from one beast to another, and changing their shape by ingenious vivisection, he produces an array of grotesque humanoids which even attain rudimentary speech. None of them he regards as a success, consigning them to caves in the jungle so that their presence will no longer remind him of his failures. There they develop a community of sorts, chanting the laws he has imposed on them, but rarely obeying them; for, as the doctor claims, the beast flesh is forever creeping back. Only the threat of a return to 'The House of Pain' (his vivisection room) can persuade them to maintain some semblance of order. However, when one of them acquires a taste for blood, the fever spreads rapidly. Moreau himself is killed by a she-puma which escapes half-mutilated from his compound, and with the death of their master the remaining Beast Folk degenerate rapidly.

The critics of the day failed almost universally to observe the underlying *motifs* of the novel, choosing to see it simply as a rather repellent horror story. Latterly, its allegorical qualities have been recognized, together with its blasphemous intent. Moreau has come to be seen as the Creator figure which Wells sought to depict, and the Beast Folk as an allegory of mankind, through whom the animal instinct is forever surging to the surface. *The Island of Dr. Moreau*, 1896

MORLOCKS, THE : The machine-minding, underground race come upon by the Time Traveller in the distant future. They are short, of nauseating appearance, chinless and pale, with huge, lidless pinkish-grey eyes. In their dark caverns they operate vast machines, although the purpose of these is not revealed. Coming to the surface only at night they prey on the effete Eloi whom they use as a source of meat.

The Morlocks seize the Time Machine and conceal it within the statue of a white sphinx. They make several attempts to overpower the Time Traveller, who succeeds in repelling them with the light of matches and kills several with an iron bar. Others perish in a blazing wood during their attack. The Morlocks are seen as the final evolution of the former working class, consigned to spend their days underground by the élitist culture which they originally served. *The Time Machine*, 1895

MWRES, ELIZEBE θ : Daughter of a Wind Vane Trust official at the close of the twenty-first century. She loves Denton, an air landing-stage attendant, but her father is determined that she should marry the man of his own choice, the middle-aged Bindon. Eighteen years old at the story's outset, Elizebe θ (whose name in earlier English would have been spelt 'Elizabeth Morris') is hypnotized in an ultimately unsuccessful attempt to discourage her affection for her lover. Together they escape from the enclosed future city of London to wander among the ruins of Surrey towns, but a brief acquaintance with life in the open and an attack by dogs persuade them to return to their original environment.

After marriage they live reasonably comfortably for a period, unaware that Bindon is engineering their downfall. He uses his influence to ensure that Denton fails to secure permanent employment, until the couple are obliged to enrol for a lifetime of drudgery with the Labour Company. Their baby daughter, 'Dings', dies; and Elizebe θ, who is delegated to metal-work, fears that she is degenerating to the same level of coarseness as her slatternly workmates. She and Denton are finally saved by a last-minute change of heart by Bindon, who, learning he is dying of cancer, bequeaths her a legacy which enables them to resume their former way of existence.

The story is set in the same future as *When the Sleeper Wakes*, which it preceded in publication by two years. The dystopian quality of the society portrayed is developed substantially in the novel, but there is sufficient body in the short story itself to indicate Wells's darker interpretation of human prospects at the time of writing. 'A Story of the Days to Come', 1897

MYAME, ABNER : A Baptist schoolmaster and guardian of Edward Albert Tewler after his mother's death. A thin, large-headed man, deep-voiced and adorned with profuse black side-whiskers. His small private school benefits from Tewler's presence, by virtue of Myame's appropriating the boy's money to build extensions and provide other facilities. He is incensed when Edward Albert contacts his father's former employer, Whittaker, whose enquiries reveal Myame's financial irregularities. He forbids any of his other pupils to speak to Tewler, but, under pressure from

Whittaker, arranges a mortgage to provide for repayment of the sum involved. Fundamentally an honest man, he has viewed the availability of Tewler's cash as a God-given opportunity to improve the school; he is guilty more of naïvety than any criminal intent. *You Can't Be Too Careful*, 1941

N

NARRATOR, *A Modern Utopia* : Introduced at the opening of the book as 'the Owner of the Voice', he is described as 'a whitish plump man, a little under the middle size and age, with such blue eyes as many Irishmen have, and agile in his movements ... His front is convex' (as far as it goes it could easily be a description of Wells himself at the time of writing). With his companion, the Botanist, he arrives unexpectedly in Utopia in the course of descending the Lucano Pass in the Alps. In effect, the pair have entered a parallel world which circles a sun lying beyond the star, Sirius. It is also a mirror-image of Earth, to the extent that the geographical localities remain the same and the people are subtly transformed counterparts of the terrestrial population.

No real attempt at characterization is made in the book and its appeal lies entirely in its exposition of a rational world state and its impact on the visitors. The first revelation is that, unlike the earlier literary utopias, which were secreted on islands or in hidden valleys, this particular society is indeed worldwide. Its prosperity is based on the intelligent and controlled use of science and technology, a possibility which the narrator sees as fully applicable to his own planet, given the wits and will :

'The plain message physical science has for the world at large is this, that were our political and social and moral devices only as well contrived to their ends as a linotype machine, an antiseptic operating plant, or an electric tram-car, there need now at the present moment be no appreciable toil in the world, and only the smallest fraction of the pain, the fear, and the anxiety that now makes human life so doubtful in its value. There is more than enough for everyone alive. Science stands, a too competent servant, behind her wrangling underbred masters, holding out resources, devices, and remedies they are too stupid to use. And on its material side a modern Utopia must needs present these gifts as taken, and show a world that is really abolishing the need of labour, abolishing the last base reason for anyone's servitude or inferiority.'

In keeping with this devotion to applied science, the machines and architecture of Utopia astonish the visitors with their complexity and grandeur. Medicine, too, has enjoyed its place in the great advance. The Utopians are healthy and free of disease. A prohibition on breeding among criminals, alcoholics, mental degenerates and social recalcitrants has improved the genetic strain, and the greater part of the population remains fit and active until advanced old age.

The government of Utopia is conducted on a voluntary basis, by a ruling élite known as 'Samurai'. Sworn to an ascetic lifestyle, their ranks are open to anyone over the age of twenty-five who is in good health and adequately educated. They are Utopia's only administrators, and also its only voters, the ancient principles of democracy being regarded as inefficient and outmoded. For one week in the year, every Samurai is obliged to take himself off to a barren part of the countryside for a period of meditation and spiritual renewal. Chastity is demanded of him, but not complete celibacy.

The world state is also a comprehensive welfare system, providing either directly, or through its local and regional governments, health and education services, care for the elderly, low-cost housing and public transport. It places many obstacles in the way of inherited wealth.

To aid the process of worldwide administration, a massive central index containing the fingerprints and personal details of every citizen of Earth is held in Paris. An individual's changes of address and other movements are also recorded. Wherever he might be, he can be found and identified without delay. To combat the argument that such practices would place restrictions on individual liberty and constitute a gross invasion of privacy, the following rationale is provided : 'The old Liberalism assumed bad government, the more powerful the government the worse it was, just as it assumed the natural righteousness of the free individual. Darkness and secrecy were, indeed, the natural refuges of liberty when every government had in it the near possibility of tyranny, and the Englishman or American looked at the papers of a Russian or a German as one might look at the chains of a slave.'

Because the Utopian government is intrinsically good, its

efforts to keep track of its citizens can be seen as no more than an allegory of paternal concern. Its altruism extends to the active development of a kinetic society, in recognition of the dangers a purely static state of well-being holds for any organization of human beings. The current utopian state is seen as merely one point in a long progression of stages serving the causes of evolution and the enhancement of intelligence.

The narrator meets his own double in Utopia, and a somewhat self-conscious discussion ensues. In the meantime, the Botanist, whose criticisms of Utopian mores have been used to voice the objections of the closed-minded to a revolutionary society, has recognized the double of a woman with whom he is ineffectually in love on his own world.

With the same suddenness that found them originally translated to Utopia, the pair are returned to the streets of everyday London, appalled at the dirt, poverty and debasement of human aspirations. This scene effectively ends the narrative, but Wells added an appendix entitled 'Scepticism of the Instrument', being a shortened version of a paper which he had first read to the Oxford Philosophical Society on 8th November, 1903. (This in its turn had been derived from ideas expressed in his article, 'The Rediscovery of the Unique', which was published by editor Frank Harris in the *Fortnightly Review* for July, 1891.)

The appendix is a characteristically Wellsian attack on the assumptions of logic and is described by the author as a denial of 'the absolute validity of Logic', his principal assertion being that *'the forceps of our minds are clumsy forceps, and crush the truth a little in taking it'*. (In this statement Wells had unwittingly forecast a parallel development in sub-atomic physics— the advent two decades later of Heisenberg's 'Uncertainty Principle', which argued that the movements of particles could never be accurately measured, since they would be influenced by the electrical forces of the actual instruments attempting to measure them.)

Wells's basic objections to the assumptions of logic were threefold : firstly, that logic depends on the disregarding of individuality and on the assumption that unique objects are actually identically similar. These are then grouped under one term, the significance of which tends to become intensified. Secondly, the only way logic can freely handle negative terms is to approach them as if they were positive. Finally, he queried the acceptance of dimensions and planes, suggesting that if there was any validity in the image of a three-dimensional jelly in which the mind's ideas were suspended, the kind of reconciliation required in logic that all things should be in accordance on a single plane was not only unnecessary but also impossible—since they could never come together on one plane. He continued the appendix with a dissertation on the long-standing argument regarding Determinism as against Free Will.

The book, highly praised by such diverse personalities as Henry James, his philosopher brother William James, and Joseph Conrad, is particularly noted for its style of presentation. Wells himself described it as 'a sort of shot-silk texture between philosophical discussion on the one hand and imaginative narrative on the other'. He arrived at this approach after considering and setting aside such forms as the Socratic dialogue and the kind of discussion novel associated with Mallock and Peacock. His frequent footnotes citing earlier utopian writings are evidence of his wide knowledge of the subject. Although he was to update his vision of an ideal society in the later *Men Like Gods* (1923), it has been generally recognized that *A Modern Utopia* is the most 'beautifully seen and beautifully thought' of any such work conceived during the last hundred years. *A Modern Utopia*, 1905

NARRATOR, 'LITTLE MOTHER UP THE MÖRDERBERG': A novice at mountaineering, who nevertheless insists on his mother accompanying him on a difficult climb up the Mörderberg in the Alps. His fellow Englishmen in the hotel doubt the wisdom of his ascent, as do the guides he hires, but he persists. Having attained the summit, both he and his mother are swept over a precipice by an avalanche, but land unharmed miraculously cocooned in snow. Unabashed by the experience, he claims a record time for the descent. 'Little Mother up the Mörderberg', 1910

NARRATOR, *The War of the Worlds*: Chronicler of an alien invasion, he is a writer specializing in speculative philosophy, who lives with his wife on Maybury Hill, near Woking in Surrey. The first Martian cylinder falls on Horsell Common, close to his home, and he is soon to learn of the deadly attributes displayed by the alien invaders. He takes his wife to Leatherhead to stay with cousins, on the false assumption that she will be safe there, and returns to find the Martians extending their territory against all resistance. He shelters an artilleryman in his house for a night, before setting out again for Leatherhead. Deflected from his route, he witnesses the destruction of Weybridge and a desperate fight beside the Thames at Shepperton, where the river literally boils under the attack of the aliens' heat-ray and one of their number is killed by a lucky shot.

Shortly afterwards he finds himself encumbered by a demented curate who becomes more of a dangerous liability as the days progress. He is finally obliged to silence him for ever with a meat chopper after they have been trapped for a week in a house in Sheen on the outskirts of London. The building has collapsed on the impact of the fifth Martian cylinder which has dropped close-by.

After a near encounter with a Martian handling machine that carries off the curate's body, he escapes in the direction of Putney where he again falls in with the artilleryman. While he is impressed with the Gunner's dreams of resistance, it is soon evident to him that the man lacks the character to carry them out. Proceeding alone towards Fulham, he discovers the Thames, and much of the surrounding land, clogged with a luxuriant red weed—an attempt, he assumes, by the invaders to convert the conquered territory into a semblance of Mars. London is deserted; those inhabitants who neglected to flee have died in the poisonous black smoke, fired in cannisters from the fighting machines (the destruction of the capital is related by his brother —*see under* The Medical Student, *page 148*). When he comes at last to where the seventh cylinder has descended on Primrose Hill, he is amazed to find the Martians either dying or already dead, struck down by bacteria to which they have no immunity.

For several days he wanders in a delirium, knowing that Leatherhead has been destroyed and presuming his wife killed. However, on returning to his home after being cared for by chance acquaintances, he rejoices to find her there alive and well. In an epilogue, he tells of the great benefits to science yielded by an investigation of the Martian machines. The secret of flight now belongs to Man, together with many other advances. He warns against the possibility of a further attack and speculates on a successful Martian invasion of Venus. More philosophically, he dwells on the psychological effect on humanity, brought about by the invasion, and the knowledge that it is not alone in the Cosmos. His judgement of the Martians he has already given —in the introduction to his tale : 'And before we judge them too harshly, we must remember what ruthless and utter destruction our own species has wrought, not only on animals, such as the vanished bison and dodo, but upon its own inferior races. The Tasmanians, in spite of their human likeness, were swept out of existence in a war of extermination waged by European immigrants, in the space of fifty years. Are we such apostles of mercy as to complain if the Martians warred in the same spirit?'

It is possible to see the story as an oblique attack on British Imperialism and its gun-boat diplomacy. In view of his later writings on the subject, it is clear that Wells disapproved of the colonialist ethos wholeheartedly. *The War of the Worlds*, 1898

NORBERT, DR.: The 'intolerable psychiatrist' of *The Croquet Player*, who buttonholes Frobisher at Les Noupets and reveals that the tale he has heard from Finchatton of a mass haunting in the Fenland marshes is a delusion. Norbert, a powerful, glaring and untidily-dressed man, given to wild gesticulations, subjects Frobisher to his own views of the causes of growing violence in the world, to an extent that the latter suspects that the psychiatrist also has become infected with Finchatton's sickness. Modern man, he suggests, has broken 'the frame of the present', so that the human past stands revealed in all its brutality and horror—and the spirit of the caveman has been released : 'He has never died. He is anything but dead ... Only he was shut off from us and hidden. For a long time. And now we see him here face to face and his grin derides us. Man is still what he was ... Man, sir, unmasked and disillusioned is the same fearing, snarling, fighting beast he was a hundred thousand years ago ... The brute has been marking time and dreaming of a progress it has failed to make.'

Norbert's outburst reflects one aspect of Wells's own views, which he came to express frequently in his final works, and which in effect echoed the tenor of some of his very earliest stories. *The Croquet Player*, 1936

NORMANDY, THE HON. BEATRICE : The woman whom George Ponderevo eventually comes to love after she has already given herself over to the protection of Lord Carnaby. She first meets George at Bladesover House when she is eight and he twelve. There, two years later, they indulge in some very juvenile kissing and petting, but she betrays him by lying about a fight he has with her half-brother and as a result he is packed off to Chatham. They are not to meet again for some two decades. Beatrice is the daughter of a courtesy Baron, who has died 'of general disreputableness' before his own father; consequently she is raised in relatively humble circumstances. In maturity she is attractive, with disorderly, naturally curling brown hair, a pale complexion, and yellowish-brown eyes which on occasion may turn impishly dark. There is about her an air of softness, both in voice and manner.

The pair are re-united when Beatrice comes to stay with her step-mother, a neighbour of George's uncle at Crest Hill. She rides over with Carnaby to call on Edward Ponderevo and at first fails to recognize George. When alone, she confesses that she had long felt guilty about the childhood betrayal. She shows much interest in George's flying experiments, in spite of nearly being hit by his glider while she is on horseback; but her interest in the man himself appears to wax and wane. She nurses him in her step-mother's home after he has crashed in a tree and agrees to marry him, at the same time suggesting vaguely that there will be difficulties to be overcome (George is unaware of her relationship with Carnaby). On hearing that he has business in Africa, she promises to wait for him.

He returns financially ruined, and although she becomes his mistress for a brief fortnight, she is adamant that there can be no question of their marrying. She admits her liaison with Carnaby, confessing that she has been spoilt by the luxurious life and could not be happy as the wife of someone without wealth. Also, she regards herself as soiled; Ponderevo must be content with the two weeks of deep love which she has given him. At their last parting she hints vaguely at the use of a narcotic, a possibility which George subsequently suspects may explain her otherwise mysterious alternating moods. *Tono Bungay*, 1909

NORVEL : Director of Education in Rud Whitlow's world government and a man who, like others in the Group, grows in stature as his responsibilities increase. His educational aims are a reflection of Wells's frequently reiterated concepts. He organizes an effective world survey of schools, only to discover the paucity of mental direction endured by the greater part of humanity. 'Norvel found himself involved in a gigantic extension of the old structures of thought, research and instruction, in the evocation and training of vast armies of teachers, in the application of film and aerial to school use and the establishment throughout the world of millions of those community centres that manifestly had to replace the schools and home instruction of the past.' *The Holy Terror*, 1939

NUNEZ : The sighted man in 'The Country of the Blind'. A South American mountaineer, he becomes separated from the English party he is guiding and stumbles quite literally into a lost valley where the entire population has been sightless for many generations. Taking for granted the old adage : 'In the country of the blind, the one-eyed man is king', he assumes he will enjoy a unique advantage. In fact, he is regarded as deranged :

' "Why did you not come when I called you?" said the blind man. "Must you be led like a child? Cannot you hear the path as you walk?"

Nunez laughed. "I can see it," he said.

"There is no such word as *see*," said the blind man, after a pause. "Cease this folly, and follow the sound of my feet." '

A romance ensues with the girl Medina-Saroté, but the elders of the community withhold their consent because of Nunez's pretensions to sight. However, they come to the conclusion that his derangement is caused by two strange growths on either side of his nose; if he will agree to their removal, they are convinced his sanity will be restored, and then he may marry. Although Nunez initially accepts the proposal, he concludes on the eve of the operation that the sacrifice would be too great in spite of his love—and he escapes from the valley. Well over a decade after he had written what is seen as his finest short story, Wells added a new ending, more in keeping with the sociological ideas he was then attempting to propagate. In general, the result was to decrease the tale's effectiveness, and it is the original version which is normally read. 'The Country of the Blind', 1904

O

OSTROG, 'BOSS' : Head of the Wind Vanes Control and the man responsible for wakening Graham from his two-hundred-year sleep. He has pale blue eyes beneath a broad forehead, an aquiline nose and resolute mouth; despite his upright bearing, it is obvious from the sagging flesh of his face that he is old.

Ostrog's mental state verges on megalomania, and his obsession to wield power is the motivation behind Graham's resurrection. His influence over the Labour Companies is surreptitious and he has armed them in secret. He plans a revolt against the White Council, who have run the world ostensibly on Graham's behalf. Having awakened the Sleeper, the Labour Boss attempts to manipulate him as a figurehead. Initially successful, he overthrows the Council and begins to rule in Graham's name, while the latter is still acclimatizing himself to the world of the future.

Only when Graham is convinced by Ostrog's niece, Helen Wotton, that her uncle has the makings of a despot, does he decide to intervene. He leads the people against the Labour Companies and attacks the aerial landing stages where the Boss's reinforcements from Africa are due to arrive. Ostrog, appearing defeated, flies before the pursuing Graham; but his fate, and the outcome of the entire revolt, is left uncertain, the story ending in Graham's death when his aircraft is caught in an explosive blast. *When the Sleeper Wakes*, 1899

P

PADISHAH, SIR MOHINI : The turbanned 'Piccadilly swell' whose precious diamond is swallowed by one of the eponymous birds of 'A Deal in Ostriches'. The action takes place during an ocean journey to Brindisi, during which the five birds are auctioned individually by their owner, Potter, to hopeful bidders who aspire to ownership of the Hindoo's jewel. The resulting proceeds are considerable, and the story ends on a note of doubt whether the diamond was ever swallowed at all. 'A Deal in Ostriches', 1894

PALACE, BRYNHILD : Wife of a successful author who finds herself, against her more cherished inclinations, drawing ever farther apart from her husband. She is tall, slender and fair-haired, with a broad serene face and kind brown eyes which frequently assume an expression of perplexity. Twelve years younger than Rowland, she married him when she was still immature and has developed the habit of placing him on a pedestal. Even after several years of marriage she feels he is too critical of her.

Consequently, she views with some amusement his growing preoccupation with self-publicity, realizing that he is less sure of himself than he is at pains to appear.

For a time Brynhild has remained content to be seen as an attractive appendage to Palace's rising career; the outline of her story records a shift away from this dependency towards a growing awareness of her need for self-sufficiency as an individual. Nevertheless, she remains attached to him throughout the narrative, and constantly troubled by the knowledge that he recognizes that she does not fully understand him. The evidence suggests that neither does she fully understand herself, for she reflects at considerable length on the lot of women without coming to any positive conclusion, except that things should be changed.

In the opening section of the novel she remains in the background, evincing the qualities of the 'quiet lady' which is the rôle she has assigned to herself. As if in recognition of this retreat, the narrative over-passes her to dwell on Palace's attempts to improve his public appeal, culminating in his hiring of the obsequious Immanuel Cloote. (While Brynhild remains the central character, much of the plot involves Palace's individual experiences, as noted in his entry below.)

In the course of her self-appraisal, Brynhild adopts an air of detachment which adds to her general attitude of vagueness. Thus, on the occasion of a house party, when Rowland makes an ass of himself during a game of charades, and later disappears into the garden with Cythera Label, she locks her bedroom door against him. But she is never quite certain whether she should repeat the act, or even if her husband is aware that she had performed it in the first place. At the same gathering she meets the retiring writer, Alfred Bunter, whom she recognizes as being as misplaced as herself. She endeavours to draw him out, and they discover a mutual sympathy.

Once Rowland places his future public career in the hands of Cloote, whom Brynhild detests, she is left very much alone. She responds to a cry of distress from Bunter, accepting the confession of his true identity and the need for his escape from his wife, Freda Lewis. He admits that he may also be responsible, by default, for the death of his brother-in-law, Gregory, who fell down a disused mineshaft in Cardiff while in a drunken stupor. Bunter neglected to alert any rescue services, being more concerned with disappearing beyond the grasp of a possessive wife. In the outcome, Mrs. Lewis first identifies the corpse as her brother's, but later claims it to be that of Bunter/Lewis, possibly in an attempt to shield him.

Bunter goes to pieces on Cloote's revelation of his past, and Brynhild makes love with him, more as an act of comfort and solace than anything else. She deceives Rowland into the natural assumption that he is the father of the ensuing child.

Brynhild and Bunter meet no more, at least not for many years. In the meantime, he succeeds in proving his innocence and finds seclusion in Dubrovnic. Brynhild continues with Palace and bears him several of their own children. She finds in motherhood at least a compensation for, if not an idealistic fulfilment of, her dreams. She develops 'an increasing social confidence and dignity'. Palace in the meantime, as befits his aim, progresses ever 'upward and on'.

The novel can be regarded as lightweight, indicating signs of undue haste and a desire by the author to complete it without delay. A profligacy of loose-ends is wound up in a page and a half! The quality of Brynhild's introspection suggests that Wells was still attempting to explore the type of feminine thinking which had already been out-of-date for more than a decade. Nevertheless, the book records his continuing championship of the woman's cause, to which he had contributed significantly in earlier and more effective works. *Brynhild*, 1937

PALACE, ROWLAND : A successful author in the intellectual sphere, and a man of 'acute sensibilities and incessant anxieties'. Intellectually, his pose is to 'acquiesce in everything and believe in nothing'. His first book, *Bent Oars*, meets with acclaim in both Britain and America. During his early career he has taught English and History, having graduated from Cambridge. He meets Brynhild when he is thirty-two and she twenty.

The opening of the story sees Palace almost obsessively concerned with his public image. He feels he has made a fool of himself by appearing in the robes of a bard at a local May Day festival, where a number of unflattering press photographs were taken. He is also worried by the challenge to his reputation posed by the rapidly rising writer, Alfred Bunter. He consults both his agent, Blatch, and his publisher, Schroederer, in an effort to interest them in greater publicity, but neither is willing to undertake the task. Subsequently he hires Immanuel Cloote as his promotions manager and is reasonably satisfied with his work, although he is less than impressed with his personality.

Palace enjoys the adulation of his reading public, particularly the attentions of several young women in his immediate circle. He indulges in a prolonged flirtation with Lady Cythera Label, but there is no evidence of the liaison developing beyond that stage. Clearly he believes that Brynhild's child is his own. The close of the story relates his departure for a grand tour of the literary capitals of Europe, accompanied by the effusive Cloote. *Brynhild*, 1937

PARCHESTER, THE REV. MR.: Only one of the countless mass of humanity who witness a fleeting vision of God in His glory when a single note is inadvertently blown on the instrument reserved for the playing of the Last Trump. The effect on Parchester, who is a popular preacher and highly appealing to ladies of a genteel persuasion, is dramatic. For a brief period he recognizes the hypocritical nature of his behaviour; but no one, including his Bishop, is particularly inclined to bear with his confession. He turns at last to the consolation of one of his female admirers and arrives home later fully restored to his normal self. The story ends on a cynical note, in keeping with the book in which it originally appeared, *Boon*. 'The Story of the Last Trump', 1915

PARHAM, MR.: The Senior Tutor of St. Simon's, Oxford, who as Lord Paramount of England unleashes a world war. Also a publicist and historian, he is by his looks a pale, mild-mannered man, but given to the expression of reactionary and imperialistic views. His attitude to the concept of an international republic, for example, being: 'Your world peace, when you examine it, flies in the face of the fundamental institutions—the ancient and tested institutions of mankind—the institutions that have made man what he is.' He is also obsessed by the need to encircle Soviet Russia.

The opening of the novel sees Parham accepted into the circle of the business entrepreneur, Sir Bussy Woodcock, whom he seeks to influence towards his own personal view of world betterment. Woodcock entertains Parham with visits to race meetings and sailing excursions, to the envy of other Oxford dons. Parham's metamorphosis into the Lord Paramount of England occurs at a small séance where a visitant from Mars manifests itself. In effect Parham appears to coalesce with the spirit and henceforward regards himself as being of exalted status.

In his new rôle, Parham makes his debut at the Albert Hall in

London, during a meeting of the Amalgamated Patriotic Societies, where he calls for the foundation of the League of Duty Paramount. Within weeks he has given similar addresses to Eton and Harrow Schools and has been cheered for twenty minutes by the members of the Stock Exchange. He invades the House of Commons to dismiss its members, the next day joining the King in a Garden Party at Buckingham Palace. Having achieved a national following by his patriotic pronouncements, he assembles his Council, to which his devoted follower Nanette Pinchot becomes 'reporter'. The Lord Paramount has now taken control of the country.

He begins to initiate the policies advocated by the ineffectual Parham, namely: the encirclement of Russia, the re-establishment of the monarchy in Germany, the restoration of European predominance in China and the conversion of Britain into a militant state. In all this he rejects any American influence. Reviewing the position of his armed forces, he selects General Gerson as his military *Éminence Grise*. With him he conducts trials of poison gas and discusses the logistics of an attack on Russia. In the area of gas warfare a super-weapon, Gas L, has been developed, manufactured from basal substances found only under the seabed off Cayme, in Cornwall, the supposed site of Lyonesse. These mineral deposits are controlled by Sir Bussy, who has as yet played little part in Lord Paramount's endeavours.

A grand tour of Europe is undertaken to universal acclaim, Paramount promising much to various leaders: France expresses interest in Syria and North Africa, Germany shares the determination to conquer Russia, while Italy is offered Greece and the Balkans, together with the Crimea. The Italian leader is shown as a caricature of Mussolini, launching into a diatribe on the glory of power. As a result of these negotiations a propaganda excuse is employed to justify the declaration of war on Russia; at the same time Japan, acting in collusion, institutes a blockade of China. A number of American vessels attempt to violate the blockade and are duly sunk, precipitating an ultimatum from the United States.

The war developments are viewed with growing alarm in Britain and civil unrest and criticism become rife. The Empire, too, expresses an unwillingness to support the Lord Paramount's cause. Canada refuses to join in a war against the U.S., both South Africa and Australia displaying a similar attitude. Even the

European allies are tardy in their enthusiasm for such a venture, with the exception of Italy. India is torn by continual internal conflicts.

Exhausted by the strain of his responsibilities, Paramount is revitalized by drugs and special exercises under the supervision of his personal physician, Sir Titus Knowles, and he determines to assert his authority over the wayward Canadians. The greater part of the British fleet is despatched across the North Atlantic, where by accident it engages in a devastating battle with its American counterpart. Neither side is victorious, but both fleets are almost completely eliminated. This conflict proves the flash-point for a dissolution of the European alliance and the participants turn on one another, Germany and Italy uniting to fight France whom Britain is obliged by treaty to assist. Turkey attacks the Arab lands, while Canada allies itself more closely with the United States. London, Paris, Hamburg, Berlin and Rome are all heavily bombed. An insurrection in Dublin proclaims the independence of Eire.

In opposition to Paramount's militaristic policies, anti-war riots break out in Britain, many citizens being arrested and shot. At this point Sir Bussy attempts to intervene but is curtly dismissed by Gerson. In desperation Paramount decides to resort to the use of Gas L, and in company with Gerson he leads an assault on Woodcock's stronghold in Cornwall where the supplies are held. In a confrontation with the financier, the general attempts to shoot him, inadvertently shattering the giant glass distillery in which the gas is manufactured. All are enveloped in the ensuing explosion, only to find themselves and the world returned to a state of normality once the cataclysm has abated. The fantasy has come to an end.

The novel was regarded by its author as 'a rather boisterous caricature not of the personality but of the imaginations of a modern British imperialist of the university type'. It lampoons a number of leading figures of the day, including one of Wells's favourite targets, Winston Churchill, particularly in regard to Churchill's attitude towards the Soviet Union. It is also interesting as a second attempt by Wells to employ a séance as the basis with which to initiate a tale, the first being *Christina Alberta's Father*. (Another such occult gathering, also significant to the plot, was related in *Love and Mr. Lewisham*.) Parham's misadventures were choicely illustrated in the first edition by the noted cartoonist, David Low, whose later graphic attacks on the factual European dictators were to become renowned. *The Autocracy of Mr. Parham*, 1930

PARLOAD : A young solicitor's clerk who lodges near Leadford's home in the Midlands pottery town of Clayton. Tall, fair-haired and gawky, he is given to infectious enthusiasms of which the most prominent is astronomy. He and Leadford share a common interest in the advancement of socialism, but the latter finds Parload's championship of science dull. Together they plan to organize a series of socialist meetings on a plot of nearby waste land but their intentions are delayed by the coming of the comet —an event which Parload follows nightly through his opera glass. *In the Days of the Comet*, 1906

PARSONS : An apprentice at the Port Burdock Drapery Bazaar, and a contemporary of Mr. Polly. A devotee of English Literature, and not averse to being something of a character at the bar of a country inn, he is dismissed after a glorious tussle arising from his attempt to dress a shop-window in a more original style and refusing to abandon his feat of enterprise. *The History of Mr. Polly*, 1910

PEMBROSE, MRS. : A martinet widow whose powers of organization appeal to Sir Isaac Harman when he appoints her manageress of the hostels he has built to please his wife. Lady Harman develops an almost immediate aversion to her, being first struck by her extreme pallor. Besides being pale, her complexion is freckled, and she has small hard blue-grey eyes, a protruding chin, and a voice of 'wooden resonance and a ghost of a lisp'. She holds herself erect and guardedly alert—in essence a thoroughly authoritarian personality. Her attitude to the running of the hostels is utterly at odds with Ellen Harman's. She believes in the strict obedience of even stricter rules and professes no sympathy at all with the women's rights movement. Lady Harman is obliged to intervene when she begins ousting any girl who provides her with the slightest grounds for disfavour. *The Wife of Sir Isaac Harman*, 1914

PENTSTEMON, UNCLE : An ancient relative of Mr. Polly—given to pithy comments of a resolutely undiplomatic nature. His clothing appears to date from another age, and includes a long cylindrical top hat which he refuses to take off indoors. 'Time had removed the hair from the top of his head and distributed a small dividend of the plunder in little bunches carelessly and impartially over the rest of his features . . .' He is distinctly unimpressed with the Larkins sisters, and also, for that matter, with Mr. Polly. Nor are his views on marriage of much comfort to the newly-wed. All the family hold him in something aproaching awe, as much as he 'drats' them all. *The History of Mr. Polly*, 1910

PETERS, GAVIN : An American foreign correspondent who encounters Gemini Twain in Stockholm and travels with him as far as Riga in Latvia. He contacts Stella Kentlake by letter during a visit to London, and later meets both her and Dione Twain to relate his experiences with Gemini during the Nazi invasion of Poland. His appearance arouses Stella's dislike—tightly-waved coppery hair, dead white skin, eyes which refuse to meet hers and long thin hands which he holds 'as though they were in readiness for the keyboard of a piano'. Nevertheless he is able to describe much of Twain's progress in his effort to reach Russia before his disappearance and confesses that he owes his life to him. *Babes in the Darkling Wood*, 1940

PHILIPS, MADELEINE : An actress who joins her friends, Mrs. Bowles and Mrs. Geedge, on a caravanning trip, in the course of which they cross paths with the runaway Bealby. The boy is overwhelmed by her beauty, and she knows it—she has become used to such reactions on the part of the opposite sex. Nevertheless, she treats him kindly and devotes more time to him than her companions are disposed to spare. She obviously entertains some form of romantic attachment for Captain Douglas, and when he appears unexpectedly her affection for him plunges Bealby into love-lorn despair. *Bealby: A Holiday*, 1915

PINCHOT, NANETTE : The young widow of an English merchant in Mauritius who becomes the Lord Paramount's devoted secretary. 'Dusky, with a curiously beautiful oval olive-tinted face', she is well-versed in psychic matters and is profoundly moved by Mr. Parham's translation into a super-being. Convinced of his destiny, she remains his loyal supporter even when the tide of the world war he has unleashed has turned against him. *The Autocracy of Mr. Parham*, 1930

PLANTAGENET-BUCHAN, MR. : An urbane, Europeanized American

who is the first guest to appear at Mrs. Rylands's Italian villa. A 'very exquisite little gentleman' in his sixties, he has a finely modelled face punctuated by a small beard and conveys an overall impression that 'a Velasquez portrait had left its proper costume upstairs and dressed for dinner'. He is intrigued by the prospect of meeting the 'Utopographer', Sempack, and proves his main contestant in the discussion featured in the early part of the novel. *Meanwhile*, 1923

PLATTNER, GOTTFRIED : A modern-languages teacher of Alsatian extraction who is precipitated into the fourth dimension by an explosion during a school chemistry experiment. He finds himself in a strange twilight land superimposed over the school's surroundings which he can still also dimly perceive. Equally disconcerting are the sad, tadpole-like creatures he encounters; later he comes to realize that they are human souls. After several days in limbo, he returns to reality by accidentally exploding the remains of the powder originally responsible for his predicament. Subsequently, it is discovered that his body has been reversed as a result of revolving through the fourth dimension—his heart now beats on his right side. 'The Plattner Story', 1896

PLESSINGTON, AUNT : Related to the Popes on her husband's side, her husband being Mr. Pope's brother. A tall lean woman who wears 'hats to show she despised them' beneath 'carefully dishevelled hair'. Her principal intention in life is to 'get on', motivated by an urge which she interprets as akin to Bernard Shaw's 'life-force'; she sees little in the purpose of existence bar the necessity for 'shoving'. Her husband, Uncle Hubert, suffers no such urgent compulsions—he is a complacent Oxford don.

Aunt Plessington has instigated a movement which occupies much of her time and energy (a familiar pursuit among several of Wells's ageing female characters), its aims being to benefit the lower social orders by restricting their consumption of alcohol and various unnourishing foodstuffs. She arouses Trafford's disaffection by her reactionary opinions and is rarely welcome in his household. She is also referred to on several occasions in *The Wife of Sir Isaac Harman*. *Marriage*, 1912

POLLOCK : Assistant to an English explorer in West Africa who has the misfortune to shoot and wound a Porroh man, a member of a tribe bearing a reputation for superstitious vengeance. Finding himself subsequently stalked, and the victim of frequent near misses, Pollock employs a known killer to rid him of his assailant. In due course he is presented with the Porroh man's head; but try as he might, he cannot rid himself of the grisly relic. Although he leaves the actual head behind in Africa, it continues to haunt him, even on his return to London, and he eventually cuts his throat. 'Pollock and the Porroh Man', 1895

POLLY, ALFRED : The epitome of Wells's struggling 'little men', and of all of them the possessor of the greatest, if eccentric, imagination. His mother died when he was seven, and he was educated first at a National School and later at a private establishment until he was fourteen. To put it charitably, his education was a mess. His acquired vocabulary is so lacking that he is obliged to invent an idiosyncratic version of his own. Among his choicer expressions are 'Sesquippledan verboojuice', 'Cultured Rapacacity', 'Zelacious commerciality' and 'benifluous influence'. Replicating Wells's own experience, he begins his working life as a draper's apprentice, befriended by Parsons who is shortly dismissed following a fight precipitated by his revolutionary method of window dressing.

Drifting through a succession of drapery jobs, Polly enjoys a welcome respite on the death of his father, who has been cared for by Harold Johnson, and the receipt of a modest legacy. At the funeral he meets his three female cousins, the Larkins girls, and the ancient and tetchy Uncle Pentstemon. Some odd compulsion prevails on him to propose to Miriam Larkins, but not before he has indulged in an idyllic dalliance with an attractive schoolgirl, Christabel, whom he finds sitting on a wall during one of his bicycle rides. His marriage ceremony is noted for its garbled responses (*see under* Clergyman) and is conducted under the watchful eye of a family friend, Mr. Voules, lest the bridegroom succumb to a change of heart. Polly subsequently rents a shop in the small coastal town of Fishbourne, where he remains for fifteen years in a progressively more stultifying situation. His eccentricities are met by hostility from his fellow shopkeepers, notably Rusper the ironmonger; his marriage proves childless and unsatisfying, and he is plagued with chronic indigestion. By the age of thirty-seven, which is the point at which the story opens, his only consolation is the public house, his bicycle, and the multitude of books which have brought him escape from the overwhelming dreariness of his real life.

the two are thrown more and more into each other's company, finally to fall deeply in love.

The affair gives rise to a growing scandal, largely at the instigation of Altiora Bailey who cannot forgive Remington for deserting the Liberal cause and who, being but a mediocre writer herself, is envious of Isabel's ability. When Remington is obliged by the extent of the rumours to confess the association to his wife, Isabel attempts to save his reputation by agreeing to marry Shoesmith, an admirer of both the lovers and an early school acquaintance of Remington. But the thought of such an outcome affects her health and she is contemplating suicide when she receives a note from Remington, who is not far short of a similar condition of distress. They elope to the Continent, eventually to live in Italy where she bears their child.

The personality of Isabel, for all her mental alertness and capability of meeting Remington on the same intellectual plane, reveals an inner core of weakness—she lacks the strength to face life without him—unlike his wife who, while unable to attain the same levels of thought, proves she can survive losing him. Remington's dilemma is to determine which of the two will be most hurt by the decision he is obliged to make. He throws away his career, and all that each member of the trio has worked for, to save the weaker of his two loves. *The New Machiavelli*, 1911

RIVERTON : A newly-commissioned army subaltern who secures the affections of Eleanor Scrope. He has a pleasant, slightly freckled fair face, and 'very honest blue eyes'. His mouth, chin and the line of his brows are finely modelled. The son of a doctor, he has taken a Natural Science Tripos at Cambridge, where he first meets Eleanor. He encounters Bishop Scrope, more or less by coincidence, on the eve of his departure for the Front, when his manner meets with the latter's approval. *The Soul of a Bishop*, 1917

ROOTHING, BOBBY : A slender young man who occupies the same lodgings as Preemby after the latter's metamorphosis into Sargon, King of Kings. He is struggling to become a writer, after a harsh upbringing during which he was frequently locked in a cupboard by the aunt who looked after him. Consequently he abhors loss of liberty and is determined to help Preemby escape from the mental asylum where he is later detained. In this he succeeds,

H

and secretes a now ailing Sargon in a boarding-house at Dymchurch on the South Coast.

He cables Christina Alberta in London and meets her for the first time when she comes with the solicitor Devizes to visit her father. He proposes to her after Preemby's death and is eventually accepted only to be rejected later, although the couple remain close. The story ends with a meditation by Bobby on his projected novel and the quality of mind of such women as Christina Alberta. *Christina Alberta's Father*, 1925

RUFOUS MAN, THE : A fellow club-member of the novelist Joseph Davis who, during the course of an after-lunch discussion on the nature of cosmic rays, suggests that they may be deliberately directed at Earth by a scientifically advanced civilization on Mars, with the intention of changing man for the better. The idea seizes the imagination of Davis and provides the central talking point of the story. *Star Begotten*, 1937

RUSPER, MR. : An ironmonger acquaintance of Mr. Polly at Fishbourne. A man possessed of a curiously egg-shaped head which provokes Polly on occasions to suggest he 'boil it'—a remark not entirely understood by Rusper, but certainly not lost upon his wife. He also suffers from a defect of the palate which manifests itself by a regular 'kikking' sound. His principal action in the story is an inglorious tussle he engages in with Polly after the latter has swerved his bicycle into the goods displayed outside Rusper's shop. Both men are subsequently bound over to keep the peace. *The History of Mr. Polly*, 1910

RYLANDS, CYNTHIA : The central character of a novel in which the threat of the British General Strike of 1926 and the menace of Mussolini's fascist régime in Italy dictate much of the action. She is in the course of entertaining a house party at her villa, Casa Terragena, in Ventimiglia, when the story opens—a small, fragile woman with dark hair and 'pretty arms'. She is also in an advanced stage of pregnancy. Among her house guests are the intellectual expatriate American, Plantagenet-Buchan, the reactionary Colonel Bullace, and the renowned writer and utopian, Sempack. Female members of the company include the eligible divorcee, Lady Catherine Fossingdean, and the headstrong Puppy Clarges.

Since the book takes the form of a Wellsian dialogue piece, its early pages are very much occupied with a discussion between the men and in which Cynthia plays little part. In interludes which depict her private thoughts she is shown to be devoted to her husband, attracted by his intelligence and sensitivity, but disappointed by his lack of action. She is therefore all the more upset to come across him making sexual advances to Puppy Clarges, a girl known for her coarseness and promiscuity. Much distressed, she runs into the garden, only to be confronted by Lady Catherine and Sempack in a close embrace. Later the writer attempts to comfort her, endeavouring to explain Philip's behaviour in terms of the male sex-drive, but she remains unconvinced.

Eventually the party separate, Miss Clarges having already departed abruptly—to the puzzlement of the head servant, the normally imperturbable Bombaccio. Rylands and Bullace leave for England to adopt their respective stances for the forthcoming strike. Lady Catherine follows them shortly, while Sempack embarks on a walking tour. Left alone to herself, Cynthia becomes reconciled to Philip's indiscretion and finds comfort in his letters. Later she is joined by Mrs. McManus, an Ulster-born nurse who cares for her during her confinement. Their relative calm is disturbed one night by sounds of a violent pursuit, and by the discovery of an exhausted Signor Vinciguerra who has collapsed outside the villa while fleeing from a gang of Blackshirt thugs.

The two women secrete the former minister in a bedroom, without the knowledge of Bombaccio whom they suspect (incorrectly) may also be a fascist supporter. Once he has recovered, they drive him across the French border somewhat comically disguised in the nurse's clothes—he has particular trouble with her shoes. The final part of the book is taken up almost exclusively with Philip's accounts of the General Strike and culminate in the birth of the Rylands' child.

A number of themes are interwoven in the novel, from the practical demonstration of the outcome of fascist ideology to the self-enquiry of a, then, modern woman as to how she can be of use to society outside her immediate family. To a certain extent it also dwells on the pursuit of sexual gratification in terms of wasted energy; but its chief interest now probably lies in its discussions and reports on the General Strike. In a 'Preface Dedicatory' Wells explains that the idea for the story came to him on seeing an unknown woman seated in the celebrated garden of La Mortola, near Ventimiglia. *Meanwhile*, 1927

RYLANDS, PHILIP : The wealthy and apparently somewhat effete husband of Cynthia who eventually returns to England to take a more responsible rôle in the crisis period of the General Strike. At the opening of the novel he gives the impression of being intellectually restricted. He has served well in the First World War and is planning to stand for Parliament, but his mind appears to lack any militance. However, his interest in the discussions at the Casa Terragena surprise his wife and her re-appraisal of him is only clouded by his brief entanglement with Puppy Clarges.

Since much of his wealth is derived from his share in the family collieries, he begins seriously to consider the justification of the miners' grievances. He quarrels violently with his uncle, Lord Edensoke, who fully supports the miners' lock-out. His long letters to Cynthia on the progress of the strike include many satirical references to the activities of Winston Churchill and are also enriched by several amusing pictorial sketches (actually drawn, as was his wont, by Wells himself). The book is as much a chronicle of Philip's growing awareness of the active part he should play in ensuring a more just society as it is a portrait of Cynthia's exploration of her own intellectual processes. *Meanwhile*, 1927

S

SARNAC : See 'Smith, Harry Mortimer'.

SARNAC'S LISTENERS : Five inhabitants of the ideal world of two thousand years hence to whom Sarnac relates his dream of being Harry Mortimer Smith. Respectively they are Sunray, who is Sarnac's lover and resembles Hetty Marcus of the dream, and two couples : the brother and sister, Radiant and Starlight, and two sisters, Willow and Firefly. Sunray is a writer and illustrator of stories set in the ancient past, while Radiant and Starlight educate animals; they are a dark handsome pair of Southern origin. Willow and Firefly are both fair-haired and work as electricians.

In many respects the company reflects the Utopians of *Men Like Gods*. They are clean-limbed and healthy, and go naked even in the mountains where they are holidaying. What little is said of their society sets it along utopian lines. Together they explore the ruins of a town which dates from the twentieth century, the 'Age of Confusion', and it is after this excursion that Sarnac falls asleep and dreams. Each of the listeners makes occasional comments as he relates his experience of a former life. *The Dream*, 1924

SATAN : The interloper in heaven who argues with God during the Prologue to *The Undying Fire*. Recalling their original wager regarding Job, he suggests that with the passage of millennia the whole of mankind must now be Job's descendants. He calls for a new test to ascertain whether afflicted Man will lose his faith and curse God. Decrying human progress, he asks, should he win the new wager, that an end be put to Man. He is given leave to try the race to the full, to see 'if he is indeed no more than a little stir amidst the slime, a fuss in the mud that signifies nothing . . .' *The Undying Fire*, 1919

SAWBRIDGE, GEORGINA : The elder, unmarried sister of Lady Ellen Harman, and an undesirable influence so far as Sir Isaac is concerned. As a child she has attended a day-school at Penge where, according to her mother, she became opinionated and unladylike, 'besides developing her muscular system to an un-refined degree'. Being an ardent suffragette, she constantly argues with Sir Isaac and infuriates him by challenging his attitudes on many matters. She interests Ellen in the 'Votes for Women' movement and supplies her with literature which Sir Isaac would prefer destroyed. Her most offensive action, in his eyes, is to obtain two tickets from him for a Liberal party reception, and then to pass them to suffragette friends who disrupt the occasion by physically assaulting a leading dignatory. *The Wife of Sir Isaac Harman*, 1914

SAYER OF THE LAW, THE : A white-haired member of the Beast People whose responsibility it is to intone the creed and code of behaviour which Moreau has imposed on his creations, even though he regards them as failures. The muddle-headed man-beasts dutifully repeat the articles of the Law, while continuing to break them:

'"Not to go on all-Fours; *that* is the Law. Are we not Men?" ...

"Not to eat Flesh nor Fish; *that* is the Law. Are we not Men?" ...

"Not to chase other Men; *that* is the Law. Are we not Men?" '

The Sayer also dies in the drunken affray instigated by Montgomery when he finds that Moreau has been killed. *The Island of Dr. Moreau*, 1896

SCHROEDERER : Rowland Palace's publisher, and a realist in his business. A massively-built man, with a large face beneath abundantly curly hair, he regards authors as mere material to be arranged on his list to the increasing profitability of his firm. His marketing policy is to establish a uniform line of dust-jacket designs which the public will come to associate with good reading regardless of the writers' names. When the avid reader admits to buying Schroederer's books, 'there would be an end to authors and their airs and graces'. (Wells, in company with many of his profession, entertained mixed feelings towards his publishers— he experimented with more of them than any of his contemporaries.) Schroederer is as unconcerned with Palace's obsession for publicity as the writer's literary agent, Blatch. In the publisher's view, the Age of the Great Man has passed; people now read *books*, not *writers*, and Palace had better reconcile himself to the fact. In the course of their conversation he confides that he has contracted the new writer, Alfred Bunter, a name virtually unknown to Palace, but a man who will feature prominently in the attentions of his wife. *Brynhild*, 1937

SCOTT-HARROWBY, PROFESSOR : Incumbent of the Chair of Latent History at Camford University who is assailed by the Voice of the invisible visitant and questioned on his interpretation of human history. The Voice admits it belongs to an extraterrestrial being who has watched humanity during the greater part of its progress. It quizzes the professor regarding the seeming lack of direction which has overtaken civilized man and, since it cannot read minds, invites him to explain what is now happening inside human heads and what the educational establishment can do about it. Scott-Harrowby rises only in-adequately to the challenge. *The Camford Visitation*, 1937

SCROPE, EDWARD—BISHOP OF PRINCHESTER : The Anglo-Catholic dignatory whose secession from the Church is prompted by two visions induced while he is under the influence of a drug. A well-built man in early middle-age, he possesses a pale clean-shaven face, brown hair and light-blue eyes. Born the only son of a well-connected vicar, he had a sheltered upbringing and until adult-hood was 'able to take life exactly as in infancy he took his carefully warmed and prepared bottle—unquestioningly and beneficially'. His career has spanned an early incumbency of the Church of the Holy Innocents, St. John's Wood, London, a period as the bishop suffragan of Pinner, in Middlesex, and finally his appointment as bishop of the industrial diocese of Princhester in 1910. His elevation to bishop suffragan was initially opposed by Queen Victoria because of a press leak which anticipated the event; however, she relented after the intercession of Scrope's mentor, Bishop Likeman.

The opening of the story finds the Bishop in a state of mental exhaustion some four years following his move to Princhester. He has found the area's harsh industrialism a challenging con-trast to the more urbane atmosphere of the South, and he is perturbed by the condition of labour unrest which he en-counters. He is also tormented by certain doubts regarding the nature of the Trinity and by the arguments advanced in a critical book, *The Core of Truth in Christianity*, by the Rev. Chasters. The outbreak of the First World War disturbs him further and he suffers considerable insomnia aggravated by his attempts to forego smoking.

Scrope resolves to consult his physician in London and on the way he stays overnight at the home of a county hostess where he meets Lady Agatha Sunderbund. He finds her vitality and enthusiastic reception of his views refreshing, and he contrasts her personality favourably with the more aloof attitude of his wife, Lady Ella. He leaves with the keen anticipation that she will become what in effect will be his first real woman friend.

On arriving in London he discovers his regular doctor *in absentia*, to be replaced by Dale, a young man of disconcerting appearance who argues that a rest would hardly be the solution in the Bishop's case and recommends more radical treatment. He provides Scrope with a drug which he warns him will relieve his condition but will also enlarge the vistas of his mind. Passing the night at his London club, Scrope swallows a few drops from Dale's phial and later experiences his First Vision. He becomes aware that he is in the presence of the Angel of God, and expresses the doubts which are burdening his soul :

' "I want . . . to know about God. Slowly through four years I have been awakening to the need of God. Body and Soul I am sick for the want of God and the knowledge of God. I did not know what was the matter with me, why my life had become so disordered and confused that my very appetites and habits are all astray. But I am perishing for God as a waterless man upon a raft perishes for drink, and there is nothing but madness if I touch the seas about me. Not only in my thoughts but in my under thoughts and in my nerves and bones and arteries I have need of God." '

The Angel dismisses the convoluted arguments of many religions, revealing a view of God as He can be comprehended on the human scale, that is as King of all Mankind. It is sufficient for Scrope to appreciate Him in these terms; and the climax of the Vision is a brief sight of the Deity.

On recovering his normal self Scrope consults Bishop Likeman, telling him of the Vision and of his persuasion that he should leave the Church to propagate a new, more universal creed. Likeman advises him that his proposed heresy will only disturb his former followers and asks him to make no decision for at least three months. With the passing of time, Scrope's insomnia and perplexity return, and he experiences difficulty in explaining his doubts to his wife or any of his five daughters, with the exception of Eleanor, the eldest. Consequently he takes a second dose of the drug and sees his Second Vision. In this the Angel explains to him that it was necessary for him first to apprehend God and desire Him—the purpose of the First Vision —but that now he is to be shown how the time is arriving when the nature of God will be manifested throughout the Earth. In the Angel's company Scrope is taken around the world, listening in to the talk of many people on the subjects of war, kingship, race hatred, science, and the desire for a world state (in essence, a prolonged series of individual Wellsian arguments).

The effect of the Second Vision is to provoke the Bishop into an open denunciation of the orthodox Church and all monarchies at his next confirmation service, when he impulsively amends the words of the Benediction to expand the Trinitarian description of God by adding 'King of Mankind'. The inevitable result of the outburst is his resignation and an agonizing rebuke from Likeman. The majority of his family are at a loss to comprehend his action and only Eleanor supports him. Subsequently he receives a long letter from Lady Sunderbund offering to finance him in his new mission, in which she is determined to be his loyal disciple.

Scrope visits London to obtain a further supply of the drug, following Lady Ella's disposal of the phial, and finds his usual physician, Dr. Brighton-Pomfrey, back in residence. The doctor is alarmed on hearing that Scrope has taken a drug provided by Dale, who has since been killed, and dismisses the visions as mere hallucinations—many others of his patients have resorted to bizarre behaviour as a result of Dale's medication, even to the extent of exalted ladies wishing to do war work. However, since Dale left no notes, the secret of the drug is lost. Scrope realizes that if he is to have a further vision, it must be self-induced.

With the loss of his stipend he returns to London, setting up his family in a small house in Notting Hill before retiring personally to the Norfolk coast for a period of recuperation. In his absence, Lady Ella prays devoutly that the sea air will enable him to recover his senses but she finds him adamant as ever when he rejoins her. In the meantime, Lady Sunderbund's discipleship has progressed to the stage of planning a vast temple and designs for costumes which would surround Scrope with an atmosphere of splendour—the very reverse of the simple appearance he wishes to present as the essence of the New Faith. In a tearful interview she is told that she has prepared for him nothing but a gorgeous toy which he feels bound to reject, although by doing so he recognizes that his means must now remain impoverished. On his way back to Notting Hill he encounters Eleanor in a park where she is waiting to rendezvous with Riverton, a young officer whom she has met at Cambridge and with whom she has fallen in love.

Doubting the wisdom of his daughter becoming engaged to a fiancé who may well be lost at the Front, Scrope nevertheless gives the couple his blessing. He goes on to explain fully to his wife and family the full meaning of his conversion which, in effect, constitutes his Third Vision. Their understanding and acceptance bring the tale to its close.

The book is the second of the three which mark the brief 'religious' period through which Wells passed towards the end of the First World War, the others being the non-fictional *God The Invisible King* (1917) and the novel, *The Undying Fire*. Excepting the final book, Wells came to regret his dalliance in this area. In his autobiography he declared that his 'deistic phrasing' made no concessions to doctrinal Christianity. He regarded his religiosity as artificial and 'a flaming heresy' and considered himself as coming no nearer to Christianity than Manicheism. Referring to this period of 'terminological disingenuousness' he was to say: 'I wish, not so much for my own sake as for the sake of my more faithful readers, that I had never fallen into it; it confused and misled many of them and introduced a barren detour into my research for an effective direction for human affairs'. *The Soul of a Bishop*, 1917

SCROPE, ELEANOR : The eldest daughter of Edward and an ardent supporter of his new Vision of Faith. Dark-complexioned as her mother, but less slender, she has fine eyes and a broad brow. Hockey and tennis have developed her shoulders so that her build has become sturdy. She is studying at Newnham College, Cambridge, and has successfully completed the first part of the Moral Science Tripos at the time of her father's First Vision. Her reaction to Scrope's extraordinary confirmation sermon is characteristic: 'Daddy . . . the things you said and did that afternoon were the noblest you ever did in your life. I wish I had been there . . . It was like light and order coming into a hopeless dark muddle. What you said was like what we have been trying to think—I mean all of us young people. Suddenly it was all clear.'

When her father is agonizing over the family's reduced circumstances, she confronts him with her romance with Riverton, declaring herself ready to be hurt if the young man becomes a war casualty. The end of the story shows her anticipating a scholarship to the London School of Economics. *The Soul of a Bishop*, 1917

SCROPE, LADY ELLA : Wife of Edward and a daughter of the Fifth Earl of Birkenholme. She is a tall, dignified woman, but given to a certain cold reserve—even 'stoniness'. On her husband's appointment to the diocese of Princhester, she seems to him to change markedly. She appears 'stiller and more restrained; a certain faint arrogance, a touch of the "ruling class" manner which has marked her character in the past disappears. Prin-

216

chester has made her think more deeply and 'put a new and subtler quality into her beauty'. Lady Ella is profoundly distressed by Scrope's secession from the Church and for a time her attitude to the Bishop is noticeably chilling. She accepts the family's removal to Notting Hill, in London, resentfully but with resignation. Later, after Scrope's explanation of his position to his daughters, she softens towards him, and her own allegiance to the Church becomes doubtful. This change in her demeanour is due in no small measure to Scrope's break with Lady Sunderbund. *The Soul of a Bishop*, 1917

SCROPE, OTHER DAUGHTERS : The four younger sisters of Eleanor —namely, Clementina, Miriam, Daphne and Phoebe. They play only a small part in the tale, and no real physical descriptions are given. None seem to be affected by the same doubts as Eleanor before their father's secession from the Church. Clementina had been due to join her elder sister at Newnham, but this intention has to be shelved after Scrope's resignation. Instead, there are plans for her to study at London University, while the three younger girls are sent to Notting Hill High School. Clementina, Miriam and Daphne all engage in voluntary war work by providing comforts for the wounded. Scrope finds the youngest, Phoebe, the most like Eleanor. All four accept their father's new interpretation of the Kingdom of God once he has fully made it clear. *The Soul of a Bishop*, 1917

SEA LADY, THE : The erstwhile mermaid who comes to land in search of a lover. She is first encountered in the sea off Folkestone, on the South Coast, where she simulates the act of drowning. Her cries for help attract the attention of Adeline Glendower who is visiting her friends, the Buntings. She is 'rescued' by a Bunting son and brought ashore, where she reveals her disinclination to return to her natural habitat. Mrs. Bunting insists that the mermaid stays with the family and arranges for a wheelchair and a discreet maid to be put at her disposal. She virtually accepts her as a third daughter until she discovers the true reason for her leaving the sea.

Unbeknown to her hosts, who have given her the name Miss Waters, she is in search of Harry Chatteris, whom she has seen on the shore and for whom she has developed an infatuation. Chatteris is acquainted with the Buntings, being a prospective parliamentary candidate for the local constituency. He is a physically attractive and engaging man whose earlier career has not been without blemish. He is also the fiancé of Adeline Glendower, who comes to regret that she ever responded to the mermaid's appeal for assistance.

Once he has met Miss Waters, Chatteris succumbs to her limpid appeal, unaware of her ability to put the object of her desire under a spell. As a result, his engagement with Adeline Glendower is now at risk, and the girl confides in Mrs. Bunting that her guest is attempting to entice her fiancé away. The mermaid has already confessed her designs to Melville, another friend of the Buntings who is also associated with Chatteris. She tells him that there are better dreams in existence than those merely entertained by men, and her confidant is shocked to realize how ruthless she can be in achieving her ends. It is clear to Mrs. Bunting that she can no longer be entertained in the family home. Arrangements are therefore made for her to take up residence with her maid in a nearby hotel.

Having abandoned her original excuse for staying ashore— that of wishing to find a soul—the Sea Lady continues to pursue Chatteris, who is now troubled by his disloyalty to Adeline. Although a plain girl in physical terms, Miss Glendower has given him her loyal support and considerable political and campaigning help in the constituency. In recognition of this, he decides after a discussion with Melville that the mermaid is not for him. No sooner has he reached this conclusion, than her magical appeal draws him to her in the night. He carries her in his arms to the beach in the knowledge that he is going to his death.

Swimming out with her until she is able to pull him down, he demonstrates the price a mere mortal may have to pay at the behest of an immortal.

Wells sub-titled the tale 'A Tissue of Moonshine', and it is clear that he intended it to be taken very lightly. It contains few of the elements of social criticism which are usually to be found in his stories and can be regarded more as a simple fable. He had just begun to live below Folkestone at the time of writing, and almost the entire action of the story is set in that town. The first American edition of the book was illustrated by Lewis Baumer. *The Sea Lady*, 1902

SELENITES, THE : The underground lunar civilization discovered by Cavor and Bedford in *The First Men in the Moon*. A highly-organized, but stratified society, many of the workers being 'shaped' by physical means for the tasks they are ordained to perform (the human science of ergonomics in reverse—tailoring the worker to fit the job as opposed to the contrary process). Thus selenite heralds, instead of blowing trumpets, are graced with drawn-out fluted lips. Knowledge is stored in the head rather than in books, the vastest brain-case of all belonging to the Grand Lunar, and requiring many helpers to support it.

Although basically humanoid in appearance, selenites tend to give the impression of insects reared up on their hind-legs. They are devoid of noses and ears. As a chief source of food they herd mooncalves, huge white, slug-like beasts some two hundred feet long and eighty feet in girth. *The First Men in the Moon,* 1901

SEMPACK : The 'Utopographer in the Garden' and the dominant character in the early part of *Meanwhile.* He is large, gawky, with a face 'that ought to be weeded'. His bones appear to his hostess, Mrs. Rylands, to 'run positively wild under his skin as he talked'. He is a renowned writer and dreamer for the future, advancing the Wellsian argument in his guise as a Thinker for Mankind; but he is reluctant to take an active part in the crisis which is about to overtake Britain and is criticized for his inertia. Among his critics are Philip Rylands and Lady Catherine Fossingdean, the latter attracting him to indulge in some brief love-making. He attempts to defend Philip's indiscretion with Puppy Clarges, but fails to convince his distraught hostess. Later he receives a visit from Philip after he has been knocked down by a bus, and again when he is recuperating at his home in Dorset. *Meanwhile,* 1927

SEYFFERT, BELINDA : The companion of V. V. Grammont during the latter's visit to England, and an effusive interrupter of conversations. Also an American, she is somewhat older than V.V., less attractive and noticeably stout. Her manner of speaking, and her constant interruptions, prove too much for Dr. Martineau, who notifies Sir Richmond Hardy that if he is obliged to spend much longer in her company he will be decidedly rude to her. However, she is not without sensitivity, and consigns herself sufficiently to the background to allow V.V. and Hardy to spend a generous part of their time together alone. *The Secret Places of the Heart,* 1922

SHALFORD, EDWIN : The proprietor of the Folkestone Drapery Bazaar who accepts Kipps as an apprentice when the boy is fourteen. A small, bad-tempered but energetic man, he has a long, shiny bald head, a pointed aquiline nose and a neat beard. His business is one of the largest in Folkestone and he is quick to extol to Kipps the virtues of the 'system' he has personally developed. A thorough-going martinet, he bullies his staff continuously, being particularly harsh with the apprentices. He also affects an idiosyncratic manner of speech, omitting all articles and pronouns, and abbreviating words wherever possible. Never appreciative of Kipps, he dismisses him when, having completed his apprenticeship, the young man stays out all night in the company of the playwright Chitterlow. *Kipps*, 1905

SHOESMITH : A fellow student of Remington at City Merchants School where they embark on a new style of magazine, a venture much influenced by another boy, Cossington, later to become a press baron in the Northcliffe style. Remington and Shoesmith become acquainted again in adult life, when the latter becomes a dedicated, but sometimes cautious, supporter of Remington's political ideas. His main contribution to the story, however, is his offer to marry Isabel Rivers as a means of alleviating the scandal erupting around her affair with Remington. While first accepting him, and admiring the characteristic generosity of his act, she comes to realize the hopelessness of such a solution and contemplates suicide. In the outcome, she elopes with Remington four days before the proposed marriage, abandoning Shoesmith to the derision of society. *The New Machiavelli*, 1911

SKELMERSDALE, MILLY : Briefly the mistress of William Benham when he first comes to London after graduating from Trinity College, Cambridge. She is a young and pretty widow, black-haired, with a mobile mouth, hazel eyes, and 'a pathetic history'. Benham first meets her at the home of a friend, where he is intrigued by her manifest lack of interest in paintings. Her love of music is a different matter, and she entices him to her flat to hear her play an antique Clementi piano, and to be seduced. It is Benham's introduction to love-making, which he finds 'very wonderful and delicious', but he also regards the affair as 'shabby and underhand'. Milly charms him with her subtlety and tenderness; however, she disconcerts him by her lapses into vulgarity and by having some very odd friends. Although she clearly loves him, he resolves to end the relationship, aware that his mother is becoming suspicious and that his own peace of mind is in jeopardy. *The Research Magnificent*, 1915

SKELMERSDALE, MR. : A young village grocer who, falling asleep on Aldington Knoll, in Kent, awakes in a genuine Fairyland. Among other enchantments, which include being plied with gold by elves, he is beguiled by a fairy girl who begs him not to leave; but only on his return via a swamp to the real world does he realize the extent of his feelings for her. Evidence that he has not simply dreamed the whole episode is provided by the time factor —he has been gone some three weeks. The experience affects his attitude towards his fiancée and their engagement is broken, leaving him to moon about the knoll in the unrealized hope that he might again find entrance to the magic realm. 'Mr. Skelmersdale in Fairyland', 1901

SKINNER, ALFRED NEWTON : A notably unwashed individual to whom Bensington delegates the supervision of the 'Boomfood' farm where the wonder-drug is put to experimental use. A big-faced man, graced by the twin defects of a squint and lisp, he affects clothing noteworthy for 'a manifest shortage of buttons'. When his wife escapes from the giant wasps and rats infesting the farm at Hickleybrow, Skinner's fate remains undisclosed, although it is hinted that he has probably fallen victim to one or other of the menaces. *The Food of the Gods*, 1904

SKINNER, MRS. : Wife of the manager of the Hickleybrow experimental farm who, in her flight, carries off a jar of the growth-inducing drug 'Herakleophorbia', later to be fed to her grandson. A tiny, dirty old woman, whose nose obscures the greater part of her face, she seeks refuge with her daughter, Mrs. Caddles, at the village of Cheasing Eyebright, where the young Caddles is in due course to become the local giant. *The Food of the Gods*, 1904

SLAUGHTER, OLIVE : A young girl courted by Arnold Blettsworthy while he is at Oxford. Slender, fair-haired, with 'amethystine' eyes, she is more given to kissing than intelligent conversation. The pair frequently ride out on their bicycles to quiet parts of the adjoining countryside where they can expect to be undisturbed. Their engagement ends when Blettsworthy surprises Olive, *déshabillé*, in the arms of his partner, Lyulph Graves. Later she is reported to have married a local pork butcher by whom she has many children. *Mr. Blettsworthy on Rampole Island*, 1928

SMALLWAYS, BERT : The chief survivor of a series of potentially disastrous events in *The War in the Air*. Born the son of a former Kentish coachman, he displays early a lively mind, capable of an education which it fails to receive—in essence, he is a Wellsian 'little man'. As a youth he is much taken to bicycling, graduating later to a motor-cycle which eventually catches fire during a ride with his sweetheart Edna. After a series of odd jobs, he leaves the home of his brother Tom to take up residence, and work with Grubb, who 'hired out quite the dirtiest and unsafest bicycles in the whole South of England and conducted the subsequent discussions with astonishing verve'. When the business fails, he contemplates a singing act with Grubb, but finds himself accidentally in sole control of Butteridge's balloon, carrying the secret plans of the latter's successful flying machine across the Channel.

Shot down over the German airfield from which the invasion of North America is about to be launched, he is initially mistaken for Butteridge and taken aboard the flagship of Prince Karl Albert. Placed in the charge of the young Luft-lieutenant Kurt, he is obliged to confess his true identity to the prince's secretary, which puts an end to his preferential treatment.

He witnesses a great sea battle between German and American warships in the Atlantic, and the capitulation of New York after selective strategic bombing. However, the ordinary populace of the city rebel against their authorities' surrender and raid the invaders' airships, precipitating an act of reprisal which reduces Broadway to ruins. During an attack by the defenders' flying-machines, the flagship's engines are shot away, and it drifts before gale-force winds to the Arctic fringes of Canada. Smallways, who is now regarded as no more than 'ballast', justifies his continuing presence on board by joining Kurt's repair team.

Eventually Karl Albert is rejoined by the remainder of his fleet, to engage in a disastrous conflict with the superior air-force of the Chinese–Japanese alliance which has attacked all the original combatants simultaneously. His flag-ship is destroyed, although he and one other officer survive the crash at the brink of the Niagara Falls. Smallways himself, having been left behind, watches the conflict from Goat Island, where he is later joined by the prince and his underling. But whereas he had hoped that they might now accept him as a comrade in adversity, they continue to adopt the same autocratic manner towards him. As a result, he shoots the prince, largely in self-defence, and the other survivor is drowned in the Falls in an effort to escape.

Smallways leaves the island by means of a repaired Asian aircraft, and finds his way eventually to the U.S. President to whom he delivers a copy he has made of Butteridge's secret design. He is appalled to hear that the whole world is now at war, with internal as well as international strife encompassing the globe. In the years to come there will be famine, followed by the plague, before a unified world state can be won. In the meantime, Smallways finds his way back by a devious route to England, to be reunited with Edna and his brother Tom.

The novel is a noted forecast of civilian bombing and other repercussions of modern warfare. In its ultimate forecast of a unified world, it illustrates the direction in which Wells's mind was turning during his second decade as a writer. *The War in the Air*, 1908

SMALLWAYS, TOM : The elder brother of Bert in *The War in the Air*, with whom the novel both opens and closes. A greengrocer by trade, and a dubious observer of progress. He admires his brother's adventurous inclinations, but his wife Jessica is more cautious. He survives the war and is encountered by Bert at the end of the story. The epilogue sees him thirty years on, discussing the conflict and its causes with his young nephew. *The War in the Air*, 1908

SMITH, MRS. HARRY (I) : See 'Marcus, Hetty'.

SMITH, MRS. HARRY (II) : See 'Kimpton, Milly'.

SMITH, ERNEST : The elder brother of Harry and some twelve years his senior. He has already left home to work at a garage in London and chauffeur hired cars before Harry is old enough to appraise him. He returns to Cherry Gardens for his father's funeral and evicts John Julip from the house when the latter suggests that he now live with his widowed sister. Ernest has a low opinion of his uncle, judging correctly that Julip would be more a burden than a help to Martha Smith. Later, when hired to drive a publisher, he is surprised to find his sister Fanny accompanying him. She writes to Ernest, giving her address, which prompts Harry to visit her. Ernest is killed at the Front a few weeks before the end of the First World War. *The Dream*, 1924

SMITH, FANNY : Harry's eldest sister who shocks her parents by eloping with a married man. Five years older than Harry, she is a 'conspicuously lovely' girl whose eyes can be alternatively sky-blue or dark with anger or excitement so that they seem almost black. She has a winning smile and clear appealing laughter, but she is acutely aware of her ignorance. Developing a passion for knowledge, she begins to read voraciously and is concerned that Harry also should learn as much as he can. Defeating her mother's intention to send her into service, she finds work as book-keeper to a pork-butcher, but she becomes increasingly dissatisfied with her life at home. Finally she disappears, and her family learns that she is allowing herself to be kept by—it is later revealed—Newberry, a director of the publishing house where Fanny is instrumental in securing Harry employment once they have been re-united in London.

She enjoys a life of some luxury under Newberry's patronage; she is very obviously devoted to him. There are many indications that he will marry her when he is eventually free. In the meantime she sees Harry regularly, delighted by his rapid progress in his career. She warms to his wife Hetty and is horrified by her subsequent infidelity; but Harry has deliberately exaggerated the extent of Hetty's lapse. Her feelings towards his second wife Milly are significantly cooler, but she recognizes her virtues. When Hetty is attempting to escape from Sumner, Fanny helps by conveying her messages to Harry. *The Dream*, 1924

SMITH, HARRY MORTIMER (SARNAC) : A publishing executive whose life in the early part of the twentieth century is experienced in a dream by a neuro-physiologist living two thousand years in the future. At the opening of the story the dreamer, Sarnac, suffering from overwork, is holidaying in the mountains with his lover, Sunray. They become friendly with four other holiday-makers (described in an earlier entry as 'Sarnac's listeners') and together they explore the ruins of a small town and a railway tunnel which date from the 'Age of Confusion'—our own time. The town's inhabitants died in a poison-gas attack which had the effect of mummifying many of their bodies; the ruins and corpses have been preserved as an eerie monument to the last war in human history. During their exploration Sarnac stumbles and cuts his hand. That night in the local guest-house he dreams feverishly of gas warfare and entombed men. The following afternoon he falls asleep again, to dream the entire life-history of Harry Mortimer Smith. Sarnac's account of his dream on awakening, with occasional comments from the listeners, occupies the remainder, and major part, of the novel.

Smith is born in the 'urban district' of Cherry Gardens, some two miles from the sea in Kent. He is the youngest surviving child of the family, having a much older brother, Ernest, and two sisters, Fanny and Prudence, the last playing little part in the narrative. Two further siblings have died in infancy. His earliest memories centre around his father's dingy shop and the dark basement kitchen where he spends much of his time. His education is meagre (Sarnac digresses with an explanation of the prevailing educational system, and he frequently punctuates Harry's tale with descriptions of the social *mores* and institutions of the era).

As a boy, Harry is often sent to fetch fruit and vegetables from the estate of Lord Bramble, the employer of his uncle, John Julip, who works as a gardener. These are later sold in his father's shop, but the lad is unaware that they are stolen until he is questioned on one occasion by Lord Bramble's butler and Julip is dismissed. As a result, the family fortunes decline even further, culminating in Mortimer Smith's accidental death. In the meantime Fanny has run off, to be kept by a publisher in London, while Ernest also has moved to the capital as a garage hand and driver. He refuses to allow Julip to sponge off his widowed mother.

Martha Smith, Prudence and Harry find accommodation at Matilda Good's boarding-house in Pimlico, an area in London adjoining Westminster. Matilda and Martha are friends of old, and in return for help in the management of the house, Martha and her children live rent-free. Problems arise when Martha's curiosity and unyielding sense of propriety prompt her to disapprove of some of the lodgers, but Matilda overrules her objections. The widow is similarly unbending in forbidding Harry to visit Fanny when Ernest discovers her whereabouts. Harry disobeys his mother openly and often calls to see his sister. He has found work, first as an errand-boy, and later as a chemist's assistant. Fanny helps to obtain him a post with the publishers,

Crane & Newberry, where her lover is a director. There his editorial flair and shrewd appraisal of graphics earn him rapid promotion.

Harry's mother dies when he is sixteen, and two years later the First World War begins. Enlisted, and about to leave for France, he spends a day at Cherry Gardens, for a final walk on the Downs which he crossed many times with his father. He meets Hetty Marcus, a farmer's daughter, who is about to join the Women's Auxiliary Army Corps; she is indulging in a comparable flight of nostalgia. They pass the afternoon together and, perhaps because of their respective moods and the uncertainty of the future, they fall in love. Harry is wounded in the arm during the war, he and Hetty marrying during his brief spell of sick leave. On demobilization he learns she is pregnant, but the estimated date of the child's birth proves he cannot be the father.

Hetty confesses that she was seduced for a single night by an officer, Sumner, and begs forgiveness. But Harry can see no way of accepting her betrayal; he divorces her, subsequently marrying Milly Kimpton, with whom he had previously been friendly at Crane & Newberry. She makes a loyal and solicitous wife, but fails to give him the companionship he enjoyed with Hetty. Because of his experience with Hetty, it is important to Smith that Milly should have a child, and in due course she bears him a son. They take a house in London close to Regent's Park, where, some two years after their parting, Harry again encounters Hetty. In the interval she has felt obliged to wed Sumner, only to become desperately unhappy. Her husband gambles and drinks excessively; he is also involved in the blackmail of bookmakers. Reduced to poverty, she appeals to Harry to help her make a fresh start in Canada.

Smith realizes that he still loves his former wife, regretting his earlier harsh treatment of her. He agrees to buy her new clothes and assist in her flight from Sumner. The plan is successful, with Fanny acting as an intermediary. On the day before she is due to embark at Liverpool, Hetty and Smith return to the Downs where they first met. She asks him to go with her to Canada, to be told that he wishes it so; but his work and loyalty to Milly are now his overriding concern. On the journey back to London Hetty is recognized by an acquaintance of Sumner, a chance event which is later to have fatal consequences. Three days out, she cables Harry from the ship to say that all has gone well.

In a street close to his office Smith is confronted by Sumner and the man encountered on the train, who identifies him. When they then call at Crane & Newberry, Harry sees Sumner alone, refusing to reveal Hetty's whereabouts and ignoring the other's threats. The following week, Sumner again waylays him in the street and, although drunk, shoots him several times before running off. There are no witnesses, so that Harry is able to convince the police that the gun is his own and that it was triggered accidentally. Taken home, he dies while imagining that Hetty is leaning over him—to awaken as Sarnac, with Hetty replaced by Sunray.

At the conclusion of the tale the master of the guest-house remarks that it was less a dream than a genuine memory of a former life. Starlight agrees : 'What do we know of the stuff of memory that lies on the other side of matter? What do we know of the relations of consciousness to matter and energy? ... Science increases and the power of man grows, but only inside the limits of life's conditions. We may conquer space and time, but we shall never conquer the mystery of what we are, and why we can be matter that feels and wills ... Life and death alike are within the crystal sphere that limits us for ever ... Maybe life from its very beginning has been spinning threads and webs of memories about us. Some day we may learn to gather in that forgotten gossamer, we may learn to weave its strands together again, until the whole past is restored to us and life becomes one. Then perhaps the crystal sphere will break. And however that may be, and however these things may be explained, I can well believe without any miracles that Sarnac has touched down to the real memory of a human life that lived and suffered two thousand years ago.'

Wells regarded the story as 'social criticism from a new angle', an examination of the waste and injustice of his own day as it might be viewed in an enlightened future perspective. As in *Tono Bungay*, his description of work in a chemist's shop is drawn from his own early experience as a pharmaceutical assistant at Midhurst, in Sussex. *The Dream*, 1924

SMITH, MARTHA : The wife of Mortimer and mother of Harry. Originally a good-looking woman, of regular features, she wears an expression which becomes increasingly one of resentment as she ages prematurely. Narrow-minded in the extreme, she adopts an inflexible attitude towards her daughter Fanny's elopement, later forbidding Harry to see his sister when Fanny's address is known. After her husband's death she moves her family to Matilda Good's boarding-house in London. There her bigotry is in further evidence when she spies on Matilda's lodgers, suspecting an apparent husband and wife—probably rightly—of being unmarried, at least to each other. Embittered by her children's failure to live up to her rigid and implacable standards, she loses hold of life and dies of pneumonia when Harry is sixteen. *The Dream*, 1924

SMITH, MORTIMER : The father of Harry, and a greengrocer at Cherry Gardens where his family live above and beneath his shop. A rather clumsy man, with large mild eyes, greatly magnified by spectacles which he has bought at random from a pawnbroker. He treats young Harry in a kindly manner and appears to favour him above his other three children. He takes the boy out for long walks on the Downs, discussing the mysteries of Nature and the habits of animals : 'Every sin we 'as to answer for, great or small. But an animal don't 'ave to answer. It's innocent. You *'it* it or else you leave it be . . . Except for dogs and some *old* cats . . . I've known some *sinful* cats, 'Arry.'

Smith's business is hardly a success, and he resorts to selling stolen produce provided by his brother-in-law Julip from Lord Bramble's estate. After Julip's dismissal the pair turn to drink, while the shop becomes neglected. Smith's depression is not improved by Fanny's elopement; three weeks after her disappearance he is killed by a motor-car when he inadvertently steps off the pavement without looking. *The Dream*, 1924

SMITHERS, MR. : A fellow student of Lewisham at the Normal School of Science. Square-headed and characterized by his hard grey eyes, he is an avowed disbeliever in the spirits of the dead, missing few opportunities to taunt the ageing Lagune who is a known spiritualist. Eventually Lagune invites him to a séance as a test of his scepticism. Accompanied by Lewisham he succeeds in exposing the medium as a fraud, much to Lagune's consternation—and also to that of Lewisham, who discovers that the trickster is the step-father of his first love, Ethel Henderson. *Love and Mr. Lewisham*, 1900

SPINK, LUCINDA : The most prominent of Theodore Bulpington's many aunts, and the one who oversees his adolescent progress in London. Noted for her lack of humour, she is a thin and spindly spinster whose social conscience has promoted her to the front rank of the Fabian Society and to an elected seat on the London County Council. Theodore's presence is permanently required for Sunday tea at her home in Church Row, Hampstead (a street where Wells himself once lived), and there she is given to harangues on his apparent lack of direction in life. She demands an account of his reading habits and other aspects of his leisure time. On odd occasions she reminds Theodore of his mother, but Lucinda has little of Clorinda Bulpington's more placid and sensuous appeal. *The Bulpington of Blup,* 1932

STANLEY, ANN VERONICA : The youngest daughter of an authoritarian and uncommunicative solicitor, she is twenty-one when the story opens and studying biology at Tredgold Women's College. Beneath black hair, her facial features are particularly subtle and fine, her lips forming an expression somewhere between contentment and a hint of a smile. An archetype of the new Wellsian woman, she is 'vehemently impatient' to pursue the fullness of life and 'wildly discontented' with the encumbering restrictions placed on her freedom by her father with the support of her aunt. These range from his refusal to allow her to frequent the social events of her choosing—particularly invitations from her friends, the Widgetts—to the outright prohibition of her attending Imperial College where she would benefit from the progressive science teaching of the renowned, if Godless, Russell.

Following a major crisis, during which she finds herself more or less a captive in her own home, she leaves Morningside Park to take lodgings in London. In this she is helped by a loan from Ramage, a man of business with whom she enjoys, from her point of view, a close but uncomplicated friendship. Ignoring parental pleas for her immediate return, she enrols at Imperial College and passes her leisure hours in the socialist/bohemian milieu, centred around Mr. Goopes, absorbing the prevailing Fabian debates, and indulging in informal and increasingly intimate dinners with Ramage. Her growing interest in Capes, her biology demonstrator, is one more complication in her new free way of life.

Tiring of incessant talk, she determines to throw herself behind the feminist cause by means of positive action; and while not entirely convinced that the acquisition of the vote alone will significantly improve a woman's lot, she takes part in a suffragette raid on the House of Commons at the instigation of Kitty Brett and is consequently sentenced to a month's imprisonment. In the deprivation of her cell she reconsiders her stance for living and the problems it has engendered. Having sent back half of Ramage's loan after a misjudged attempt on his part to seduce her, she has angrily burnt the money which he had promptly returned. Left with no alternative finance, she decides to live again at home, effecting what compromises she can with her father. She also decides, on the assumption that her feelings for Capes are unrequited, to allow herself to become engaged to Manning, an egotistical civil servant and the author of dreadful verse.

While Stanley allows her to continue at Imperial, her constant proximity to Capes convinces her of the impossibility of a marriage with Manning who seems to desire no more than to place her on a pedestal. Warm-blooded by nature, a fact which shocks her ascetic friend Miss Minniver, she declares her love for Capes and he, after some soul-searching, reciprocates. Since he is already married, but separated, they have no other choice but to elope, putting an end to his teaching career. Four years later, he has achieved success as a playwright and Ann Veronica is expecting their first child. While it is not specifically stated, it appears they have become legally married in the interval. Her story ends in a reconciliation with her father and aunt.

Ann Veronica has come to be regarded as perhaps the most alive of all Wells's feminine creations, and it is known that much of her personality was drawn from life. Her desire to be an equal partner in marriage in place of a passive adornment is a clear reflection of the rôle which Wells had begun to champion on behalf of the opposite sex. His open advocacy of such freedom for women was met by a hostile reception in many areas of the Establishment. The novel was banned from libraries and efforts were made to hound Wells himself from literary and social life, although he found allies in such diverse characters as Bernard Shaw and G. K. Chesterton. In spite of, or possibly because of, the furore, the book sold well. The story was adapted for the stage by Ronald Gow, and directed by Peter Ashmore at the Piccadilly Theatre, London, in 1949. *Ann Veronica*, 1909

STANLEY, MOLLIE : The sister of Ann Veronica's father, who lives with them both at Morningside Park. In earlier life she was engaged to a clerk in holy orders, but his stipend prohibited marriage at the time and he died before it could be improved. On the death of her sister-in-law she determines to become a second mother to her niece. Nevertheless, she falls almost entirely under the domination of her brother, and only after some hesitation can she go behind his back to help Ann Veronica in small ways after the latter's flight to London. At the end of the novel she, in company with Mr. Stanley, acquiesces in the union between Ann Veronica and Capes. While her old-fashioned up-bringing and sense of dignity still compel her to what she regards as a proper air of rectitude, she is impressed by the quality of the Capes's home and their obvious success, although she greets the news of Ann Veronica's pregnancy in an air of ambivalence. *Ann Veronica*, 1909

STANLEY, PETER : A solicitor specializing in company business and the father of Ann Veronica. Fifty-three years of age, he is thin, neuralgic, worried-looking and hard-mouthed. A widower with five adult children, he is cared for by his unmarried sister, Mollie, and spends much of his leisure time in the practice of microscopic petrography, becoming a renowned amateur maker of rock samples. Puritanical by nature, he is keenly aware of the proprieties of an upper middle-class existence, and displays an unyielding autocratic attitude towards Ann Veronica who is his youngest child. An older daughter, Alice, married against his will, an action which has perhaps hardened him further. His refusal to allow Ann Veronica to attend an Art Students' Ball brings to a head a crisis which results in her taking a room for herself in London.

His written appeals to her to return home prove of little avail, and not until she has spent a month in prison, as a consequence of suffragette activities, does she comply with his wishes. Even then the peace is short-lived, for she is soon to elope with her biology demonstrator, Capes. Some four years are to elapse before Stanley sees her again, when with his sister he accepts a dinner invitation after a chance encounter with Capes at a meeting of the Royal Society. Impressed by the character and ability of his son-in-law, whom he has not met before, he acquiesces in the union with cautious grace. *Ann Veronica*, 1909

STEENHOLD : A wealthy supporter of Rud Whitlow whom he first meets at Camford University. Half American in origin, he is attracted by Rud's advocacy of a common revolutionary movement in Britain and the U.S.A. He makes one of his flats available as a meeting place for the nucleus of the Ruddite Group. Having once been a heavy drinker, he later turns to a diet of carrots and water. He has also, briefly, been a member of Lord Bohun's Popular Socialist Party, but left because of its blatant anti-Semitism. Along with Bodisham and Chiffan, he becomes one of Whitlow's most trusted intimates, joining the Council of the Party of Common-Sense. He is killed by a bomb while defending Rud's headquarters in the Netherlands during an attempted seizure of power by Marshal Reedly, the commander of the Allied armies during the final world war. *The Holy Terror*, 1939

STRATTON, STEPHEN : The narrator of an autobiography which he addresses to his son. He, in turn, is the son of the Rector of Burnmore, in Surrey; and spends much of his youth visiting the Christian family at Burnmore House (a factual landmark). He and Lady Mary Christian become the 'Passionate Friends' of the title; but she refuses to marry him because of his lack of means. On her marriage to the wealthy financier Justin, Stratton is disconsolate, and, at the age of twenty-one, leaves for South Africa to fight in the Boer War. He sees distinguished service in that conflict, being twice mentioned in despatches, and returns to England after some four years' absence. In the meantime his father has inherited land and retired.

Stratton begins to move more in Establishment circles. He talks with the Prime Minister, Evesham (who plays a larger rôle in *The New Machiavelli*), and inevitably he again encounters Lady Mary. They begin an affair which is soon discovered by Justin, whose immediate reaction is to take his wife off to Ireland. Stratton eventually locates their whereabouts, but they return before he reaches them. Back in London he is assaulted by Philip Christian and later summoned to the home of Lady Mary's cousin, Lord Tarvrille. There he is told of Justin's intention to ruin him unless he agrees to go abroad.

The next few years he spends travelling in Europe, the Orient and finally the United States, where he goes into partnership with a rich young American, Gidding. They plan an ambitious publishing venture to make available the world's classics of science and philosophy in popular and cheap editions, the purpose being to further the idea of a world state. Much of Stratton's reminiscences of his travels is laced with his thoughts on this subject.

Earlier on a return visit to Europe, and while staying with his cousin, the Fürstin Letzlingen, in Germany, he renews an acquaintanceship with Rachel More whom he had first met when she was seventeen. Her matured intelligence attracts him, and he responds to the affection which she continues to hold for him. They marry and in due course raise three children. In 1909 he receives an unexpected letter from Lady Mary who, having heard of his marriage, assumes that it is now safe for them to correspond, although Rachel is less than enthusiastic at the prospect.

Two years later the former lovers are reunited by chance in the Swiss Alps, a meeting which is maliciously reported to Justin by Lady Mary's companion, Stella Summersley Satchel. Unbeknown to Stratton, Lady Mary insists on switching hotel bedrooms with Miss Satchel so that she can be closer to him; and although this is no more than a gesture of friendship, it prompts her husband to begin divorce proceedings. The couple meet for a final time in London, when Lady Mary, distressed by the upset their liaison has caused both their families, announces that she will spend the rest of her life in seclusion. In the event, she commits suicide immediately afterwards, leaving Justin and Stratton with the realization that between them they have killed her.

The story reflects Wells's continuing preoccupation with the problems of marriage which he entertained during that period and which he had already explored in *The New Machiavelli* and *Marriage*. He was to pursue it further in the following year with *The Wife of Sir Isaac Harman* before the First World War directed his attention elsewhere. It is also a further examination of the destructive nature of sexual jealousy, emphasized by Justin's willingness to allow his marriage to go unconsummated until he learns of his wife's love for Stratton. *The Passionate Friends*, 1913

STUART, NETTIE : Daughter of a head gardener and early sweetheart of Leadford, their respective mothers being second cousins. Dark-haired and dark-eyed, she has an air about her of quiet gravity which extends even to her smiles. She first becomes close to Leadford while they are both in their late teens, but she comes to realize that they have few tastes and ideas in common. She is puzzled by his letters which 'after one or two genuinely intended displays of perfervid tenderness, broke out towards theology, sociology, and the cosmos in turgid and startling expressions'.

She later succumbs to the advances of Edward Verrall, the son of a local landowner, with whom she elopes although there is little intention of his marrying her. After the comet's passing she confesses to Leadford that she is in love with both him and Verrall, but allows herself to be persuaded to remain with the latter. For a period she and Leadford correspond, eventually becoming lovers at the beginning of the fourth year of the new era when, in the age of enlightenment, their relationship is freely accepted by Verrall and Leadford's wife, Anna. *In The Days of the Comet*, 1906

STUBLAND, ARTHUR : The father of Peter whose last-minute alteration to his will—to name four guardians—complicates the early education of his son and Joan. Born into a Quaker family of West-of-England stock, he spent much of his early life in questioning the many prohibitions of his family's faith. His emancipation in this respect was greatly assisted by his elder sister, Phyllis, who 'brightened' his Sunday afternoons. Educated at Cambridge, he elected to study Art, with the intention of becoming an architect. In the event, the only house he ever designs is the home built for himself and his wife Dolly.

Arthur experiences some difficulty in assimiliating Dolly's mental processes, particularly when she queries the purposes of their respective aims. This dichotomy of interests leads him to indulge in a brief affair—a liaison which is met by a conventional reaction on Dolly's part. On their reconciliation, he takes her to Capri, where both are drowned; but before leaving he names three further guardians for Joan and Peter in addition to Oswald Sydenham : his sisters, Phyllis and Phoebe, and Lady Charlotte Sydenham. *Joan and Peter*, 1918

STUBLAND, DOLLY : The wife of Arthur and a woman whose conclusion that she is not contributing enough to life irritates her husband. The daughter of a country vicar, she remains at home to care for her widowed father while her two brothers pursue their education at Oxford; although later she spends a year at the Royal College of Science and while there first meets Arthur. At the time she is an attractive, dark-eyed 'leggy' girl of a somewhat sceptical nature. Even during their honeymoon, on a tour of various parts of the Continent, she begins to puzzle Arthur by her expressed doubts as to whether they should be wasting their time sightseeing when there was important work to be done at home.

Always fond of her cousin, Oswald Sydenham, she is strongly tempted to elope with him to Africa after she learns of Arthur's affair. She eventually declines his offer when Arthur assures her that his extra-marital dalliance is over. It is during their second honeymoon on Capri that their boat is capsized. For a while she swims resolutely in an effort to reach the shore, thus surviving her husband, but she is finally overcome. The disclosure some time later by witnesses that she outlived Arthur brings her own will into force, naming Oswald sole guardian of Joan and Peter.
Joan and Peter, 1918

STUBLAND FRIENDS : Acquaintances of Joan and Peter who play small but often significant rôles in their story. Among them is Winterbaum, a dark-eyed, fuzzy-haired youth whom they both meet at their first school and whom Peter fights for the favours of Joan. They meet again as undergraduates at Cambridge, and Winterbaum—now with a moustache—later escorts Joan to various London nightclubs. He is killed early in the First World War.

Another is Wilmington, who professes unlimited devotion for Joan but whom she finds unamusing. He is a brilliant mathematician and enlists as a gunner at the outbreak of war. He writes regularly to her from the Front, expressing the rapid disillusionment he feels with the poor abilities and lack of dedication of his fellow officers. He, too, is killed, by a shell in 1916. Also a casualty is the near-pacifist, Bunny Cuspard, who gives Joan her first lover's kiss. A light-hearted young man, who enjoys playing the Wellsian toy-soldiers game of 'Little Wars', he finds the reality of the trenches in France altogether too fierce. He dies as a member of the British forces transferred to Dublin in 1916 to quell the Irish Uprising.

One friend who does become a pacifist is Gavan Huntley. Blond-haired and blue-eyed, he is a successful novelist and a critic 'eminently unpopular with actor-managers'. Too arrogant to be much of a companion, he is nevertheless attracted to Joan; but he is interested in 'the feminine of all ages'. He works as a farm-hand during the war, contributing stridently to the pacifist press, but avoiding sending any of his writings to the patriotic Joan.

An acquaintance from Peter's schooldays, Troop, is a good-looking, healthy fellow who excels at sports and adopts a liberal attitude, albeit limited to the narrow sphere of his own activities. Coming from an army background, he joins up immediately at the beginning of the war, an example which Peter is rapidly persuaded to follow.

Finally there is the Indian, Mir Jelalludin, a young Muslim with a finely-modelled face and 'beautiful teeth'. Joan finds him intriguing, much to Peter's dismay; and he endeavours to dissuade her from associating with the Asian. However, when Peter is in trouble with an enemy air-ace above the Front, it is Jelalludin—serving with the French Flying Corps—who shoots the German fighter down. *Joan and Peter*, 1918

STUBLAND, JOAN : Ostensibly Peter's foster sister, who later discovers they are actually no more than cousins and that she is free to marry him. She is the daughter of Dolly's dissolute literary brother and a young woman who died of child-bed fever soon after giving her birth. The only member of the family who appears at all concerned about her illegitimacy is Lady Charlotte Sydenham, who endeavours at one stage to keep her hidden away. During childhood she becomes very attached to Peter, enjoying the usual petty squabbles and acts of competitiveness. She shows a talent for dancing when very young.

During her enforced separation from Peter, at Lady Charlotte's instigation, Joan is deposited in a gloomy household, to be cared for by a woman whose chief preoccupation is the vast variety of disorders which can assail the human body. Graphic descriptions of cancers, tumours and gory operations provide the bases for the most terrifying dreams : 'It was like pouring drainage over a rosebud'; and incredulous thoughts of hell are implanted in the young girl's head at the same time. Fortunately, the return of Oswald Sydenham from Africa rescues Joan from any further of Lady Charlotte's attentions, and her education is then continued along enlightened lines. At the age of nineteen she is effectively made mistress of the house, under the guidance of Oswald's housekeeper.

In adolescence she is a high-spirited, lanky girl, with dark hair and eyes, and a penchant for indulging in fantasies of being the mistress and inseparable companion of kings. By the time she goes to study at Newnham College, Cambridge, she has become visibly 'a young lady' and adult conversation is open to her. She joins the University Fabian Society and other serious-minded groups, where she meets a number of male admirers, although none whom she finds she can like as much as Peter. Strangely, however, it is during this period that she finds Peter's presence under

Oswald's roof in the vacations almost intolerable. Her reaction to his affair with Hetty Reinhart is to prompt her to consider taking a lover herself, but she finds no one of whom she is sufficiently fond.

After learning the truth of her parentage, Joan realizes that it is Peter she wants; however, it is some time before she can break down the barrier of reserve that has risen between them. Only when she openly confesses her love while he is on leave from the Flying Corps is the problem overcome. After their marriage she continues her war-work, driving cars for the Ministry of Munitions, and planning to build houses once the conflict is at an end. *Joan and Peter*, 1918

STUBLAND, PETER : The young man whose experiences from childhood to early adulthood form the central feature of the story, together with those of his cousin Joan. (His parentage and early orphaning are described in the entries for *Arthur* and *Dolly* above.) Following the death of his parents, he and Joan are initially cared for by his aunts, Phoebe and Phyllis, who take over the family home as the two most available of the children's four guardians. He has already formed a deep affection for his third guardian, Oswald Sydenham, a former navy midshipman who won the V.C.—but lost half his face—during the bombardment of Alexandria. Oswald serves in the Consular Service in Uganda and is content for the time being to leave the orphans in the hands of their aunts.

The first part of Peter's childhood is almost idyllically happy. The household is unconventional and the children attend a local school which is run on progressive lines. Only one event really disturbs their peace before they begin at the School of St. George and the Venerable Bede, and that is their enforced christening under the direction of their fourth guardian, the formidable and reactionary Lady Charlotte Sydenham, who takes them to a nearby church on the pretext of an afternoon's outing. Joan believes Peter is about to be drowned in the font, having just seen some kittens disposed of in similar fashion the same morning.

On the advice of her solicitor, Lady Charlotte is persuaded to intervene further, a few years later, by taking Joan and Peter off without consulting the aunts. The girl she puts into the care of the sister of her maidservant, a slovenly and morbid woman, considering that a female bastard has no entitlement to a proper

237

education. Peter she sends to a badly-managed boarding-school where he is bullied and so unhappy that he eventually runs away. Reaching the bridge over the Thames at Maidenhead, he steals a boat which is later found drifting empty and it is assumed that he has been drowned. In fact, he succeeds in reaching his home, where he is determined to stay. With the aid of their own solicitor, Phoebe and Phyllis also succeed in retrieving Joan, but not before she has succumbed to measles.

At this juncture it becomes clear that Dolly Stubland survived her husband by some half an hour and that, by virtue of her will, Oswald is rightfully the children's only guardian. He has arrived back in England to fulfil his responsibilities, only to be distressed by the poor attitude of the British to their empire, and even more disconcerted by the educational standards of the schools which he visits in his search for suitable places for his wards. He muses at length along Wellsian lines about the need for an entirely new approach to education. Eventually he places Peter at White Court Preparatory School and subsequently at Caxton, a college well endowed with science laboratories and with an enlightened approach to the teaching of mathematics. Joan, for her part, is sent to Highmorton School, some ten miles from Oswald's house in Hertfordshire.

During their adolescence, Oswald is loath to preach at Joan and Peter, although he does talk to them on many topics, from his experiences in Africa and his view of the Empire to his ideas about education. Their mutual detestation of each other's friends, even at this stage, causes occasional rifts between the young people, but on the whole they remain close. Both share a horror of killing animals, an emotion reinforced by the only occasion when Peter shoots a rabbit and is obliged to finish off the wounded creature by hand.

Having distinguished himself by winning prizes at Caxton, Peter studies at Trinity College, Cambridge. There he sees less of Joan, for they mix in different circles. Also, he has begun an affair with Hetty Reinhart, a spirited woman several years his senior whom Joan cannot abide; she feels that he is cheapening himself in the arms of an adventuress. By now, Peter realizes that he can no longer regard his foster sister as his junior, which he has tended to do in the past, although there is actually no more than eighteen months between them. At Cambridge they are of equal maturity.

Shortly before the advent of the First World War Oswald takes

Peter on a visit to Russia, an expedition which leaves many vivid impressions in the latter's memory : the long train journeys through Holland and Germany, the Sunday morning crowd upon the Unter den Linden, the vast expanse of Russia, the black-and-gold shops of Petrograd, the massive walls of the Kremlin and 'the first glimpse of that barbaric caricature, the cathedral of St. Basil'. There is much discussion during the trip and Oswald frequently finds himself comparing Peter with his young Russian counterparts. Peter, in his turn, can see little essential difference between the cities of one nation or another. He finds Russia a land of dull tragedy as against England's dull comedy, but to him it's 'all the same old human thing. Even the King and Tzar look alike . . .' He considers that there is little evidence of the majority of people taking life in earnest :

'Oh, I don't *see* the ideas at work ! Except as a sort of flourish of the mind. But look at the everyday life. Wherever we have been—in London, Paris, Italy, Berlin, here, we see every man who can afford it making for the restaurants and going where there are women to be got. Hunger, indulgence, and sex, sex, sex, sex . . . We're too little. These blind impulses—I suppose there's a sort of impulse to Beauty in it. Some day perhaps these forces will do something—drive man up the scale of being. But as far as *we've* got—!'

With his return to London, Peter finds Joan indulging in 'the nightclub round'. Encountering her in one such establishment, he suggests that it is no place for decent people, a conclusion which she has already reached herself. He proposes that they abandon their respective partners—in his case, Hetty—and accompany each other home. Joan is on the point of agreeing when her need to assert her independence overcomes her better inclinations.

On the very eve of war Peter joins Hetty in Italy for a holiday by the Lake of Orta. All around mobilization is taking place, and when war is actually declared he feels obliged to return to England to enlist, resisting Hetty's appeals that he should stay. His indignation that the Kaiser should have plunged Europe into conflict reflects the prevailing mood of his country during the opening stages of the hostilities, a mood he shares with Oswald. Peter insists on joining as a private, with the intention of working his way up through the ranks—a decision of which Oswald, who is himself attempting to secure a commission, disapproves. Peter's career as an infantryman, however, takes him no nearer the Western Front than Hampshire, for he decides to transfer to the Royal Flying Corps, in which he is commissioned.

During training he revels in the exhilaration of flight and is a rapid learner. Within weeks he is in action over France, for a time flying above the enemy lines on several successful bombing missions, but without personal combat. His first real encounter with an enemy aircraft proves to be his last, since he has the misfortune to come up against a German air-ace who wounds him and disables his plane. He is only saved from the threatening *coup de grâce* by the intervention of Mir Jelalludin who shoots the pursuer down. Peter just succeeds in regaining the allied lines before crash-landing. His injuries include a smashed shoulder-blade, and he is repatriated for a long convalescence. During his initial period of unconsciousness in a field hospital, he has a vision of God in which he accuses the Almighty of mismanagement, to be told in reply that if he wishes to change the world the effort must be his. He should exert himself.

Oswald, too, has been seriously wounded while working with a corps of African labourers behind the Front. Hit by splinters from a bomb explosion, he is now a very sick man. Both he and Peter are reunited with Joan in Hertfordshire where they recount their various experiences. On his recovery, it is clear that Peter is unlikely to fly again, but his war service continues in an observation balloon attachment on the Western Front. Before he leaves home, he has arrived at an understanding of his true feelings for Joan and they are quickly married. Again Peter is unfortunate. His balloon is set on fire by tracer bullets, and as he parachutes down he is shot several times. These later injuries preclude him from any further form of active service, for he is permanently lamed. He continues with the Flying Corps in a junior administrative post at the London Headquarters. He plans after the war to qualify as a doctor, with a view to devoting himself to medical research. With Joan he decides to take a small flat close to his office, and the closing scene of the story is occupied with their farewell to Oswald.

In the face of his coming loneliness Oswald prepares a long 'valediction' for his wards which might be described as the apotheosis of his philosophy. He reviews his attitudes to British society and its institutions, holding the war to be the result of an educational breakdown. He sees in the League of Nations perhaps the only hope for the establishment of a World Republic. Joan and Peter, he declares, have a great inheritance; it is up to them and their generation to revitalise England and justify its place in a new world :

'Listen when the old men tell you facts, for very often they know. Listen when they reason, they will teach you many twists and turns. But when they dogmatize, when they still want to rule unquestioned, and, above all, when they say *'impossible'*, even when they say *'wait—be dilatory and discreet'*, push them aside. Their minds squat crippled beside dead traditions . . . That England of the Victorian old men, and its empire and its honours and its court of precedences, it is all a dead body now, it has died as the war has gone on, and it has to be buried out of our way lest it corrupt you and all the world . . .'

Wells regarded the novel as one of his most ambitious, and he was disappointed by its relatively poor sales. One reason for its low selling figures was the war-time paper shortage which resulted in an unusually high publication price. He wished it to be a 'great' novel on the subject of education and planned for a section covering Peter's public-school experiences. However, the story had already become so long (it is exceeded in length only by *The World of William Clissold*, and then only marginally), that he was obliged to exclude it. The gist of that section can be found in his non-fictional study of Sanderson, the Headmaster of Oundle, *The Story of a Great Schoolmaster* (1924). He also considered the novel complementary to *Mr. Britling Sees It Through*, as a portrait of the English spirit during the War and in the face of the need for reconstruction. He regarded it as the finer of the two endeavours. *Joan and Peter*, 1918

STUBLAND, PHOEBE : Arthur's younger sister who, with his other sibling Phyllis, cares for Joan and Peter immediately following the tragedy at Capri. She is an effusive woman, given to flamboyant outbursts of her opinions and the writing of purple prose, of which the title of her novel *Hail Bambino and the Grain of Mustard Seed* gives some indication. Another Wellsian female advocate of women's suffrage, she regards her joint-guardianship of the two orphans as an opportunity to enjoy the advantages of maternity 'without the degradation'. Her distaste for men is evidenced by her physical assault on Lady Sydenham's solicitor after the children's abduction, and her view of Lady Charlotte herself is little better : 'Feminine ! No ! She is completely a Man-made Woman. Quintessentially the Pampered Squaw. Holding her position by her former charms. A Sex Residuum. Relict. This last outrage. An incident—merely. Her course of action was dictated for her. A Man. A mere solicitor... The flimsiest creature! An aspen leaf—but Male. Male.' *Joan and Peter*, 1918

STUBLAND, PHYLLIS : The elder aunt of Peter and a woman with 'an abnormal sense of humour'. With her sister Phoebe, she is appalled by Lady Charlotte Sydenham's enforced christening of her wards and is instrumental, with the family solicitor, in retrieving them after their virtual kidnap by their fourth guardian. It is she who finally reveals to Joan the true nature of her parentage. *Joan and Peter*, 1918

SUMMERSLEY SATCHEL, STELLA : The companion of Lady Mary Justin who witnesses her employer's unexpected reunion with Stephen Stratton in the Swiss Alps in 1911. She is 'a blond businesslike young woman with a stumpy nose very cruelly corrugated and inflamed by a pince-nez that savagely did much more than its duty by name'. She has evidently harboured a strong resentment of Lady Mary and is quick to report her meeting with Stratton to Justin, an action which leads to his institution of divorce proceedings and his wife's suicide. The same character appears in Wells's later novel *The Wife of Sir Isaac Harman*, in the rôle of Lady Harman's secretary toward the end of Sir Isaac's life. *The Passionate Friends*, 1913

SUMNER, FRED : The second husband of Hetty Marcus and the murderer of Harry Mortimer Smith. A weak man, he is fair-haired, with a blotched complexion, watery-blue eyes and a straw-coloured moustache. His height and build are much the same as Smith's. He seduces Hetty while he is serving as an officer in the First World War and Smith is away at the Front. Although the liaison is a one-night affair, a child is conceived which, because of the time interval, Smith realizes cannot be his. After her divorce Sumner marries Hetty, but she soon discovers that he is a drunkard and a wastrel. He is also involved with a gang which preys on bookmakers. A crisis is reached when Hetty's mother is obliged to sell her farm to meet his debts, and Hetty approaches Smith to help her escape to Canada. After her departure, Sumner is convinced that Smith is hiding her. He calls on him at his office, and, getting scant response, later shoots him in a fit of drunken jealousy. In his dying moments Smith insists that he has accidentally shot himself, thus allowing his killer to go free. *The Dream*, 1924

SUNDERBUND, LADY AGATHA : A wealthy American widow whose devotion to the New Vision of Bishop Scrope finally proves an embarrassment. She is tall like Scrope's own wife, but without the same calm and quietude—in short, she is 'electric'. Black-haired and blue-eyed, she displays smiles and a complexion which are 'an established brightness' exceeding 'the common lustre of things'. She dresses expensively, frequently adorning her hair with jewellery. Her manner of speech is effusive and is distinguished by 'a pretty little weakness of the r's' which has probably been acquired abroad. She first meets Scrope on his move to Princhester, rapidly becoming an avid devotee of his work and attending all his services.

Many discussions ensue between the Bishop and Lady Agatha and he finds her an eager disciple following his break with the Church. She wishes to finance him in a grand crusade, commissioning an architect to design what Scrope intends should be a simple meeting house in London where he may propagate his message. In the event the architectural plans reveal an immense temple of brobdingnagian proportions, and a thoroughly disconcerted Scrope realizes that Lady Agatha's enthusiasm is inappropriate to his cause. Reluctantly—for her financial support would enable him to keep his family in its former style—he advises her of his decision. She finds it difficult to understand his need for simplicity and is astonished at his rejection of the impressive pseudo-ecclesiastical vestments she has designed for him. In response to his conviction that he should wear quite ordinary clothes her reply is characteristic : ' "O'dina'y clothes a' clothes in the fashion. You would have to go to you' taila for a new p'eaching coat with b'aid put on dif'ently, or two buttons instead of th'ee . . ." ' On parting she weeps and begs his forgiveness for her misinterpretation of his needs. *The Soul of a Bishop*, 1917

SWANSDOWN, HAROLD : See 'Betterave, W. B.'.

SYDENHAM, LADY CHARLOTTE : Dolly Stubland's cousin who endeavours to exert her reactionary views in the matter of the upbringing of the orphans, Joan and Peter. She is the largest woman that the infant Peter has ever seen, heavily costumed in all manner of garments, each of which bears additional sewn-on appendages. Her features are square, considerable and freckled, her eyes hard and blue. From one cheek she has growing 'a little tussock of sandy hair' which instantly captures the boy's attention. Her voice is loud, harsh, slow and arrogant—in the manner of 'the ruling class of those days'.

Her first effort of domination in the story is to have the children forcibly christened during what was intended to be an afternoon outing, an act which was expressly in defiance of their late parents' wishes. Later she abducts the pair, forcing Peter into an appalling boarding school from which he runs away, and putting Joan in the charge of her maid's sister who is morbidly unsuitable for the task. When Lady Charlotte is obliged to relinquish her joint-guardianship of the children, so that they become the sole responsibility of her nephew Oswald, she still endeavours to exert an influence—but with little effect. She then directs her attentions to opposing the suffragettes, raising money towards buying guns for Ulster in a reaction against the proposed Home Rule Bill, and advocating the persecution of all Germans (with the exception of royalty) found in Britain on the outbreak of the First World War. Hardly surprisingly, she is disgusted at Peter's marriage to Joan, knowing the girl to be illegitimate. *Joan and Peter*, 1918

SYDENHAM, OSWALD : The nephew of Lady Charlotte and eventually the sole guardian of Joan and Peter Stubland. At the age of twenty he won the Victoria Cross during the bombardment of Alexandria when, as a naval midshipman, he picked up an Egyptian shell and threw it overboard. The missile exploded as it left his hands, destroying one side of his face, including an eye. Initially, his mutilation led him to contemplate suicide, for he could not imagine any woman wanting him, but with time he comes to accept his appearance. He even finds that some women seem to be attracted to him because of his disfigurement. Nevertheless, he prefers to shun society and joins the Consular Service in Africa, an occupation in accord with his keen sense of the value of the British Empire.

He comes to England only occasionally, usually staying with his aunt—a woman uncharacteristically subdued by his presence. When he first encounters Peter and Joan they are infants. They both warm to him immediately, affectionately addressing him as 'Nobby'. Reluctantly he agrees to become their godfather, in the briefest of ceremonies which consists of no more than a mutual introduction. He has long had an affection for Peter's mother, Dolly, a sentiment which she reciprocates; and when he hears of her husband's infidelity he asks if she will return with him to Uganda. Much tempted, she eventually disappoints him, once she is assured by Arthur Stubland that his affair is over.

Back in Africa, Oswald learns that his godchildren have been orphaned and that he is one of their four guardians. Assuming that the other three will manage adequately, he resolves to remain where he is for the time being. He reappears in the narrative when it is discovered that he is, in fact, the children's only guardian, a trust which he originally regards as an imposition, until he realizes that he loves them. He then becomes devoted to their welfare. To begin with, his ideas on their education are nebulous—he finds it difficult to direct them into ways which he has still to define to his own satisfaction. He consults many headmasters in his search for appropriate schools, often disillusioned by the paucity of outlook he finds in 'educational' minds. He is also shocked by the lack of interest in their Empire which is shown by the majority of his countrymen at home.

Finally he selects two schools which he feels are the best in the circumstances, but by no means ideal. He experiences the same problems when it comes to the choice of universities; and in the end he sends Joan to Newnham and Peter to Trinity, both at Cambridge. With the outbreak of the First World War his dedication to the Empire impels him again to join the services. After a number of setbacks he finds a place in the supervision of an African corps of labourers behind the lines, but he is badly wounded by a bomb blast. Invalided home, he suffers a chronic deterioration in health which persuades him of the urgency of his responsibilities to his wards. He admires the dedication and courage with which Joan and Peter have thrown themselves into the war effort, but he is distressed by what he regards as their innocence in a fateful world.

Oswald accepts Peter's injuries less phlegmatically than his own, believing that it is tragic that the young should have to suffer as a result of the omissions of their elders. Now very ill, he prepares his 'valediction'—a statement whereby he seeks, in a sense, to refurbish his own faith while reassuring those whom he loves. His delivery of this peroration brings the story to a close.
Joan and Peter, 1918

T

TARVRILLE, LORD : A cousin of Lady Mary Justin and a sympa-
thizer with the plight into which she and Stephen Stratton have
fallen as a result of their affair. He is able to convince Stratton
that he will be financially and socially ruined by Justin unless he
agrees to go abroad and persuades him of Mary's helpless position, after which he allows them a brief parting in his London
home. *The Passionate Friends*, 1913

TAXIDERMIST, THE : A character who reveals the secrets of his
trade in what is essentially a brief, but intriguing, monologue. He
concludes by recalling the extinct, and even non-existent, birds
he has created, and the mermaid he produced which was
destroyed as a blasphemy by an irate itinerant preacher. 'The
Triumphs of a Taxidermist', 1894

TED, THE MAN WITH THE GLASS EYE : The narrator of 'The Lost
Inheritance', who tells of his eccentric rich uncle and the profusion of unreadable books he produced. The last of these was
given to Ted to read; but having failed to do so, he never
discovers that it contains the will nominating him as sole heir.
Thus the inheritance passes to an unlovely relative who had never
been obliged to suffer the uncle's tedious company. 'The Lost
Inheritance', 1897

TEDDY : Mr. Britling's secretary at Matchings Easy before he joins
the army in the early stages of the First World War. The son of
a Kilburn solicitor, he has a generous quantity of dark hair and
very fine dark blue eyes. (Throughout the narrative he seems
never to have been given a surname.) First reported wounded and
missing on the battlefield, his death is assumed after a long period
without news. His arm has been torn by shrapnel and requires
amputation, following which he eventually returns safely to
England, much to his wife, Letty's, joy. *Mr. Britling Sees It
Through*, 1916

TEMPLE : A former science student who has travelled abroad for some five years before returning to meet Findlay, with whom he had once fallen out over a woman. The wrong still rankles, and after a drunken evening, under the pretence of a friendly sparring-bout, Temple beats Findlay to death with the earbone of a whale which the latter has used as a doorstop. 'The Bulla', later retitled 'The Reconciliation', 1895

TEWLER, EDWARD ALBERT : Wells's last attempted portrayal of the proverbial 'little man' held back by a blinkered upbringing, a mediocre education and the strictures of a reactionary society. Tewler is born into lowly circumstances, left without a father at an early age and spoiled by a hopelessly inadequate mother until her death when he is in the throes of a puberty for which he has been woefully ill-prepared. He is given over as ward to the devout, if narrow-minded, care of Myame, a schoolmaster who directs his attention more to the expeditious use of Edward Albert's money than the boy's well-being.

Tewler appeals to Whittaker, his father's former employer, who helps him to enter the Imperial College of Commercial Studies and arranges for him to lodge at Mrs. Doober's boarding-house. There he falls under the influence of Chamble Pewter, a sceptically-minded bigot who more or less shapes Tewler's outlook for the rest of his life. He becomes suspicious of 'ideers', books, science and any novelty of thought and argument. At the boarding-house he also meets Evangeline Birkenhead, who rushes him into a betrothal (with the assistance of her father and Philip Chaser) when she discovers that he has inherited property in Scotland. Tewler, however, is a rough and clumsy lover, so ignorant of sexual technique that she soon finds him physically repellent. Only her pregnancy, and the undisguised persuasion of her police inspector father, persuade Tewler to marry her.

Originally a pale and undersized boy, of delicate and undistinguished features, Edward Albert acquires a more presentable appearance as he matures, although he does not cease growing physically until he is thirty. By the time of his marriage he is approaching average proportions and his profile has become more firm. But, as indicated, his sexual awakening has been much impeded—the description consigned to one of his boyhood friends is equally applicable to him : '. . . on the rack between the insanity of Nature cranking away at one end and the insanity of the social order cranking away at the other'.

Evangeline deserts him soon after the birth of their son Henry, and Tewler subsequently marries Mary Butter, the resigned divorcee employed as housekeeper who has become devoted to the baby. They move from London to the South Coast resort of Brighthampton, where in the pretentious surroundings of Morningside Prospect Tewler takes up golf and does very little else bar acquiescing in the predominantly right-wing attitudes of his neighbours. On the outbreak of the Second World War, he joins the Home Guard, and distinguishes himself by killing several Germans, more in a frenzy of fear than valour, during a Dieppe-style attack on the town. In his absence for his investiture with the George Cross at Buckingham Palace, his wife is fatally injured in a bombing raid, and he is subsequently married for a third time—to a widow he meets at a health-farm. By the story's close he remains as unenlightened as throughout his history, lamenting on his son's apparent break with him and failing utterly to comprehend its causes. From first to last his byword has been : 'You can't be too careful.'

The story is Wells's final novel, and an indication that even very late in life his gift for comic scenes was not entirely lost. But there is evidence of creative fatigue—in the marriage service with Evangeline, the clergyman employs the almost identical garbled offertory which enlivened *The History of Mr. Polly* three decades earlier. In the personality and haphazard progress of Tewler many comparisons with Kipps are obvious; but the general intent of the book is more wide-ranging. Wells wrote of *Homo Tewler* as a disorganized forebear of what he hoped might one day emerge as *Homo sapiens*, dismissing the latter title as inappropriate to modern man. The novel concludes with a characteristic evocation of the future possibilities of the race, and with an appendix illustrating how the primates represent an early branching in biological evolution and can hardly be considered as the most refined species in the natural order. *You Can't Be Too Careful*, 1941

TEWLER, MRS. EDWARD (I) : See 'Birkenhead, Evangeline'.

TEWLER, MRS. EDWARD (II) : See 'Butter, Mary'.

TEWLER, MRS. EDWARD (III) : Formerly a widow of independent means whom Edward Albert meets at a hydropathic centre in the Peak District during the Second World War. After several casual meetings brocaded with autobiographical reminiscences, they decide to overcome their individual loneliness and achieve some solace in mutual comfort and reassurance. She does her best to establish good relations with Tewler's son Henry, but with no recorded success, despite her punctiliousness in observing a posthumous respect for his dead step-mother. *You Can't Be Too Careful*, 1941

TEWLER, HENRY : Son of Evangeline and Edward Albert, unwanted by his mother and passed almost immediately into the care of Mrs. Butter (later to become Mrs. Tewler II). His devotion to books meets with his father's disapproval and his 'ideers' are dismissed accordingly. He resents Tewler's third marriage, and, after serving in the forces during the Second World War, he moves to Wales where it is assumed he has become a socialist. His break with his father is attributed in the latter's reasoning to his having fallen prey to agitators. *You Can't Be Too Careful*, 1941

TEWLER, MRS. RICHARD : The mother of Edward Albert, she is widowed four years after her only son is born. She becomes overprotective in her motherliness, leading a life of 'intensely concentrated anxious happiness'. Seeking solace in the Baptist Church, she meets Mrs. Humbleday while frequenting Baptist Social Afternoons and they become close friends. She is rather shocked by Mrs. Humbleday's broadmindedness and is alarmed at the thought of the areas of temptation soon to be laid open to her growing son. Consequently she places great faith in the guidance of Mr. Myame, a schoolmaster and fellow Baptist, consigning Edward Albert to his care. A dedicated hypochondriac in her final years, she dies technically of pneumonia, but probably from a surfeit of patent medicines when Tewler is thirteen. *You Can't Be Too Careful*, 1941

THIRP : Director of the World Police under Rud Whitlow and officially the head of the Ministry for the Preservation of the Revolution—a title bearing suspiciously sinister connotations which his career is to justify all too well. He is unlike his fellow directors in the youthful World State, in that he appears totally indifferent to the concept of social reconstruction which is taking place around him. He has a habit of disappearing to remote corners of the Earth, either in protection of his agents or in pursuit of exotic atmospheres. With Whitlow's growing paranoiac tendencies, Thirp becomes more an instrument of terror than the chief upholder of the law and his organization degenerates into the equivalent of Himmler's Gestapo, although he tries to distract his chief by a vain attempt to interest him in women. He is finally assassinated by one of his agents to whom he promised promotion and subsequently disappointed. *The Holy Terror*, 1939

THOMAS : A footman at Shonts and sworn persecutor of young Bealby. His uninvited attentions are ultimately rewarded with a jab in the chin from a toasting-fork, and it is this action which drives Bealby into flight upstairs where he collides with the rear of the Lord Chancellor. But like the butler, Mergleson, Thomas appears genuinely concerned when he believes that Bealby may be trapped and starving in a secret passage. *Bealby: A Holiday*, 1915

THREE PURSUERS, THE : The master and his two servants who ride into the valley of spiders in pursuit of his eloping woman and her lover. There they encounter great drifting balls of web housing poisonous spiders with a span a foot across. It seems evident that the runaways have already succumbed to this unexpected menace; and only after a desperate struggle do the master and one of his men escape, the latter to be killed when the former requires his horse. No setting is given for the tale, but by the general description it would appear to be either Mexico or somewhere in South America. 'The Valley of Spiders', 1903

TIME TRAVELLER, THE : The late-Victorian inventor who gives an account of his journey into the future for the benefit of his less than credulous friends. Little physical description is provided save that he has a broad head, grey eyes and a normally pale face. His story opens with an after-dinner discussion on the nature of time and his insistence that it should be possible to travel through it. He demonstrates his argument by showing his guests a small model of a time machine which disappears when he sets it in motion, an incident that is dismissed as a conjuring trick. Notwithstanding, he leads the company to the Time Machine itself and invites them to return in a week, during which he announces that he intends to experiment personally in time travel.

When the party reassembles, they are shocked by the sudden

arrival of their host, dishevelled and in the last stage of exhaustion. He then tells them graphically of his experience in the future. His description of his outward journey is imbued with a sense of wonder—how, as he begins to accelerate the machine, 'night followed day like the flapping of a black wing'. When he increases speed the surroundings become blurred, but he is able dimly to see buildings rise and fall and the landscape shift and change.

Finally he comes to rest in the year 802, 701 A.D., overturning his machine on impact. He finds himself in what appears to be a universal garden, complete with dilapidated palaces and, closer by, a white sphinx-like statue with outspread wings. He has barely recovered from his fall when he is approached by the first of the Eloi, frail beautiful people who spend a life of idyllic, but purposeless, ease. He learns they live communally in the palaces, sustained by fruit with which the garden abounds. Their language is simple and he is soon able to communicate with them, but they show surprisingly little interest in their visitor.

Since his arrival the Time Traveller has been puzzled by a series of vents which are set at intervals in the ground, and from which a dull throbbing can be heard. He descends one of these when he discovers, in panic, that his machine has been dragged inside the sphinx and the statue's doors barred. In the subterranean world giant engines are at work; and although he has only matches to illuminate his way, he can just make out dining-halls and tables set with meat. Having fallen asleep, he is awakened by the Morlocks who attempt to overpower him but are repelled by the light of his match. Their appearance nauseates the Traveller who has not anticipated this underground race of chinless, pink-eyed humanoids. Only after a struggle does he succeed in climbing back up the shaft.

Returned to the surface, he is reunited with Weena, an Eloi girl he has rescued from drowning and with whom he has exchanged flowers. Together they investigate the Palace of Green Porcelain, which proves to be a vast decaying museum where the majority of exhibits have long since crumbled to dust. He does, however, find a box of matches miraculously preserved. There follows a nightmarish episode during which the couple are attacked by the Morlocks while they are asleep in the open. The Traveller kills many of them with an iron lever he has salvaged from the museum, and others die in a blazing wood set alight by his camp-fire, but eventually Weena is carried off.

With the girl's abduction the Time Traveller arrives at a full understanding of the nature of the society he has come upon. Earlier he had speculated on the degeneracy of the Eloi, assuming them to be the remnants of civilization. His encounters with the Morlocks lead him to the realization that they, too, are the equally degenerate descendants of Man—the last representatives of a working class compelled to labour underground by an élitist establishment from which the Eloi have descended. He recognizes with horror the source of the meat which he had seen on the Morlocks' tables.

When daylight arrives, the Traveller finds that the Morlocks have set out to trap him; the doors of the sphinx stand open, revealing the Time Machine within, but although they close when he enters he succeeds in escaping through time. His flight takes him to the remote future where all signs of human life are gone. The sea has encroached upon the land and the shore-line is infested with giant crabs. Fascinated, he moves even further ahead : 'So I travelled, stopping ever and again, in great strides of a thousand years or more, drawn on by the mystery of the earth's fate, watching with a strange fascination the sun grow larger and duller in the westward sky, and the life of the old earth ebb away. At last, more than thirty million years hence, the huge red-hot dome of the sun had come to obscure nearly a tenth part of the darkling heavens. Then I stopped once more, for the crawling multitude of crabs had disappeared, and the red beach, save for its livid green liverworts and lichens, seemed lifeless.'

With this sombre vision of the tail-end of terrestrial vitality the Time Traveller returns to meet his guests and recount his tale. All he has to verify his account is his own dishevelled state and the two flowers given him by Weena. The following day he sets off again—and never returns. In a moving epilogue one of his friends speculates on his fate : 'One cannot choose but wonder. Will he ever return? It may be that he swept back into the past, and fell among the blood-drinking hairy savages of the Age of Unpolished Stone; into the abysses of the Cretaceous Sea; or among the grotesque saurians, the huge reptilian brutes of the Jurassic times ... Or did he go forward, into one of the nearer ages, in which men are still men, but with the riddles of our own time answered and its wearisome problems solved? ... He, I know—for the question has been discussed among us long before the Time Machine was made—thought but cheerlessly of the Advancement of Mankind, and saw in the growing pile of civilization only a foolish heaping that must inevitably fall back upon and destroy its makers in the end. If that is so, it remains for us to live as though it were not so ... And I have by me, for my comfort, two strange white flowers—shrivelled now, and brown and flat and brittle—to witness that even when mind and strength had gone, gratitude and a mutual tenderness still lived on in the heart of man.'

The Time Machine was the first of Wells's novels and is based on an earlier serial, 'The Chronic Argonauts', which he wrote for *The Science Schools Journal* in 1888 and broke off after three instalments because he was unable to finish it. He then painstakingly rewrote the story several times before it was serialized in its final form in W. E. Henley's *The New Review* in 1894 and published as a book in the following year. Its critical reception was highly favourable and marked the turning-point in Wells's struggle to establish himself as a professional writer. It is still regarded by many as his finest work and his most effective piece of social criticism. Certainly its suggestion that the future of progress was not assured, and that Man could end up degenerate, shook many of its first readers—as did the almost savage dichotomy it drew between the ruling and the working classes. Its powerfully evocative images and flights of imagination raise the narrative at times above the level of mere prose; 'No poet, so far as I know', the critic Walter Allen has said, 'ever wrote an epic based on Darwinism. *The Time Machine* is the nearest thing we have.' *The Time Machine*, 1895

TRAFFORD, MARJORIE : A young woman of twenty at the beginning of the novel who has just completed her studies at Bennett College, Oxford. She is tall, slender and athletically-built, graced with an abundance of copper-red hair, a broad brow and steady, grey-blue eyes. But her mouth might be 'noticeably soft and weak' were it not that it is 'conspicuously soft and pretty'. She leaves Oxford to holiday with her parents, the Popes, in Kent, where after some persuasion she succumbs to the overtures of the writer, Will Magnet, finally agreeing to marry him. That intention, however, is rapidly dismissed on the precipitous arrival of Trafford.

In her adolescence Marjorie has nursed a diversity of ambition. Her sympathy for others is quickly aroused, but she is also imbued with a keen sense of her own place in the world and of her general worthiness as a citizen. She has entertained thoughts of becoming the first woman Member of Parliament, whilst on more fanciful occasions she has seen herself as the mate of some barbaric Bornean chief. It is this latter element, perhaps, which allows her to be swept away by Trafford, with whom she elopes as soon as she is twenty-one. The marriage causes a family rift and it is some years before she is able to resume a relationship with her father. She continues to see her socialist-minded Aunt Plessington in London, although that ageing relative finds little favour in Trafford's eyes. The couple set up home in a small terraced-house, during the furnishing of which Marjorie's expensive tastes become apparent (she has already confessed to Trafford that she has accumulated a number of debts while a student). Nevertheless, she is allowed free access to her husband's bank account, although her continuous overspending leads to disharmony in the marriage. The situation improves when she becomes pregnant, but with the birth of her daughter, after a prolonged and difficult labour, it again deteriorates and she is forced to surrender her chequebook. With time on her hands, she contemplates taking up public speaking, particularly in support of the feminist movement towards a greater participation in politics. She feels herself becoming increasingly isolated as a mother largely confined to her home.

A second 'honeymoon' in Switzerland after the arrival of their next child provides some alleviation of the Traffords' marital problems, and on their return her husband foregoes his work in crystallography to enter business. Success comes quickly, but it is paralleled by Marjorie's demands for an increasingly higher standard of living and her urge to move house at short intervals. With the birth of two further children she considers her family complete, but the physical strain on Trafford, coupled with his growing preoccupation with social matters, makes it impossible for him to continue. He insists that Marjorie accompany him to Labrador for a year, where in the harsh climate she discovers in herself a resourcefulness and strength of personality which she had hitherto not suspected. Both these traits become more pronounced while she nurses Trafford after an accident. They spend the long icy evenings in argument and self-analysis, to return to England with an enhanced mutual understanding and a determination to renew their marriage on this more positive foundation.

The story can be regarded as Wells's next major attempt after *The New Machiavelli* to probe the complexities of a marital relationship. In it he also sought to illustrate, as he had done to a lesser degree in *Love and Mr. Lewisham*, his conviction that marriage and a family should not be contemplated until a man has won monetary success—even if that be at the expense of his true vocation. It is generally considered that the book suffers as a result of the suspension of action in its second half when it becomes an outright dialogue novel, but many of its earlier pages bear evidence of vivid description and flashes of humour. *Marriage*, 1912

TRAFFORD, RICHARD : The husband of Marjorie, whom he more or less first overwhelms when he literally descends out of the sky (a minor aeroplane crash) into the garden of the vicarage where her family are holidaying at Buryhamstreet in Kent. A dedicated scientific researcher, he is tall, good looking, and with a buoyant air which readily appeals to Marjorie. His father, a surgeon, died when Trafford was three, and his mother, fearful of spoiling him as an only child, despatched him to a boarding school young. Thereafter he studied at the Royal College of Science and at Cambridge. By the age of twenty-six he is already a minor professor and is eventually to become a member of the Royal Society.

Trafford is compelled to remain at Buryhamstreet until his friend, Sir Rupert Solomonson, who was injured in the plane crash, recovers. In the course of a few brief days he and Marjorie fall in love, much to the disapproval of her father, Mr. Pope, who surprises them embracing. He meets her again on his return to London, when they decide to elope. After their honeymoon in Italy it soon becomes evident to Trafford that his income is no match for Marjorie's extravagance. He is forced to go into business to provide for a growing family, but becomes increasingly dissatisfied with both the work and his marital circumstances. Determined to sever himself from his life in London—temporarily, at least—he endures a year of hardship in Labrador during which he feels free enough to discuss with Marjorie many of the challenges facing modern man. The final chapters of the novel are almost entirely occupied by these dialogues which serve to bring the couple closer together. At their conclusion he has decided to abandon his former career and to write : 'I've grown —into something different. It isn't how atoms swing with one another, or why they build themselves up so and not so, that matters any more to me. I've got you and all the world in which we live, and a new set of riddles filling my mind, how thought swings about thought, how one man attracts his fellows, how the waves of motive and conviction sweep through a crowd and all the little drifting crystallizations of spirit with spirit and all the repulsions and eddies and difficulties that one can catch in that turbulent confusion. I want to do a new sort of work now altogether . . .' *Marriage*, 1912

TRUMBER, MR. : An English don at Camford, who is addressed by the visitant's disembodied voice during a dream and is disconcerted to find that it continues once he is awake. A small, downcast man, who speaks rapidly and wetly, he enjoys casting aspersions on the work of major poets and praising the lines of nonentities about as insignificant as himself. He does not take kindly to the Voice's view of his bias, and confides as much to his friend, Bream, the vicar of St. Hippolytus. *The Camford Visitation*, 1937

TWAIN, MRS. DIONE : Wife of the magistrate and mother of Gemini, who refers to her unfailingly as 'Dione M'am'. In her mid-forties, she is tall, slender and finely-featured, reminding Stella Kentlake on their first meeting of some dynastic Egyptian woman. Somewhat unapproachable, she dislikes her husband not only for his unyielding autocratic manner, but also for the—to her—discomforting sexual demands he has placed on her since their marriage. For a time she attempts to find solace in the Christian Scientist religion, but comes to see it as no more than a device for escaping from the stresses of real living.

She develops a close bond with Stella during Gemini's absence on the Continent and throughout his subsequent illness, defying her husband by visiting the psychiatric clinic in Sweden where their son is being treated. She writes a long letter to Stella's uncle, Robert Kentlake, seeking his help and expressing her profound mistrust of the Freudian methods of the clinic's head. (Her arguments are precisely those of Wells himself, who was never less than suspicious of Freudian techniques. By inclination he was more in sympathy with the approaches of Jung and Adler, as can be seen in his 1940 thesis for a Doctorate of Science in London University : *A Thesis on the Quality of Illusion in the Continuity of Individual Life in the Higher Metazoa, with Particular Reference to the Species Homo Sapiens*, included in '*42 to '44: A Contemporary Memoir upon Human Behaviour during the Crisis of World Revolution* (1944)). *Babes in the Darkling Wood,* 1940

TWAIN, JAMES (GEMINI) : A young clerk in the Penguin Press offices and the lover of Stella Kentlake, with whom he is briefly living in a Suffolk cottage when the story opens in 1939. In his mid-twenties, tall, with brown unruly hair, a resolute mouth and disarming brown eyes, he walks with a severe limp—the result of an early accident which has rendered him ineligible for military service. Of keen intelligence—he is also a book reviewer—he views life with the enthusiasm and self-centredness of the young, but also with apprehension at the imminent prospect of war. He and Stella argue, affectionately, over a broad sweep of subjects, sometimes alone and on occasions in the company of Balch, an elderly writer, and of the local vicar, Morton Richardson. Their discussions are frequently overheard, if barely understood, by their inquisitive housekeeper, Mrs. Greedle. They discover a huge block of alabaster in the garden of a sculptor, Kalikov (later to be interned during the war), and see in it a model of the world—uncut, bloodshot, crushing the grass. They agree their purpose in life is to perceive the shape encapsulated within the block—a vision of the unrevealed better world—and then to chisel it out.

The lovers are separated by the harsh intervention of Gemini's father and Stella's uncle, Major Hopkinshire. Defying his father's instruction to see Stella no more, Gemini is expelled from the family home. He rents a dingy room in London, from which he writes long letters to Stella, dwelling at length on Cottenham C. Bower's recent book *The Expansion of Sex*. He finds an evening of solace in the bed of Mary Clarkson, the friend from whom they rented the cottage, but entertains mixed feelings about his disloyalty to Stella.

Resolved to see something of Russia before war closes in, he makes his way to Poland via Stockholm, where he falls in with an American journalist, Gavin Peters. The two witness the Nazi advance on Warsaw and suffer much hardship, including aerial attacks on their train before they part at Riga. After their escape from the train Gemini saves Peters from drowning in a narrow canal. Unable to reach Russia, he is attempting to return via Sweden when he is concussed by an ammunition explosion in Flens. The shock, coupled with the horrors of war he has seen, leads to mental illness and loss of the will to live. He is treated unsuccessfully in a Flens clinic from which he is rescued by his mother, to whom he is deeply attached although he seems at the time hardly to recognize her.

Back in England, he is slowly cured by Stella's other uncle, the Cambridge psychologist Dr. Robert Kentlake, whose style of psycho-analysis is diametrically opposed to Freudian theories. During his illness he has totally rejected Stella, partly because he has become temporarily impotent, which in itself is a result of the human degradation brought home to him in Finland and Poland (he feels the sense of Beauty has been wiped from his life), and partly because of a squalid transaction with a prostitute in Stockholm. However, he finally marries Stella and they return to Suffolk where she has since bought the cottage. There he is able to make love. They find the village community much changed with the advent of the war. Kalikov has gone, but his block of alabaster remains; as they approach it the vast slab rolls over, almost crushing them. Gemini interprets the extraordinary incident as a mute appeal, a sign that they must begin the task they have appointed themselves. The end of the novel finds him serving on a minesweeper, while Stella has become a nurse.

The story is the last of Wells's major discussion novels and a fair example of his interpretation of young people's attitudes as he approached his mid-seventies. In the Introduction he once again justifies his adoption of 'the dialogue novel of contemporary ideas', citing the Socratic Dialogue and Plato's dramas of the mind as venerable, but living precedents. In keeping with his earlier attempts at the form, the views expressed cover numerous aspects of modern life, from religion, morality and sex, to war, psycho-analysis and the halting progress of Soviet Russia.

In its closing pages Gemini refers to a debate on a new Declaration of the Rights of Man which had recently taken place in the *Daily Herald*. This was a series of articles and correspondence initiated by Wells himself and can be found summarized in his *The Rights of Man, Or What Are We Fighting For?* (1940). The Declaration was dropped by Royal Air Force planes over Occupied Europe. It served as a useful pointer to the Universal Declaration of Human Rights adopted by the United Nations Assembly in 1948. *Babes in the Darkling Wood*, 1940

TWAIN, STELLA : See 'Kentlake, Stella'.

TWAIN, WILLIAM : A forbidding London magistrate, renowned for the severity of his court conduct, and known unpopularly as 'the Cadi of Clarges Street'. The father of Gemini, his unbending attitude towards his wife and son seems little better than the treatment he accords the accused who are brought before him. Physically, he presents an urbane and dignified figure. His features resemble those of his son, but his eyes are deeper set and a severely pursed mouth gives evidence of his character. Although he bars Gemini from the family house and severs all contact with him, it is clear from his reaction to the youth's illness that he is broken-hearted by the disappointment of his own hopes vested in his son. On the other hand he threatens his wife with the Defence of the Realm Act should she attempt to visit Gemini in Sweden, and expresses his satisfaction that Gemini now appears to loathe Stella. *Babes in the Darkling Wood*, 1940

U

UGH-LOMI : A Stone Age warrior and one of 'the Sons of Uya', a tribe named after its chief. Ugh-Lomi's choice of mate fails to find favour and he is made an outcast. Establishing a retreat for his woman Eudena on a cliff-side, he goes back to kill Uya and returns with the necklace of the dead chief's wife as a gift. The couple survive various hardships and hazards, including an attack by a bear, before Eudena is kidnapped by the tribe who now believe that Uya has been reincarnated in the shape of a lion. Ugh-Lomi saves her from being sacrificed by killing the beast, but he is badly mauled and is slow to recover. Later attacked by the tribe, he shows by his prowess that he is a worthy successor to Uya and he becomes the new chief. 'A Story of the Stone Age', 1897

UNEXPECTED VOICE, THE : An unseen visitant which for a period disturbs the university town of Camford. It first makes itself heard in the dining-room of Holy Innocents College where the Master, a guest and several Fellows have gathered for breakfast. During a conversation in which it is agreed that the college needs protection from the dictation of the half-educated, the Voice utters its first words : 'Half-educated? What do you mean by education? . . .' Initially taken aback, the company later assumes that the effect must be attributed to an undergraduate's practical joke; but the Voice subsequently addresses Trumber, an English don, who relates the encounter to his friend, Bream, demanding to know why he makes distinctions about what is the right kind of poetry and what is the wrong kind—and what significance they bear in relation to biological reality.

It then accosts Scott-Harrowby, a professor of Latent History, and reveals itself as an extraterrestrial entity which has watched the earth with interest, and some affection, during most of human history. But now it is disturbed at the apparent lack of direction inside human heads and seeks to know what Camford, as a seat of learning, is doing about it. It pursues other members of the Camford community, challenging the purposes of the local communist party and pestering undergraduates to say what they think they are learning. Finally on Congregation Day in the Great Hall, it speaks to the entire college while the usual honorary titles to visiting dignitaries are being duly awarded. It sounds a dreadful warning, but the ceremony continues in spite of it; and the passage of a few months since its last appearance convinces Camford that the whole episode is best forgotten. To take seriously what the visitant has said would be to cast light on too many little personal ambitions.

The novel can be seen as a somewhat short manifestation of Wells's growing apprehension towards the end of his life that Man was about to be overtaken by some inexorable form of disaster, against which his ingenuity and resources would count for little. The mysterious voice is clearly that of Wells himself, elaborating on the earlier hints of menace he had put into fictional guise in *The Croquet Player* the year before. *The Camford Visitation*, 1937

UTOPIANS, THE : The principal characters representing the advanced culture which suffers the advent of Mr. Barnstaple and his less amenable fellow Earthlings. They include Serpentine, who explains the scientific theory behind the space-time experiment which has brought the Terrans to Utopia, and Cedar, both of whom are shot by Ridley when they attempt a parley at the castle.

Among others worthy of note are Lion, a psychologist; Urthred, who acts as a spokesman on religious and more general matters; and Lychnis and Crystal, respectively Barnstaple's nurse who is saddened by the loss of her children by drowning and her thirteen-year-old boy cousin—a talkative companion who helps to elucidate the Utopian system for Barnstaple's benefit.

Sungold appears towards the close of the novel—an ancient and auburn-bearded man who acts as Barnstaple's mentor and arranges for his eventual return to Earth. *Men Like Gods*, 1923

V

VAIR, AUBREY : A minor, somewhat ineffectual poet whose half-hearted attempt to leave his wife in favour of a certain Miss Smith is recorded in the short story 'In the Modern Vein'. Wells himself had engaged in a similar enterprise after he had married his cousin; but in his case, since he could hardly be called in-effectual, the attempt had succeeded. 'In the Modern Vein', 1894

VERRALL, EDWARD : The son of a wealthy landowner in the Potteries towns whose influence over Nettie Stuart compels Leadford to attempt his murder. University-educated, he is young, intelligent and has a reputation for gallantry. He first arouses Leadford's anger when the latter discovers him waiting to meet Nettie. Leadford subsequently attacks him physically during a workers' strike at Lord Redcar's local colliery.

Verrall persuades Nettie to elope with him to Shaphambury on the East Coast, although it is clear from the letter she writes to her mother that there is little prospect of their marrying. He and Nettie are bathing when Leadford finally tracks them down; they only narrowly escape his shots before the comet's green mist envelops them all. With its passing Verrall's relations with Leadford becomes entirely amicable, to the extent that he is able to condone Nettie's eventual sharing of both men as lovers. *In The Days of the Comet*, 1906

VINCIGUERRA, SIGNOR : The former Italian government minister who is hounded by Mussolini's Blackshirts and seeks refuge at Mrs. Rylands's villa, Casa Terragena. He is in a state of advanced exhaustion, but recovers some of his air of a middle-aged Latin gentleman after the ministrations of Cynthia Rylands and her nurse, Mrs. McManus. He abhors the suppression of democracy in his native land and the new régime's persecution of leading intellectuals. Eventually he is smuggled to safety in France by the ruse of being disguised in Mrs. McManus's clothes. *Meanwhile*, 1927

VOULES, MR. : A licensed victualler and an uncle of the Larkins sisters. A fat, short man of ruddy complexion, he gives Miriam away at Mr. Polly's wedding. Suspecting the bridegroom's wavering resolve to go through with the ceremony, he fixes him with a 'watchful, blue eye of intense forcefulness' until the service is done. At the reception he dominates the proceedings with an overbearing demonstration of good will. *The History of Mr. Polly*, 1910

W

WALLACE, LIONEL : A rising politician who is haunted by a childhood experience—either imagined or real—in which he found a white door in a street wall leading to an enchanted garden. Throughout his future life, he attempts to re-discover the door; but, with the exception of a few fleeting glimpses when he cannot pause to investigate, he fails. As the pressure of his work increases, the search for the door becomes a growing obsession; and he is eventually found dead at the bottom of a construction shaft, having walked through a door in the hoarding above it. The story has often been quoted as an archetypal 'escape from reality' parable, seen in twentieth-century terms. 'The Door in the Wall', 1906

WALSHINGHAM, HELEN : The fiancée of Kipps, whom he abandons in favour of Ann Pornick. In her early twenties, she is as pale-faced as her brother, with dark grey eyes and black hair which she styles after the manner of that shown in a painting by Rossetti. She adorns her slender figure with the kind of loose bohemian clothes that are a badge of the intellectual women of the time. To Kipps, whom she first meets when he is a student in her woodcarving class, she is 'altogether beautiful'.

Helen finds Kipps rather touching in an uncouth way, but she only begins to take a closer interest in him when he comes into his inheritance. She laments over what she regards as her family's relatively humble address; and there is a suggestion that Kipps's fortune is no small help in kindling her affections. She tries her best, in company with Chester Coote, to educate Kipps in the niceties of upper-class social life, also attempting to improve his slipshod pronunciation, to little avail. She insists that he receive and return 'calls' from her acquaintances in Folkestone, a practice which Kipps finds so daunting that he is not above running off at the first opportunity. At one social gathering he is genuinely shocked at Helen's revealing dress, further evidence to him that he can never rise to meet her aspirations. When he turns from her to Ann Pornick, Helen foregoes any suit for breach of promise; and it is she who notifies Kipps that her brother has gambled away the money entrusted to him. *Kipps*, 1905

WALSHINGHAM, MRS.: The widowed mother of Helen who is surprised to discover her daughter is familiar with Kipps when they call at the Folkestone Drapery Bazaar. Dark and slender, she appears to the apprentice to be 'rather faded, rather tightly dressed', but Kipps later finds her 'a soul of sense and sentiment' to whom he can relate with ease. Mrs. Walshingham is reticent on the subject of her late husband, other than describing him as more an artist than a business man who had been misled by his partner. Her main preoccupation is her children, whom she regards as her twin jewels : 'They are so quick, so artistic, so full of ideas. Almost they frighten me. One feels they need opportunities—as other people need air.' Helen reports her as 'overcome with grief' when her son absconds. *Kipps*, 1905

WALSHINGHAM, YOUNG : Brother of Helen and a fledgling solicitor to whom Kipps transfers the management of his affairs. Dark, with a pale face and Napoleonic profile, he is a bold thinker much given to epigrams. He has a fondness for large-sized hats. The reading of Nietzsche has influenced him profoundly, so that he suspects that he himself is an example of the 'Non-moral Overman' depicted by the German philosopher. Prone to boasting, he meets his match in the playwright Chitterlow who can speak from experience, whereas Walshingham's knowledge of life has been largely acquired from books. His abandonment of morality evidently enables him to speculate with Kipps's and his own family's capital without scruple. Having misappropriated and lost the entire fortune, he disappears. *Kipps*, 1905

WAR CORRESPONDENT, THE : The journalist who witnesses the devastation of a proud army by land ironclads—a remarkable forecast by Wells of the coming of the tank. While many of his technical details differed widely from the later reality, his basic exposition of a highly mobile, armoured fighting-machine, housing men, proved correct. 'The Land Ironclads', 1903

WARMING : A cousin of Graham, the Sleeper, who arranges for the care of his body during his long trance. Devoid of any other next-of-kin, Warming leaves his substantial fortune to Graham so that it may be preserved intact—he has no expectation of the Sleeper awakening. He also provides for a group of twelve trustees to administer the estate in Graham's name, the forerunners of what comes to be the White Council by the year 2100 A.D. A wealthy American who as a young man witnessed Graham's collapse, also makes him his heir. After two hundred years of compound interest and the skilful investment of his inheritance, Graham is revived to find himself nominal owner of half the world—and the White Council seemingly omnipotent. *When the Sleeper Wakes*, 1899

WATKINS, MR. TEDDY : A prospective burglar with designs on the valuable jewellery of Lady Aveling. He enters Hammerpond Park in the guise of an artist, complete with easel and paint-box which he is able to convert into housebreaking equipment. During his attempt in the night he is disturbed and following a fight with two apparent pursuers he fears he has been caught. They, however, are also burglars, and the twist in the story is that he is assumed to be their apprehender. Taken into the house by a grateful Lord Aveling, he disappears in the morning accompanied by the jewel collection. 'The Hammerpond Park Burglary', 1894

WEENA : An effete, Eloi girl rescued and then befriended by the Time Traveller. He subsequently loses her to the Morlocks. *The Time Machine*, 1895

WESER DREIBURG, THE PRINCESS OF : The young giantess who is fed 'Herakleophorbia' by a pupil of Redwood in the hope of overcoming her family's hereditary failing in terms of size. She grows up unaware that she is not alone in stature, until she meets Redwood's son with whom she falls in love. She accompanies him to the fortress at Chislehurst when the battle between giants and men begins. *The Food of the Gods*, 1904

WHITE : An early school-fellow of William Benham who promises his dying friend that he will arrange his papers for book publication. In this capacity he is part-narrator of the novel. No physical description is given, and all that is said of him is that he is a journalist and author, and a member of the Rationalist Press Association. He is re-united with Benham, after a long interval, when they meet in Johannesburg during the labour riots of 1913; it is in one of these demonstrations that Benham is killed. White finds Benham's papers confusing and disjointed. Even after considerable editing and selection he declares the end result 'an indigestible aggregation'. 'On this point White is very assured. When Benham thought he was gathering together a book he was dreaming, White says. There is no book in it . . .' Critics of the day seized on this statement in the opening chapter as Wells's own confession that the novel was uncertain and muddled. *The Research Magnificent*, 1914

WHITLOW FAMILY, THE : The parents and elder brothers (Samuel and Alfred) of Rud Whitlow. They are described in the barest outline. The mother is reasonably intelligent and the beneficiary of a modern education; but she has difficulty in either understanding, or coping with, her youngest son's tantrums and violent behaviour. She is still worried about his health when he pays her a much publicized visit after he has become World Trustee, but she seems equally concerned about her own nervous dyspepsia. The father is a none too successful businessman who reluctantly chastises Rud when left with no alternative. He is unwilling to maintain him at a university, but yields to Rud's almost threatening demands in this respect.

There is also an Aunt Julia, who entertains 'ideas of the most diverse sort about the bringing up of children and the lamentable foolishness with which people in general set about that business'. She suggests that Rud might benefit from psycho-analysis, but the idea is not pursued. When he comes to his position of ultimate power, her recollections of him as a boy assume a rosier hue. *The Holy Terror*, 1939

WHITLOW, RUDOLPH (RUD) : Eventual World Director who has

finally to be murdered to preserve the global state he has brought into being. Even as an infant his tantrums and screams earn him the soubriquet 'a holy terror'. As a boy he is unpopular, even with his brothers. His youthful imagination is fired by the history of wars and conquests and he is much given to fantasies in which he pictures himself as a conquistador, with Carstall (actually the head boy of his school, whom he admires) as his trusted lieutenant. In appearance he has little to commend him—a bilious white face, broad intelligent brow (most often scowling) and a debilitated physique.

Insisting on a university education, he realizes at Camford that he has a gift for intuitive oratory. He calls for a revolution although at the time he has little idea what form it might take. But he is adamant in his vision of a union between the working peoples of Great Britain and America. On a walking vacation he encounters Chiffan, who is to become a major influence in his subsequent career. Together they visit the New World Summer School, a left-wing seminar where Rud's speaking abilities again arouse interest. On the same tour they investigate the semi-fascist League of Free Democrats, finding it totally ineffectual.

Rud returns to Camford convinced of the futility of the 'revolutionary' movements he has seen so far, but with a growing confidence in his own power to move audiences. During the next two years, under Chiffan's guidance, he establishes a group of supporters who meet in London at the flat of the wealthy young Anglo-American, Steenhold. As his political acumen matures, Rud becomes aware that his vision and magnetism emanate from an *alter ego* which transcends his normal, unlikeable personality. He discovers in himself a capability for grasping outlines and a mental lucidity superior to any of his associates. He begins to shape his personal conduct to exploit these gifts.

Among his followers he recruits several members of Lord Horatio Bohun's Popular Socialist Party, an extreme right-wing organization which has enjoyed some success in the past but is now stagnating for want of effective leadership. Rud challenges Bohun by taking over his platform at Hyde Park's Speakers' Corner. A closed meeting for the airing of differences is agreed, which Bohun seeks to dominate by a show of force. In the event, his hired thugs are overpowered, and although Rud is briefly imprisoned in Bohun's headquarters, he emerges as undisputed leader of the movement which he renames the Common-Sense Party, also known as the Party of Common Man. From this point events move rapidly. Another associate, Bodisham, a genius at intricate planning, develops the concept of 'parallel independent co-operation', bringing in allies from a variety of fields : Bellacourt, who seeks federal air control, and Reedly, a brilliant but disgruntled military strategist, among many others. On the outbreak of the Second World War, the Common-Sense Party is firmly based internationally; and after a year of fighting, when the European nations have reached the point of collapse, it is the only power structure capable of assuming overall control. A last-minute attempt by Reedly to stage a coup is foiled, and Rud becomes the head of an emergent World State.

The remainder of his tale relates the many problems inherent in the administration of a global community in its early stages particularly in the educational sphere which is organized by Norvel. It also recounts the onset of Rud's growing paranoia. Deprived of a sobering influence by Bodisham's sudden death, he succumbs increasingly to introspection and a deepening suspicion of those about him. Chiffan is murdered when he endeavours to help his old friend; Bodisham's doctors are tried and killed; the trappings of a police state, under the control of Thirp, are all but complete when Rud himself is surreptitiously poisoned in the clinic of his former schooldays' idol, Carstall—the one person he is still able to trust.

Rud is a man who has always hated the established order, a power structure which he successfully sets out to overthrow. But in doing so, he also destroys the motivational force which has driven him impetuously in pursuit of his goal. Renouncing any form of sexual relationship early in his career (on the advice of Chiffan), he has cut himself off from the possibilities of love. At the pinnacle of his achievement, he remains the warped, hostile character which the beginning of the story found him.

The novel is Wells's final effort to picture the actual realization of a World State. The fact that it should have been achieved by so flawed an instrument as Rud Whitlow, among the most unsympathetic of all the author's leading characters, is a paradox which no commentator has as yet satisfactorily explained. *The Holy Terror*, 1939

WHITTAKER, JIM : The head of Colebrook and Mahogany, a London firm of china merchants where Tewler's father was employed as a repair man. Conscious of having underpaid the worker, Whittaker takes some interest in his son Edward Albert, and rescues him from the attentions of his guardian Myame after Mrs. Tewler's death. He arranges lodgings for him and helps with his entrance to the Imperial College of Commercial Studies, in Kentish Town. However, he finds Edward Albert an unattractive youth and is manifestly relieved when a legacy from a Scottish uncle relieves him from any further liability towards the boy. *You Can't Be Too Careful*, 1941

WIDGERY, DANGLE AND PHIPPS : The ill-assorted trio of admirers who assist Mrs. Milton in the hunt for her step-daughter Jessica— respectively a bank manager, a sub-editor and a music student. Their pursuit of Hoopdriver and Jessie gives rise to a number of comic incidents. Dangle proves the most energetic of the three— and the most accident prone. His eye is blacked in a fight, while other parts of his anatomy suffer during his inexperienced handling of a horse-and-fly. Widgery is the most conspicuous by his size; he is 'one of those big, fat men who feel deeply'. Phipps is revealed as 'a callous youth of few words, faultless collars, and fervent devotion'. Constrained to be friends on the insistence of Mrs. Milton, they are not above reciprocal criticism : 'Dangle thought Widgery a Philistine, appreciating but coarsely the merits of *A Soul Untrammelled* (Mrs. Milton's book), and Widgery thought Dangle lacked humanity—would talk insincerely to say a clever thing. Both Dangle and Widgery thought Phipps a bit of a cub, and Phipps thought both Dangle and Widgery a couple of Thundering Bounders.' *The Wheels of Chance*, 1896

WIDGERY, SAM : An unpleasant man, with 'a very long pock marked sheep's face', who with his wife manages the Preembys' laundry business after Mrs. Preemby's death. He visits Sargon/ Preemby in the mental hospital where he is receiving treatment and is disconcerted to find that the latter fails to recognize him. He describes Preemby as 'mad as a hatter' and endeavours to persuade Christina Alberta to leave London and to stay with him at Woodford Wells. On her angry refusal, he threatens to withhold any money due to her from the laundry. The Widgerys appear sullenly in the background at Preemby's funeral. *Christina Alberta's Father*, 1925

WIDGETT FAMILY, THE : A lively trio of brother, Teddy, and two sisters, Constance and Hetty, who attempt to introduce Ann

Veronica into their bohemian and socialist circles, much to the disapproval of the girl's father. It is at their instigation that Ann Veronica attempts to go to the Art Students' Ball, until parental opposition overwhelms her. In their company she meets Nettie Minniver, who is to influence her further towards socialist and feminist ideals. *Ann Veronica*, 1909

WILBECK, DOLORES : The elegant, vituperative and vindictive wife of Stephen, and a character more than partly drawn from real-life. Formerly an Egyptian princess by marriage, she has been convent educated in Monaco where she was born the daughter of a Scottish father and a mother of Armenian origin. Slender in build, she has a warm face, finely modelled features, and a dusky complexion which lead many to believe, erroneously, that she has come originally from Oriental stock. Wilbeck is first drawn to her by her audacious behaviour at an hotel on the Riviera and she soon monopolizes him. Tricking him into marriage by a false pregnancy, she later claims that, far from being a foetus, it is a cancerous internal growth—a condition which her doctor discounts. Nevertheless throughout the subsequent thirteen years of her marriage she regularly resorts to bouts of pain whenever circumstances suggest it would be propitious.

Dolores cannot exist as anything less than the centre of attention. Her attire is never otherwise than startling, and her conversation even more so. She is jealous and possessive to the point of insanity, inventing a host of mistresses for Stephen and going so far as to accuse him of an incestuous affair with his daughter.

All this she discusses freely with her circle of Parisian friends during Wilbeck's regular trips to England.

Among her many eccentricities is a curious set of exercises which combine Swedish drill with Yoga, and which she practises naked : 'Dolores in a state of nature holding her breath in an effort to send air by some entirely unknown route to her spinal cord and at the same time bursting to explain the esoteric wonder of it, was an exhilarating spectacle.' Her obsession with her health is characteristically taken to extremes. In a vastly amusing series of encounters with an ancient baroness at an hotel in Torquestol, she first reduces the old lady to apoplectic silence over an indelicate liaison between their respective dogs, and later gives vent to an irrational but unshakeable conviction that the woman has leprosy. Henceforth she insists on dining on the restaurant balcony, announcing that she will not risk eating in the same room as a leper.

Many other examples of her excessive manner could be given, but these must suffice. At her funeral Wilbeck is hard put to believe that she will not throw back the coffin-lid and embark on another scene.

Without doubt the most original, if least sympathetic of all Wells's female characters, Dolores Wilbeck dominates the novel and shrilly consigns her husband's philosophical musings, which also occupy much of the book, to a subsidiary place. It is a malicious portrait, perhaps only redeemed by the wit with which it is presented. *Apropos of Dolores,* 1938

WILBECK, STEPHEN: A London publisher and narrator of a chronicle which deals principally with his marriage and the personality of his wife. No real physical self-description is attempted, but he must evidently be more than merely presentable to attract such a woman as Dolores. Similarly his early years are not discussed, the first detail of his past life being the meeting with his first wife—later to become Mrs. Alice Hoopler—when he is thirty-two and on leave from the trenches to mend a broken arm. Deliberately avoiding a commission, he has attained the rank of sergeant-major since his enlistment in 1915.

At the time of their first encounter, they discover a strong mutual attraction and are married before he returns to the war. A daughter is born in his absence, but on his demobilization Alice has already become involved with Hoopler and Wilbeck sees no alternative to releasing her.

The actual opening of the narration finds him enjoying a brief interlude in Brittany before joining his second wife, Dolores, at Torquestol. This is occupied largely by a philosophical soliloquy into which the Wellsian arguments of the biologist and author, Foxfield, are introduced. Later he describes the early stages of his relationship with Dolores; and the central section of the novel recounts the events of the month following his arrival at Torquestol, interspersed with reminiscences of their life together.

Shortly after their marriage Wilbeck acquires an opulent flat in Paris which is to remain Dolores's permanent home. He, on the other hand, rapidly recognizes the need for frequent respites from her presence and takes a bachelor apartment in London, close to the publishing house which was formerly his father's. Since Dolores refuses to fly, and is so prone to either genuine or feigned sea-sickness that she will rarely cross the Channel, he effectively isolates himself by this manoeuvre. He also travels extensively, in furtherance of a series of educational books, *Way of the World*, which he hopes will present a more balanced and rational view of Man's affairs than those of his competitors.

Increasingly he finds his wife's taste and behaviour excessive. Her choice in furnishings for the Paris flat oppresses him; he is irked by her warring with, and dismissal of, their servants; he cannot abide her dog, and even less her friends, with whom she rarely discusses anything but scandal and sex; but above all it is her unremitting vocal abuse of himself on every conceivable pretext which most exasperates him. Curiously, he also derives some measure of amusement from her flamboyant egocentricity, a reflection on the duality in his own make-up. Nevertheless, his growing desire is to be rid of her for good.

Wilbeck pays a visit to the Hooplers in Southampton, to meet his daughter Lettice for the first time since she was an infant. He finds the household stifled by Hoopler's deadening influence; but he is initially impressed with Lettice, now sixteen, to whom he is obliged to represent himself as godfather. He offers to pay for her education through a London college, as a means of separating her regularly from her step-father's sway. Dolores is incensed by this development, adding Lettice to the long list of women with whom she imagines Wilbeck is having affairs in England. A climax is reached at the hotel in Torquestol when Dolores tears up a photograph of Lettice, announcing her intention of coming to London to ruin Wilbeck's life. Either by accident or design—he is never entirely certain which—he gives her an entire bottle of soluble pain-killers, in place of the required two, and she is found dead the following morning.

There follows a comic funeral scene, in which Wilbeck is loaned an odd assortment of ill-fitting mourning clothes within half an hour of the ceremony, and he follows the hearse clutching trousers several sizes too large for him. He can barely contain his laughter at the absurdity of the situation; but at the graveside itself he is overcome by emotion and weeps.

Subsequently he invites Lettice for a tour of Brittany, keenly anticipating her company. In the outcome she proves disappointing and shows little interest in the historical associations of the area. In the course of the trip Wilbeck is astonished to find himself incongruously attracted to a young Englishwoman with whom he exchanges no more than a few words. Impulsively he

271

K

follows her car around the countryside but eventually loses her. The experience unsettles him and leads him to the conclusion that he should now remain single. At the end of his narrative he is prepared to declare that if he had killed Dolores accidentally, given the chance again he would have made the act deliberate.

The novel is noted as Wells's major attempt to indulge in sophisticated wit, in comparison with the more earthy, sometimes slapstick, humour of his comic tales. To some extent it was inspired by his experience of a particular affair a few years earlier, when he had lived with Odette Keun in France before the death of his wife. It is also the last of his studies of a close personal relationship between a mature man and woman, if the term 'mature' can be applied relevantly to either Wilbeck or Dolores. In some respects its style and atmosphere recall *The World of William Clissold* and it includes some memorable evocations of the Brittany landscape. *Apropos of Dolores*, 1938

WILDERSPIN : One of three friends who suffers a terrifying experience while staying at Southsea, on the Channel Coast. After watching a firework display, they run back to their lodgings to escape a storm. But Wilderspin enters the wrong house, mistaking No. 7 for its neighbour. When he fails to reappear, his companions, together with a police constable, find him in a state of shock. He has been horrified by the sight of the badly disfigured corpse of a thief, who was struck by lightning while trying to steal gas and plumbing fittings. He also appears in the short story, 'The Thumbmark'. 'The Thing in No. 7', 1894

WILLERSLEY : A member of the London School Board who accompanies the young Remington, when he is a fellow of Trinity, on a holiday through the Alps. Having narrowly missed a fellowship himself, which would have taken him into the higher division of the Civil Service, Willersley appears old beyond his years, and is somewhat given to lecturing. He dedicates his life to social service and, while referred to occasionally later in the novel, only comes to the foreground in the early part. He witnesses, and disapproves of, Remington's first fulfilled sexual encounter—his seduction by an older Englishwoman in Locarno. His advice to his friend is that such preoccupations could prove an encumbrance to the political career to which Remington aspires, a premonition of the story's bitter conclusion. *The New Machiavelli*, 1911

WILLIAM, THE CARAVAN DRIVER : Taciturn, apparently toothless, thin-lipped and of small and uneven eyes. He takes an instant dislike to Bealby when the boy is taken in charge by the three women whom William is employed to drive. A man of base instincts and appetites, he finishes up the wine bottles remaining from a picnic and is not above helping himself to Madeleine Philips's chocolates, an act upon which he is engaged when Bealby accidentally sends the caravan horseless down a hill. William survives, but much shaken, and sets upon Professor Bowles who has come in hot pursuit. Between them they succeed in devastating what remained undamaged inside the wagon at the end of its headlong dash. *Bealby: A Holiday*, 1915

WIMPERDICK, ENOCH : An eminent convert and Catholic apologist who is a regular visitor to the Bulpington family's home at Blayport. 'A small, round fiercely smiling man, always short of breath and full of combative chuckles', his hair is dark and wiry and his eyebrows appear 'like maddened toothbrushes soaked in blue-black ink'. His manner of speech is best characterized by his frequent adjectival use of 'jahly', adapted by Raymond Bulpington as 'Cholly', and a word which Clorinda Bulpington 'jolly' well avoids. A devout upholder of things medieval, he detests 'Progress, Protestantism, Factory Chimneys and Pitiless Machinery'. His arguments, plagiarized wholesale, are to serve Theodore Bulpington well in his defence against the scientific materialism of the Broxteds. *The Bulpington of Blup*, 1932

WINCHELSEA, MISS : A school-teacher of some refinement who spends a fortnight on a travel tour in Rome, in the course of which she becomes enamoured of a studious young man. Shaken to discover his name is Snooks, she eventually loses him to one of her companions; but on visiting them some years later, she finds he can recall no interest in her and has developed into something of a bore. 'Miss Winchelsea's Heart', 1898

WINSLOW, SIDNEY : Another struggling shopkeeper of Wells's invention, whose efforts to settle with his wholesalers, appropriately named Messrs. Helter, Skelter & Grab, form the plot of 'A Catastrophe'. Winslow is at pains to persuade his wife, Minnie, of the desperate nature of the situation, but to little avail. He is saved at the last moment by a timely accident which kills both her uncle and aunt, thus providing an inheritance which will solve his financial problems. 'A Catastrophe', 1895

WINTERTON, TEDDY : A young man whose graceful movements and voice stir Christina Alberta to confess she is 'soppy' about him. He tends to behave as if he owns her, and disconcerts her father by appearing far too forward. He succeeds in seducing her, but proves totally unhelpful when she attempts to rescue Preemby from hospital. Thereafter she loses interest in him and he fades from the story. *Christina Alberta's Father*, 1925

WINTER-WEDDERBURN : The unfortunate recipient of the attentions of a blood-thirsty example of exotic flora which he tends devotedly. He escapes with his life, but in a somewhat anaemic condition. 'The Flowering of the Strange Orchid', 1894

WOODCOCK, SIR BUSSY : Described as a crude plutocrat, and an early patron of Mr. Parham before the latter's elevation to the rôle of Lord Paramount. A short thickset man, he has a ruddy freckled face with a nose 'sculptured in the abrupt modern style and a mouth like a careless gash'. He moves rapidly and impulsively—and his manners are 'voracious', his most frequent, and characteristic, exclamation being 'Gaw !'. The son of a London hansom-cab driver, he is a self-made man who has built for himself a substantial business empire.

He becomes something of a vestigial presence on the scene of the Lord Paramount's more excessive actions, returning to a central rôle when Parham attempts to invade his scientific fortress off the coast of Cornwall. In David Low's inimitable illustrations to the first edition, he is depicted as a vigorous amalgam of Winston Churchill and Lord Beaverbrook, the latter being the cartoonist's principal employer for many years. *The Autocracy of Mr. Parham*, 1930

WOODHOUSE : The assistant observer at the Avu observatory, in Borneo, who is attacked by a strange, unidentifiable flying-beast during one of his nocturnal vigils. Another of the author's excursions into the realms of terror. 'In the Avu Observatory', 1894

WOTTON, HELEN : Ostrog's niece, a physically striking girl, blackhaired and beautiful—she attempts on several occasions to engage Graham in private conversation. Finally successful, she warns him of the true nature of her uncle's designs, persuading Graham to use his popularity with the people to overthrow Ostrog. There is an element of sexual interest between Helen and Graham during their short relationship, an undertone that Wells eliminated in the retitled 1910 edition, *The Sleeper Awakes*, which also contained other revisions. *When the Sleeper Wakes*, 1899

Z

ZELINKA, KING PAUL : A nephew of the former King of Clavery who becomes monarch on the assassination of his uncle and the crown prince. A good-looking, fair-haired man with a sparse moustache, he has lived in the U.S.A. all his life, his father being exiled from Clavery for choosing a wife unacceptable to the old king. Paul is working in a factory at the opening of the scenario and his royal connections are unknown to his colleagues. He is friendly with Margaret Harting, the daughter of a noted peace advocate whose lectures Paul attends. When the news of his accession becomes public, he goes into hiding, undecided whether to accept the rôle or abdicate. He regards himself as a man of the New World and sees his Central European kingdom as part of an old and defunct order.

He is also aware of the critical political situation centred around Clavery and the adjoining states of Sævia and Agravia. A new metal, calcomite, has revolutionized the world's production lines, but its only sources of supply are South Africa, under the control of Britain, and Agravia, a new state created by the Treaty of Versailles. An agricultural nation, Agravia is unwilling to turn its economy over to the production of calcomite, a matter of vital concern to the Americans who resent Britain's monopoly of the only other source. Diplomatically, therefore, they unofficially welcome Sævia's claim to Agravia as part of its former territory. Clavery is the key to the situation by virtue of its armed strength; Sævia lacks the forces to overrun Agravia single-handed, but a union with Clavery, originally planned by the proposed marriage between Princess Helen of Sævia and the crown prince of Clavery, would overcome the deficiency. The assassination has foiled these intentions and it is assumed that the bomb which killed the Claverian king and crown prince could only have come from Agravia. The possibility of a conflict which could lead to another world war is Paul's major consideration, and the factor which determines him to accept the throne.

He arrives in Clavery to find war fever at its height, mainly incited by the supporters of Prince Michael who is next in succession to Paul. Chief among them are Baron Mitzinka and General Monza, respectively the ministers of war and foreign affairs. The widowed queen is demanding vengeance, as is Princess Helen, to whom Paul is immediately attracted. She in turn is drawn to him, but is adamant in her resolve that Sævia will invade Agravia with or without Clavery's help. Paul's dilemma is acute. Spending a day in the country incognito, he sees the results in terms of injury and suffering which the First World War has already inflicted on the nation and he dreads being responsible for their repetition. At the same time he realizes that his own life is in danger if he fails to declare war; both the press and the people are one with Prince Michael in demanding the conquest of Agravia.

In a secret meeting with the Agravian president, Himbesket (arranged by Clavery's chancellor, Hagen), Paul discovers that Michael himself organized the assassination, and that the last thing Agravia wants is war. But on his return to the capital he discovers that Sævia has begun hostilities and that Michael is attempting to seize power. At last compelled to act, Paul shoots the prince and the coup collapses. Sævia withdraws, while Agravia agrees to the mining of its calcomite under the supervision of a world control. Paul marries Helen and a union of all three countries is proclaimed. Obliged to follow Agravia's example, Britain concedes its rights in South African calcomite to the world authority, the first of many such supra-national controls which are envisaged. The scenario ends with the visit of Dr. Harting and Margaret to Clavery and a vision of a progressively more unified world.

The book was Wells's first effort to write a major film scenario (in 1928 he scripted three silent shorts for Anglo : *Bluebottles*, *The Tonic* and *Daydreams*. These were directed by Ivor Montagu and featured Elsa Lanchester, Charles Laughton and Harold Warrender). For *The King Who Was A King*, he was still thinking in terms of the silent idiom so far as dialogue was concerned, but he wrote in many details of the background music and provided novel suggestions on the use of colour. In a long introduction he described the scenario as an attempt to portray the possibilities of world peace in a popular but provoking form, seeking a mass audience for his ideas which he could not hope to reach by books alone. In view of the story's anti-monarchist arguments and its attack on commercial influence in international politics, he doubted if it would reach the screen—and it never has. However, many of the special effects he devised were later reflected in his screenplay for *Things to Come* (1935), which still retains its place among the classics of the cinema. His symbolic use of such archetypes as 'Man the Maker' and 'Man the Destroyer', linking the former with Paul and the latter with Michael's henchman, the Foreign Minister Monza, is a device since which has appeared in many films. *The King Who Was A King*, 1929

ZELINKA, PRINCE MICHAEL : Next in line to the throne of Clavery after King Paul, and a vociferous advocate of war with the adjoining state of Agravia. Dark-complexioned, tall and slightly hunchbacked, he has an intelligent if malignant face and a forceful, impatient manner. He is the true architect of the assassination of the old king and his heir, a crime which his agents have successfully misled the public into assuming was committed by Agravians. He is envious of Paul not only for the crown, but also for the hand of Princess Helen of Sævia, a potential ally. He attempts a *coup d'état* when the King refuses to declare war and is shot by him on a mountain pass at the Claverian border. *The King Who Was A King*, 1929

APPENDICES

APPENDICES

Appendix One

Bibliography of Novels

A complete chronological listing of novels, together with sub-titles, the publishers of first editions and dedications, is given below. The main characters are also noted, under whose entries an outline of their respective stories can be found in the main A–Z. In addition, three further works (indicated*), which consist largely of fiction but cannot be described as novels, are included.

1895   *The Time Machine: An Invention,*
        W. Heinemann, London. Dedicated 'to William Ernest Henley'. See under : Time Traveller, The
        The Wonderful Visit,
        J. M. Dent & Co., London. Dedicated 'to the Memory of my dear friend, Walter Low'. See under : Angel, The

1896   *The Island of Dr. Moreau,*
        W. Heinemann, London. See under : Prendick, Edward
        The Wheels of Chance: A Holiday Adventure etc.,
        J. M. Dent & Co., London. Dedicated 'to my dear mother'.

1897   *The Invisible Man: A Grotesque Romance,*
        C. Arthur Peason, London. See under : Griffin

1898   *The War of the Worlds,*
        W. Heinemann, London. Dedicated : 'to my brother Frank Wells, this rendering of his idea'. See under : Narrator

1899   *When the Sleeper Wakes: A Story of the Years to Come,*
        Harper, London. See under : Graham

1900   *Love and Mr. Lewisham,*
        Harper & Bros., London and New York. See under : Lewisham, George Edgar

1901   *The First Men in the Moon,*
        G. Newnes, London. See under : Bedford, Mr.

1902   *The Sea Lady: A Tissue of Moonshine,*
        Methuen & Co., London. See under : Sea Lady, The

The Research Magnificent,
Macmillan & Co., London. See under : Benham, William Porphyry

1916 *Mr. Britling Sees It Through,*
Cassell & Co., London. See under : Britling, Hugh, Snr.

1917 *The Soul of a Bishop: A Novel (with Just a Little Love in It) about Conscience and Religion and the Real Troubles of Life,*
Cassell & Co., London. See under : Scrope, Edward—Bishop of Princhester

1918 *Joan and Peter: The Story of an Education,*
Cassell & Co., London. Dedicated 'to P. and J.'. See under : Stubland, Peter

1919 *The Undying Fire,*
Cassell & Co., London. Dedicated 'to all schoolmasters and schoolmistresses and every teacher in the world'. See under : Huss, Job

1922 *The Secret Places of the Heart,*
Cassell & Co., London. See under : Hardy, Sir Richmond

1923 *Men Like Gods,*
Cassell & Co., London. Dedicated 'to Florence Lamont, in whose home at Englewood this story was christened'. See under : Barnstaple, Alfred

1924 *The Dream: A Novel,*
Jonathan Cape, London. See under : Smith, Harry Mortimer (Sarnac)

1925 *Christina Alberta's Father,*
Jonathan Cape, London. See under : Preemby, Albert Edward

1926 *The World of William Clissold: A Novel at a New Angle,*
Ernest Benn, London. Dedicated 'to Odette Keun, self-forgetful friend and helper'. See under : Clissold, William

1927 *Meanwhile: The Picture of a Lady,*
Ernest Benn, London. See under : Rylands, Cynthia

1928 *Mr. Blettsworthy on Rampole Island: Being the Story of a Gentleman of Culture and Refinement who suffered Shipwreck and saw no Human Beings other than Cruel and Savage Cannibals for several years. How he beheld Megatheria alive and made some notes of their Habits. How he became a Sacred Lunatic. How he did at last escape in a Strange Manner from the Horror and Barbarities of Rampole Island in time to fight in the Great War, and how afterwards he came near returning to that Island for ever. With much Amusing and Edifying Matter concerning Manners, Customs, Beliefs, Warfare, Crime, and a Storm at Sea. Concluding with some Reflections upon Life in General and upon these Present Times in Particular,*

Ernest Benn, London. Dedicated 'to the immortal memory of Candide'. See under : Blettsworthy, Arnold

1929 *The King Who Was A King: The Book of a Film,*

Ernest Benn, London. See under : Zelinka, King Paul

The Adventures of Tommy,

George G. Harrap & Co., London. Dedicated 'to Miss Margery Hick by her sincere friend and admirer'. See under : Bates, Master Tommy

1930 *The Autocracy of Mr. Parham: His Remarkable Adventures in this Changing World,*

Heinemann, London, See under : Parham, Mr.

1932 *The Bulpington of Blup,*

Hutchinson & Co., London. Dedicated 'to the critic of the typescript, Odette Keun, gratefully (bless her)'. See under : Bulpington, Theodore

1933 *The Shape of Things to Come: The Ultimate Revolution,*

Hutchinson & Co., London. Dedicated 'to José Ortega y Gasset, Explorador'. See under : Raven, Dr. Philip

1935 *Things to Come: A Film Story Based on the Material Contained in his History of the Future 'The Shape of Things to Come',*

The Cresset Press, London. See under : Raven, Dr. Philip

1936 *The Croquet Player: A Story,*

Chatto & Windus, London. See under : Frobisher, Mr.

Man Who Could Work Miracles: A Film Story Based on the Material Contained in His Short Story,

The Cresset Press, London. See under : Fotheringay, George McWhirter

1937 *Star Begotten: A Biological Fantasia,*

Chatto & Windus, London. Dedicated 'on a sudden impulse, to my friend Winston Spencer Churchill'. See under : Davis, Joseph

Brynhild,

Methuen & Co., London. See under : Palace, Brynhild

The Camford Visitation,

Methuen & Co., London. See under : Unexpected Voice, **The**

1938   *The Brothers: A Story,*
       Chatto & Windus, London. Dedicated 'to my friend J. F.
       Horrabin'. See under : Bolaris, Richard
       Apropos of Dolores,
       Jonathan Cape, London. See under : Wilbeck, Stephen
1939   *The Holy Terror,*
       Michael Joseph, London. See under : Whitlow, Rudolph
1940   *Babes in the Darkling Wood,*
       Secker & Warburg, London. See under : Twain, James
       All Aboard for Ararat,
       Secker & Warburg, London. See under : Lammock, Noah
1941   *You Can't Be Too Careful. A Sample of Life,*
       Secker & Warburg, London. Dedicated 'to Christopher
       Morley, Who Richly Deserves It . . .'. See under : Tewler,
       Edward Albert
1945   **The Happy Turning: A Dream of Life,*
       Heinemann, London and Toronto. See under : Jesus of
       Nazareth
       *The Betterave Papers,
       Cornhill Magazine, London. See under : Betterave, W. B.

Appendix Two

Bibilography of Short Stories

A listing of works, in the order in which they appear in the 1927
Ernest Benn edition of *The Complete Short Stories of H. G. Wells*,
is given below, together with the publications in which they first
appeared. Thirteen additional stories, not included in the Benn
edition, are listed at the end of this appendix.

'The Empire of the Ants'.
Strand Magazine, December, 1905.
See under : Holroyd
'A Vision of Judgment'.
Butterfly, September, 1899.
See under : God, The Lord
'The Land Ironclads'.
Strand Magazine, December, 1903.
See under : War Correspondent, The
'The Beautiful Suit'.
First published as 'A Moonlight Fable'
Collier's Weekly, April, 1909.
See under : Man in the Beautiful Suit, The
'The Door in the Wall'.
Daily Chronicle, 14th July, 1906.
See under : Wallace, Lionel
'The Pearl of Love'.
18th tale in Vol. 10 of *The Atlantic Edition of the Works of H. G.
Wells* (T. Fisher Unwin, London), 1924.
See under : Indian Prince, The
'The Country of the Blind'.
Strand Magazine, April, 1904.
See under : Nunez

'The Stolen Bacillus'.
Pall Mall Budget, 21st June, 1894.
See under : Bacteriologist, The
'The Flowering of the Strange Orchid'.
Pall Mall Budget, 2nd August, 1894.
See under : Winter-Wedderburn
'In the Avu Observatory'.
Pall Mall Budget, 9th August, 1894.
See under : Woodhouse
'The Triumphs of a Taxidermist'.
Pall Mall Gazette, 1894.
See under : Taxidermist, The
'A Deal in Ostriches'.
Pall Mall Budget, 1894
See under : Padishah, Sir Mohini
'Through a Window'.
First published as 'At a Window'.
Black and White, 25th August, 1894.
See under : Bailey
'The Temptation of Harringay'.
St. James's Gazette, 9th February, 1895.
See under : Harringay, R. M.
'The Flying Man'.
Pall Mall Gazette, 8th December, 1893.
See under : Infantry Lieutenant, The
'The Diamond Maker'.
Pall Mall Budget, 1894.
See under : Diamond Maker, The
'Aepyornis Island'.
Pall Mall Budget, Christmas Number, 1894.
See under : Butcher
'The Remarkable Case of Davidson's Eyes'.
Pall Mall Budget, 28th March, 1895.
See under : Davidson, Sidney
'The Lord of the Dynamos'.
Pall Mall Budget, 6th September, 1894.
See under : Holroyd, James
'The Hammerpond Park Burglary'.
Pall Mall Budget, 1894.
See under : Watkins, Teddy

'The Moth'.
First published as 'A Moth—Genus Novo'.
Pall Mall Gazette, 28th March, 1895.
See under : Hapley
'The Treasure in the Forest'.
Pall Mall Budget, 1894.
See under : Hocker
'The Plattner Story'.
New Review, April, 1896.
See under : Plattner, Gottfried
'The Argonauts of the Air'.
Phil May's Annual, 1895.
See under : Monson
'The Story of the Late Mr. Evesham'.
Idler, May, 1896.
See under : Elvesham, Egbert
'In the Abyss'.
Pearson's Magazine, August, 1896.
See under : Elstead
'The Apple'.
Idler, October, 1896.
See under : Hinchcliffe, Mr.
'Under the Knife'.
New Review, January, 1896.
See under : Haddon
'The Sea Raiders'.
Weekly Sun Literary Supplement,
6th December, 1896.
See under : Fison
'Pollock and the Porroh Man'.
New Budget, 23rd May, 1895.
See under : Pollock
'The Red Room'.
Idler, March, 1896.
See under : Man in the Red Room, The
'The Cone'.
Unicorn, 18th September, 1895.
See under : Horrocks
'The Purple Pileus'.
Black and White, Christmas Number, 1896.
See under : Coombes, Jim

'The Jilting of Jane'.
12th tale in *The Plattner Story and Others* (Methuen and Co.,
London), 1897.
See under : Jane
'In the Modern Vein : An Unsympathetic Love Story'.
First published as 'A Bardlet's Romance'.
Truth, 8th March, 1894.
See under : Vair, Aubrey
'A Catastrophe'.
New Budget, 4th April, 1895.
See under : Winslow, Sidney
'The Lost Inheritance'.
15th tale in *The Plattner Story and Others* (Methuen and Co.,
London), 1897.
See under : Ted, The Man with the Glass Eye
'The Sad Story of a Dramatic Critic'.
Later republished as 'The Obliterated Man'.
New Budget, 15th August, 1895.
See under : Cummins, Egbert Craddock
'A Slip Under the Microscope'.
Yellow Book, 1893.
See under : Hill, Mr.
'The Reconciliation'.
First published as 'The Bulla'.
Weekly Sun Literary Supplement, 1st December, 1895.
See under : Temple
'My First Aeroplane'.
Strand Magazine, January, 1910.
See under : Betts, Mr.
'Little Mother Up the Mörderberg'.
Strand Magazine, April, 1910.
See under : Narrator
'The Story of the Last Trump'.
First published in *Boon*, (T. Fisher Unwin, London), 1915.
See under : Parchester, the Rev. Mr.
'The Grisly Folk'.
First published as 'The Grisly Folk and their War with Men'.
Storyteller Magazine, April, 1921.
See under : Grisly Folk, The
'The Crystal Egg'.
New Review, 1897.
See under : Cave, C.

'Mr. Brisher's Treasure'.
Strand Magazine, April, 1899.
See under : Brisher, Mr.
'Miss Winchelsea's Heart'.
Queen, October, 1898.
See under : Winchelsea, Miss
'A Dream of Armageddon'.
Black and White, 1901.
See under : Man with the White Face, The

(The following stories were not included in Benn's collection)
'The Man with a Nose'.
First published as 'The Ugliest Thing in London'.
Pall Mall Gazette, April, 1894.
See under : Man with a Nose, The
'The Thumbmark'.
Pall Mall Budget, 28th June, 1894.
See under : Anarchist, The
'The Thing in No. 7'.
Pall Mall Budget, 25th October, 1894.
See under : Wilderspin
'A Misunderstood Artist'.
Pall Mall Gazette, November, 1894.
See under : Misunderstood Artist, A
'The Presence by the Fire'.
Penny Illustrated Paper. 14th August, 1897.
See under : Reid, Mr.
'The Rajah's Treasure'.
Pearson's Magazine, July-December, 1896.
See under : Rajah, The
'Le Mari Terrible'.
21st tale in the collection *Thirty Strange Stories* (Arnold, New York), 1897.
See under : Bellows, Mr.
'Mr. Marshall's Doppelganger'.
Gentlewoman, 21st August, 1897.
See under : Marshall, Mr.
'A Perfect Gentleman on Wheels'.
Woman at Home, April, 1897.
See under : Crampton, Cecil

'The Loyalty of Esau Common'.
Contemporary Review, February, 1902.
See under : Common, Esau
'Master Anthony and the Zeppelin'.
Princess Marie-José's Children's Book (Cassell), 1916.
See under : Anthony, Master
'The Queer Story of Brownlow's Newspaper'.
Strand Magazine, 1931.
See under : Brownlow
'Answer to Prayer'.
New Statesman, 1937.
See under : Archbishop, **The**

Appendix Three

Address by J. B. Priestley at Golders Green Crematorium on Friday, 16th August, 1946.

We have come together here today to say goodbye to our friend, Herbert George Wells. All of us here were privileged to know him— and some were so close to him that it is not possible for any one of us outside his family circle to express their sense of loss—and I think that all of us, knowing how great was his work and how worldwide his influence, realize that at this moment we represent millions of men and women of all races who found in him a councillor and friend. For this was a man whose word was light in a thousand dark places. Since the beginning of this century, whenever young men and women, from the Arctic to the Tropics, were determined to free themselves from mental squalor, from superstition, ignorance, cruelty and fear, there was H. G. Wells at their side, unwearying and eager to instruct and inspire. They turned to him to help them in their struggle for knowledge, insight and courage, and they never asked in vain. His literary genius was rich and rare—the best of his novels and short stories are among the finest creations of our time—but he belongs not only to English Literature, but also to world history, as a great educator and as the chief prophet of this age of transition, long foreshadowing, with pity and passion, the shape of things to come.

And now we live indeed, with our rockets and atom bombs, in a Wellsian world. We hover at the crossroads, leading either to a real world civilization or to the possible extinction of our species; and nobody would be foolish enough now to say that Wells was an idle prophet. He saw further than other men did. His unique combination of literary power and intuition, social experience, and early scientific training, gave him a profound insight into the strange historical dramas of our time. He worked with a double vision, both his own, but one long-range, the other short-range.

His long-range vision, born of his biological studies and his vivid imagination, showed him Mankind as a species, struggling through darkness and slime, cruelty and fear, towards truth and beauty, freedom and joy. So he worked with a passionate loyalty for the whole toiling, contriving, endlessly hopeful family of Mankind. His other—and short-range—vision, which made him the chief prophet of our age, and gave him the pattern of many of his best stories, was a vision of some ordinary little citizen—bewildered but hopeful, baffled but touchingly gallant—being swept along by forces he could not understand into a world of gigantic conflict and sinister chances; the very world in which H.G. found himself in these last years, old and often ailing, but still indomitable, refusing to leave his ruined terrace and the London folk he knew so well. The age of total and terrible war, against which he had warned us so often, had arrived; but he was still there to share it with us. And looking back, and remembering what little comfort his strange insight could give him, we can marvel now at his buoyancy, his vast geniality, his glorious intellectual high spirits. For, as all of us here can testify—this was no gloomy prophet, turning his back on us for his private wilderness disdaining friendship and fun. This was the man who could write *Kipps* and *Mr. Polly* and *Tono Bungay*, the man who could enrich his letters with droll little drawings, who could invent uproarious family games, whose blue eyes twinkled with mischief and whose famous voice, which never lost a kind of reedy Cockney impudence, rose higher and higher in friendly mischief; who was not only a tremendous character, but also a most lovable man. Of course, he could be prickly, rather intolerant, easily exasperated, but there was not a single streak of hard pride in his nature. When he was angry, it was because he knew, far better than we did, that life need not be a sordid greedy scramble; and when he was impatient it was because he knew there were glorious gifts of body, mind and spirit only just beyond our present reach. And always the greatness was there; the immense range of his mind, the astonishing fountains of ideas, the devastating or illuminating judgment, and the unwearying sympathy with us all, of every colour and race, in our bewilderment, despair and hope. He was a world-famous figure, the great prophet of our time, but always, from first to last, one of our friends, who only asked to talk with us truthfully, eagerly and vividly. At his worst he never diminished and hurt us. And at his best he made us feel, as he did, that we live on a star.

His body vanishes from our sight as it goes towards the consuming flames. But we shall remember him with gratitude and

on—he will live on in our hearts and still light our minds—
rust, we try to serve his vision of one world, the home of
hole human family, free at last from ignorance, cruelty and

So, remembering to hold his noblest vision as a legacy and a
rust, let us say goodbye to our friend in his own words and not
in ours : 'So far and beyond, this adventure may continue and our
race survive. The impenetrable clouds that bound our life at last
in every direction may hide innumerable trials and dangers, but
there are no conclusive limitations even in their deepest shadows,
and there are times and seasons, there are moods of exaltation—
moments, as it were, of revelation—when the whole universe about
us seems bright with the presence of as yet unimaginable things.'

Bibliography

A Select Bibliography of Studies of Wells's Life and Fiction

Beresford, J. D., *H. G. Wells* (Nisbet) 1915

Bergonzi, Bernard, *The Early H. G. Wells* (Manchester University Press) 1961

Bloom, Robert, *Anatomies of Egotism: A Reading of the Last Novels of H. G. Wells* (University of Nebraska Press) 1977

Brome, Vincent, *H. G. Wells: A Biography* (Longmans, Green) 1951

Brooks, Van Wyck, *The World of H. G. Wells* (Unwin) 1915

Dickson, Lovat, *H. G. Wells: His Turbulent Life and Times* (Macmillan) 1969

Hammond, John R., *Herbert George Wells: an Annotated Bibliography of his Works* (Garland Publishing) 1977

MacKenzie, Norman and Jeanne, *The Time Traveller: The Life of H. G. Wells* (Weidenfeld and Nicolson) 1973

Nicholson, Norman, *H. G. Wells* (Barker) 1950

Raknem, Ingvald, *H. G. Wells and his Critics* (Oslo University Press) 1962

Suvin, Darko, and Philmus, Robert M. (eds.), *H. G. Wells and Modern Science Fiction* (Bucknell University Press) 1976

Wells, Geoffrey H., *A Bibliography of the works of H. G. Wells, 1893–1925, with some notes and comments* (Routledge) 1925

Wells, Geoffrey H., *The Works of H. G. Wells, 1887–1925: A Bibliography, Dictionary and Subject-Index* (Routledge) 1926

Wells, H. G., *Experiment in Autobiography: Discoveries of a Very Ordinary Brain—Since 1866* (Victor Gollancz and the Cresset Press), 1934

Wells Society, *H. G. Wells: A Comprehensive Bibliography* (H. G. Wells Society) 1966

West, Geoffrey H. (Geoffrey H. Wells), *H. G. Wells: A Sketch for a Portrait* (Gerald Howe) 1930